what is this thing called knowledge?

- Praise for first edition:

  '. . . a valuable addition . . . a book that sets things out in a clear and elementary way, while still covering the ground properly.'
  > Finn Spicer, University of Bristol, UK

  'Clearly laid out, well organized and written by a true expert.'
  > Michael Lynch, University of Connecticut, USA

What is knowledge? Where does it come from? Can we know anything at all?

This lucid and engaging introduction grapples with these central questions in the theory of knowledge, offering a clear, non-partisan view of the main themes of epistemology. Both traditional issues and contemporary ideas are discussed in fourteen easily digestible sections, which conclude with a useful summary of the main ideas discussed, study questions, annotated further reading and a guide to internet resources.

The second edition has been revised and updated throughout and features:

- a new chapter on moral knowledge;
- a glossary of epistemology examples;
- annotated advanced further reading including more scholarly references;
- updated web resources.

Each chapter also features text boxes providing bite-sized summaries of key concepts and major philosophers, and clear and interesting examples are used throughout, making this an ideal first textbook in the theory of knowledge for undergraduates coming to philosophy for the first time.

Duncan Pritchard holds the Chair in Epistemology at the University of Edinburgh, UK. His main research area is epistemology, and he has published widely in this field, including the books *Epistemic Luck* (2005) and *Knowledge* (2009).

DUNCAN PRITCHARD

what is this thing called knowledge?

Second edition

 Routledge
Taylor & Francis Group

LONDON AND NEW YORK

● First published 2006
This edition published 2010 by Routledge
2 Park Square, Milton Park, Abingdon, Oxon OX14 4RN

Simultaneously published in the USA and Canada
by Routledge
270 Madison Ave, New York, NY 10016

Routledge is an imprint of the Taylor & Francis Group, an informa business

© 2010 Duncan Pritchard

Typeset in Berling and Arial Rounded by
Swales & Willis Ltd, Exeter, Devon
Printed and bound in Great Britain by
the MPG Books Group, Bodmin & Kings Lynn

British Library Cataloguing in Publication Data
A catalogue record for this book is available from the British Library

Library of Congress Cataloging in Publication Data
Pritchard, Duncan.
   What is this thing called knowledge?/Duncan Pritchard. – 2nd ed.
      p. cm.
   Includes bibliographical references and index.
   1. Knowledge, Theory of. I. Title.
   BD161.P749 2009
   121–dc22   2009018683

ISBN10: 0–415–55296–6 (hbk)
ISBN10: 0–415–55298–2 (pbk)
ISBN10: 0–203–09221–X (ebk)

ISBN13: 978–0–415–55296–7 (hbk)
ISBN13: 978–0–415–55298–1 (pbk)
ISBN13: 978–0–203–09221–7 (ebk)

For Mandi, Ethan and Alexander

CONTENTS

Preface to the second edition   x
How to use this book   xi

• PART I: WHAT IS KNOWLEDGE?   1

1 Some preliminaries   3
TYPES OF KNOWLEDGE   3
TWO BASIC REQUIREMENTS ON KNOWLEDGE: TRUTH AND BELIEF   4
KNOWING VERSUS MERELY 'GETTING IT RIGHT'   5
A BRIEF REMARK ON TRUTH   7

2 The value of knowledge   10
WHY CARE ABOUT KNOWLEDGE?   10
THE INSTRUMENTAL VALUE OF TRUE BELIEF   10
THE VALUE OF KNOWLEDGE   12
THE STATUES OF DAEDALUS   14
IS SOME KNOWLEDGE INTRINSICALLY VALUABLE?   15

3 Defining knowledge   20
THE PROBLEM OF THE CRITERION   20
METHODISM AND PARTICULARISM   21
KNOWLEDGE AS JUSTIFIED TRUE BELIEF   23
GETTIER CASES   23
RESPONDING TO THE GETTIER CASES   26
BACK TO THE PROBLEM OF THE CRITERION   28

4 The structure of knowledge   31
KNOWLEDGE AND JUSTIFICATION   31
THE ENIGMATIC NATURE OF JUSTIFICATION   31
AGRIPPA'S TRILEMMA   33
INFINITISM   34
COHERENTISM   35
FOUNDATIONALISM   36

5 Rationality   42
RATIONALITY, JUSTIFICATION, AND KNOWLEDGE   42
EPISTEMIC RATIONALITY AND THE GOAL OF TRUTH   43
THE GOAL(S) OF EPISTEMIC RATIONALITY   45
THE (UN)IMPORTANCE OF EPISTEMIC RATIONALITY   46
RATIONALITY AND RESPONSIBILITY   47
EPISTEMIC INTERNALISM/EXTERNALISM   49

6 Virtues and faculties   55
RELIABILISM   55
A 'GETTIER' PROBLEM FOR RELIABILISM   56
VIRTUE EPISTEMOLOGY   57
VIRTUE EPISTEMOLOGY AND THE EXTERNALISM/INTERNALISM DISTINCTION   60

● **PART II: WHERE DOES KNOWLEDGE COME FROM?**   67

7 Perception   69
THE PROBLEM OF PERCEPTUAL KNOWLEDGE   69
INDIRECT REALISM   71
IDEALISM   73
TRANSCENDENTAL IDEALISM   74
DIRECT REALISM   76

8 Testimony and memory   80
THE PROBLEM OF TESTIMONIAL KNOWLEDGE   80
REDUCTIONISM   82
CREDULISM   84
THE PROBLEM OF MEMORIAL KNOWLEDGE   86

9 A priority and inference   91
A PRIORI AND EMPIRICAL KNOWLEDGE   91
THE INTERDEPENDENCE OF A PRIORI AND EMPIRICAL KNOWLEDGE   92
INTROSPECTIVE KNOWLEDGE   93
DEDUCTION   94
INDUCTION   95
ABDUCTION   96

10 The problem of induction   101
THE PROBLEM OF INDUCTION   101
RESPONDING TO THE PROBLEM OF INDUCTION   103
LIVING WITH THE PROBLEM OF INDUCTION I: FALSIFICATION   103
LIVING WITH THE PROBLEM OF INDUCTION II: PRAGMATISM   107

11 A case study: moral knowledge — 112
THE PROBLEM OF MORAL KNOWLEDGE — 112
SCEPTICISM ABOUT MORAL FACTS — 112
SCEPTICISM ABOUT MORAL KNOWLEDGE — 116
THE NATURE OF MORAL KNOWLEDGE I: CLASSICAL FOUNDATIONALISM — 118
THE NATURE OF MORAL KNOWLEDGE II: ALTERNATIVE CONCEPTIONS — 120

● **PART III: DO WE KNOW ANYTHING AT ALL?** — 127

12 Scepticism about other minds — 129
THE PROBLEM OF OTHER MINDS — 129
THE ARGUMENT FROM ANALOGY — 130
A PROBLEM FOR THE ARGUMENT FROM ANALOGY — 131
TWO VERSIONS OF THE PROBLEM OF OTHER MINDS — 132
PERCEIVING SOMEONE ELSE'S MIND — 134

13 Radical scepticism — 137
THE RADICAL SCEPTICAL PARADOX — 137
SCEPTICISM AND CLOSURE — 140
MOOREANISM — 142
CONTEXTUALISM — 145

14 Truth and objectivity — 151
OBJECTIVITY, ANTI-REALISM, AND SCEPTICISM — 151
TRUTH AS THE GOAL OF INQUIRY — 152
AUTHENTICITY AND THE VALUE OF TRUTH — 154
RELATIVISM — 155

General further reading — 159
Glossary of terms — 163
Glossary of key examples — 179
Index — 182

PREFACE TO THE SECOND EDITION

One of the main things that I wanted to achieve with *What is this Thing Called Knowledge?* was to offer a genuinely introductory textbook which nonetheless covered the very latest developments in contemporary epistemology. Given the fast-moving nature of the debate in epistemology, this meant that one couldn't wait too long before producing a second edition for fear that this virtue of the book would be lost. A good example of the importance of refreshing the first edition is that in the relatively short time since that edition appeared, there has been a tremendous growth in free online materials in epistemology. Those working their way through this second edition are thus far better served when it comes to finding additional readings and research resources.

The second edition also sees a structural change, in that a brand new chapter on moral knowledge has been added. This chapter has been appended to the section of the book which looks at how knowledge is acquired, and is meant to offer a more concrete way of thinking about this issue. That is, while we can ask the question of how knowledge is acquired in a very general way, by looking at the different sources of knowledge, we can also ask that question by considering putative types of knowledge, like moral knowledge, and considering how they could be acquired. The new chapter has the added benefit of being able to demonstrate how reflecting on the nature and source of a type of knowledge with which we ordinarily credit ourselves can make us doubt whether there is such knowledge in the first place.

Let me close by offering a particular thanks to all the students who have taken introductory courses in epistemology with me over the years. They have helped me to refine my ideas about what a good introductory text on this topic would cover, and how it would cover it. In a very real sense, they have helped to make this book what it is.

HOW TO USE THIS BOOK

This book has been designed to make it as user-friendly as possible, so that it can guide you through the theory of knowledge with the minimum fuss. It is composed of fourteen short chapters which fall into three main sections.

The first part explores general topics in the theory of knowledge, and asks questions about, for example, what the value of knowledge is (*who cares who knows?*). The second part looks at where our knowledge comes from, and considers the role of, for instance, perception and memory in helping us to acquire, and retain, knowledge. It closes by considering a particular type of knowledge – moral knowledge – and asks what the source of this knowledge is, assuming that we have any. The third part examines the scope of our knowledge, and to that end considers sceptical arguments which purport to show that the possession of knowledge – or at least the possession of certain kinds of knowledge at any rate – is impossible.

Each chapter closes with a summary of the main points made in that chapter and some questions for discussion. For those who wish to explore the topic discussed in that chapter further, there is also a section recommending additional introductory and advanced readings. A further section identifies free internet resources that are relevant to that chapter. (If you want some general further reading on the theory of knowledge as a whole, there is a section towards the back of the book with bibliographic details.) Within each chapter you'll find text boxes which give further information relevant to what is being discussed in the main text, such as more information about a historical figure who has been mentioned.

Although terminology is avoided where possible, you don't need to worry if you come across a technical word that you don't understand, since all terminology is explained at the back of the book in a glossary. (Technical words that have corresponding entries in the glossary are identified in the text by being in **bold** at first mention.) Equally, don't worry if you can't remember the details of the examples offered, or what they show, since there is a glossary of all the main examples used in the text at the back of the book.

Finally, at the very end of the book, there is an index.

Part I

what is knowledge?

Part I

what is knowledge?

1

some preliminaries

- Types of knowledge
- Two basic requirements on knowledge: truth and belief
- Knowing versus merely 'getting it right'
- A brief remark on truth

• TYPES OF KNOWLEDGE

Think of all the things that you know, or at least *think* you know, right now. You know, for example, that the earth is round and that Paris is the capital of France. You know that you can speak (or at least read) English, and that two plus two is equal to four. You know, presumably, that all bachelors are unmarried men, that it is wrong to hurt people just for fun, that *The Godfather* is a wonderful film, and that water has the chemical structure H_2O. And so on.

But what is it that all these cases of knowledge have in common? Think again of the examples just given, which include geographical, linguistic, mathematical, aesthetic, ethical, and scientific knowledge. Given these myriad types of knowledge, what, if anything, ties them all together? It is this sort of question that is asked by those who study **epistemology**, which is the theory of knowledge. The goal of this book is to introduce you to this exciting field of philosophy. By the end of this book, you should be able to count yourself as an epistemologist.

In all the examples of knowledge just given, the type of knowledge in question is what is called **propositional knowledge**, in that it is knowledge of a **proposition**. A proposition is what is asserted by a sentence which says that something is the case – e.g., that the earth is flat, that bachelors are unmarried men, that two plus two is four, and so on. Propositional knowledge will be the focus of this book, but we should also recognise that it is not the only sort of knowledge that we possess.

There is, for example, **ability knowledge,** or *know-how*. Ability knowledge is clearly different from propositional knowledge; I know how to swim, for example, but I do not thereby know a set of propositions about how to swim. Indeed, I'm not altogether sure that I could tell you how to swim, but I do know how to swim nonetheless (and I could prove it by manifesting this ability – by jumping into a swimming pool and doing the breaststroke, say).

Ability knowledge is certainly an important type of knowledge to have. We want lots of know-how, such as to know how to ride a bicycle, to drive a car, or to operate a personal computer. Notice, however, that while only relatively sophisticated creatures like humans possess propositional knowledge, ability knowledge is far more common. An ant might plausibly be said to know how to navigate its terrain, but would we want to say that an ant has propositional knowledge; that there are facts which the ant knows? Could the ant know, for example, that the terrain it is presently crossing is someone's porch? Intuitively not, and this marks out the importance of propositional knowledge over other types of knowledge like ability knowledge, which is that such knowledge presupposes the sort of relatively sophisticated intellectual abilities possessed by humans.

• TWO BASIC REQUIREMENTS ON KNOWLEDGE: TRUTH AND BELIEF

Henceforth, when we talk about knowledge, we will have propositional knowledge in mind, unless explicitly stated otherwise. Two things that just about every epistemologist agrees on are that a prerequisite for possessing knowledge is that one has a belief in the relevant proposition, and that that belief must be true. So if you know that Paris is the capital of France, then you must believe that this is the case, and your belief must also be true.

Take the truth requirement first. In order to assess this claim, consider what would follow if we dropped this requirement. In particular, is it plausible to suppose that one could know a false proposition? Of course, we often *think* that we know something and then it turns out that we were wrong, but that's just to say that we didn't really know it in the first place. Could we genuinely know a false proposition? Could I know, for example, that the moon is made of cheese, even though it manifestly isn't? I take it that when we talk of someone having knowledge, we mean to exclude such a possibility. This is because to ascribe knowledge to someone is to credit that person with having got things right, and that means that what we regard that person as knowing had better not be false, but true.

Next, consider the belief requirement. It is sometimes the case that we explicitly *contrast* belief and knowledge, as when we say things like, 'I don't merely believe that he was innocent, I know it', which might on the face of it be thought to imply that knowledge does not require belief after all. If you think about these sorts of assertions in a little more detail, however, then it becomes clear that the contrast between belief and knowledge is being used here simply to emphasise the fact that one *not only* believes the proposition in question, but *also* knows it. In this way, these assertions actually lend support to the claim that knowledge requires belief, rather than undermining it.

As with the truth requirement, we will assess the plausibility of the belief requirement for knowledge by imagining for a moment that it doesn't hold, which would mean that one could have knowledge of a proposition which one did not even believe. Suppose, for example, that someone claimed to have known a quiz answer, even though it was clear from that person's behaviour at the time that she didn't believe the proposition in question (perhaps she put forward a different answer to the question, or no answer at all). Clearly we would not agree that this person did have knowledge in this case. Again, the reason for this relates to the fact that to say that someone has knowledge is to credit that person with a certain kind of success. But for it to be *your* success, then belief in the proposition in question is essential, since otherwise this success is not creditable to *you* at all.

• KNOWING VERSUS MERELY 'GETTING IT RIGHT'

It is often noted that belief *aims* at the truth, in the sense that when we believe a proposition, we believe it to be the case (i.e., to be true). When what we believe *is* true, then there is a match between what we think is the case and what is the case. We have got things right. If mere true belief suffices for 'getting things right', however, then one might wonder as to why epistemologists do not end their quest for an account of knowledge right there and simply hold that knowledge is nothing more than true belief (i.e., 'getting things right').

There is in fact a very good reason why epistemologists do not rest content with mere true belief as an account of knowledge, and that is that one can gain true belief entirely by *accident*, in which case it would be of no credit to you at all that you got things right. Consider Harry, who forms his belief that the horse Lucky Lass will win the next race purely on the basis of the fact that the name of the horse appeals to him. Clearly this is not a good basis on which to form one's belief about the winner of the next horse race, since whether or not a horse's name appeals to you has no bearing on its performance.

Suppose, however, that Harry's belief turns out to be true, in that Lucky Lass *does* win the next race. Is this knowledge? Intuitively not, since it is just a matter of *luck* that his belief was true in this case. Remember that knowledge involves a kind of success that is creditable to the agent. Crucially, however, successes that are merely down to luck are never credited to the agent.

In order to emphasise this point, think for a moment about successes in another realm, such as archery. Notice that if one genuinely is a skilled archer, then if one tries to hit the bull's-eye, and the conditions are right (e.g., the wind is not gusting), then one usually *will* hit the bull's-eye. That's just what it means to be a skilled archer. The word 'usually' is important here, since someone who isn't a skilled archer might, as it happens, hit the bull's eye on a particular occasion, but she wouldn't *usually* hit the bull's-eye in these conditions. Perhaps, for example, she aims her arrow and, by luck, it hits the centre of the target. Does the mere fact that she is successful on this one occasion mean that she is a skilled archer? No, and the reason is that she would not be able to repeat this success. If she tried again, for example, her arrow would in all likelihood sail off into the heavens.

Having knowledge is just like this. Imagine that one's belief is an arrow, which is aimed at the centre of the target, truth. Hitting the bull's-eye and forming a true belief suffices for getting things right, since all this means is that one was successful on that occasion. It does not suffice, however, for having knowledge any more than hitting the bull's-eye purely by chance indicates that you are skilled in archery. To have knowledge, one's success must genuinely be the result of one's efforts, rather than merely being by chance. Only then is that success creditable to one. And this means that forming one's belief in the way that one does ought usually, in those circumstances, to lead to a true belief.

Harry, who forms his true belief that Lucky Lass will win the race simply because he likes the name, is like the person who happens to hit the bull's-eye, but who is not a skilled archer. Usually, forming one's belief about whether a horse will win a race simply by considering whether the name of the horse appeals to you will lead you to form a false belief.

Contrast Harry with someone who genuinely knows that the race will be won by Lucky Lass. Perhaps, for example, this person is a 'Mr Big', a gangster who has fixed the race by drugging the other animals so that his horse, Lucky Lass, will win. He knows that the race will be won by Lucky Lass because the way he has formed his belief, by basing it on the special grounds he has for thinking that Lucky Lass cannot lose, would normally lead him to have a true belief. It is not a matter of luck that Mr Big hits the target of truth.

The challenge for epistemologists is thus to explain what needs to be added to mere true belief in order to get knowledge. In particular, epistemologists need to explain what needs to be added to true belief to capture this idea that knowledge, unlike mere true belief, involves a success that is creditable to the agent, where this means, for example, that the agent's true belief was not simply a matter of luck.

As we will see, it is in fact surprisingly difficult to give an unproblematic account of knowledge which meets this requirement. This has led some commentators to be doubtful about the whole project of defining knowledge. Perhaps there just is nothing that ties all cases of knowledge together, or perhaps there is such an essence to knowledge, but it is so complex that it is a futile task to seek an account of it.

In this book, however, we will proceed with optimism on this score. Even if an unproblematic definition of knowledge is unavailable, there are a number of plausible accounts on offer, even though none of them is entirely uncontentious. Moreover, the very practice of evaluating these different views about knowledge itself casts light upon what knowledge is, even if it does not result in a neat definition of this notion.

In any case, while the project of elucidating knowledge is central to epistemology (it is the principal focus of Chapters 1–6), it is important not to overstate its importance. As this book testifies, there is more to epistemology than the quest to define knowledge. One can examine the different ways in which knowledge is acquired and retained, for example, such as via our perceptual faculty of sight and our faculty of memory (see Chapters 7–11 on the ways in which knowledge is acquired and retained). Furthermore, there are sceptical challenges to be engaged with, challenges which purport to show that knowledge is impossible to possess *however* we define it (Chapters 12–14 deal with sceptical challenges and related issues).

• A BRIEF REMARK ON TRUTH

I want to end this chapter by commenting a little more on truth (note that I'll be saying more about truth at the end of the book). After all, the reader might be tempted to observe that it is odd that we have taken our understanding of truth as given and gone straight ahead to examine knowledge. Do we really have a better grip on what truth is than on what knowledge is?

It is true (if you'll forgive the pun) that I'm taking a certain common-sense conception of truth for granted here. In particular, I'm going to assume that truth is *objective* in the following sense: at least for most propositions at any rate, your thinking that they are true does not make them true. Whether or not the world is round, for example, has nothing to do with whether or not we think that it is, but simply depends upon the shape of the earth.

Most of us uncritically take this conception of truth as obvious, but there are some philosophers who think that this view of truth is unsustainable. I think that their reasons for rejecting this account of truth rest on a number of interrelated mistakes, and when I return to this issue at the end of the book I will explain what some of the core mistakes are. For now, however, it is enough that this conception of truth is intuitive. If you also think that it is intuitive, then that is all to the good. If, on the other hand, you don't, then I urge you to set this matter to one side until later on.

• CHAPTER SUMMARY

- Epistemology is the theory of knowledge. One of the characteristic questions of epistemology concerns what all the myriad kinds of knowledge we ascribe to ourselves have in common: *What is knowledge?*
- We can distinguish between knowledge of propositions, or propositional knowledge, and know-how, or ability knowledge. Intuitively, the former demands a greater degree of intellectual sophistication on the part of the knower than the latter. Our focus in this book will be on propositional knowledge.
- In order to have knowledge of a proposition, that proposition must be true, and one must believe it.
- Mere true belief does not suffice for knowledge, however, since one can gain mere true belief purely by chance, and yet you cannot gain knowledge purely by chance.
- In this book I will be assuming a common-sense objective view of truth which holds that (for the most part at least) merely thinking that something is true does not make it true.

• STUDY QUESTIONS

1 Give examples of your own of the following types of knowledge:
   - scientific knowledge;
   - geographical knowledge;
   - historical knowledge;
   - religious knowledge.
2 Explain, in your own words, what the difference between ability knowledge and propositional knowledge is, and give two examples of each.
3 Why is mere true belief not sufficient for knowledge? Give an example of your own of a case in which an agent truly believes something, but does not know it.
4 Think about the 'objective' and 'common-sense' view of truth that I described at the end of this chapter. Is this view of truth a matter of common sense to you? If so, then try to formulate some reasons that someone might offer in order to call it into question. If, on the other hand, it is not matter of common sense as far as you are concerned, then try to explain what you think is wrong with this view of truth.

• INTRODUCTORY FURTHER READING

Blackburn, Simon (2005) *Truth: A Guide for the Perplexed* (Harmondsworth: Allen Lane). A very readable introduction to the issues as regards the philosophy of truth. This is a good place to start if you want to learn more about this topic.

Luper, Steven (1998) 'Belief and Knowledge', *Routledge Encyclopedia of Philosophy*, (ed.) E. Craig, (London: Routledge) <http://www.rep.routledge.com/article/P051?ssid=550100850&n=15#>. An excellent, and critical, discussion of the idea that knowledge requires belief.

Lynch, Michael (2009) 'Truth', *The Routledge Companion to Epistemology*, (eds.) S. Bernecker & D. H. Pritchard, (New York: Routledge). An accessible and completely up-to-date survey of the main issues as regards the philosophy of truth.

Shope, Robert K. (2002) 'Conditions and Analyses of Knowing', *The Oxford Handbook to Epistemology*, (ed.) P. K. Moser, 25–70, (Oxford: Oxford University Press). See pages 25–30 for a good clear discussion of the need for the truth and belief conditions in a theory of knowledge, and of why knowledge isn't just mere true belief.

• ADVANCED FURTHER READING

Lynch, Michael (2005) *True to Life: Why Truth Matters* (Cambridge, Mass.: MIT Press). A very readable introduction to the issues as regards the philosophy of truth.

Pritchard, Duncan (2005) *Epistemic Luck* (Oxford: Oxford University Press). A recent in-depth discussion of the idea that knowledge is incompatible with luck.

Ryle, Gilbert (1949/2002) *The Concept of Mind* (Chicago, Ill.: University of Chicago Press). This is the classic discussion of ability knowledge, in contrast to propositional knowledge (see especially §2).

● FREE INTERNET RESOURCES

Dowden, Bradley & Shwartz, Norman (2006) 'Truth', *Internet Encyclopedia of Philosophy*, <http://www.iep.utm.edu/t/truth.htm>. A neat and comprehensive overview of the philosophical discussions regarding truth. Note that it can be a little demanding for the beginner in some places.

Glanzberg, Michael (2006) 'Truth', *Stanford Encyclopedia of Philosophy*, <http://plato.stanford.edu/entries/truth/>. A sophisticated overview of the literature on the philosophy of truth. Not for the beginner.

Steup, Matthias (2005) 'The Analysis of Knowledge', *Stanford Encyclopedia of Philosophy*, <http://plato.stanford.edu/entries/knowledge-analysis/>. Read up to §1.2 for more on the basic requirements on knowledge.

Truncellito, David (2007) 'Epistemology', *Internet Encyclopedia of Philosophy*, <http://www.iep.utm.edu/e/epistemo.htm>. Read up to the end of §2.b for more on the basic requirements for knowledge.

2

˙the value of knowledge

- Why care about knowledge?
- The instrumental value of true belief
- The value of knowledge
- The statues of Daedalus
- Is some knowledge intrinsically valuable?

WHY CARE ABOUT KNOWLEDGE?

One of the questions that is very rarely asked in epistemology concerns what is perhaps the most central issue for this area of philosophy. It is this: why should we care about whether or not we have knowledge? Put another way: is knowledge valuable and, if so, why? The importance of this question resides in the fact that knowledge is the primary focus of epistemological theorising. Hence, if knowledge is not valuable then that should give us cause to wonder whether we should re-think our understanding of the epistemological enterprise.

In this chapter we will examine this issue in more detail and discover, perhaps surprisingly, that the value of knowledge is far from obvious.

THE INSTRUMENTAL VALUE OF TRUE BELIEF

One way of approaching the topic of the value of knowledge is to note that one can only know what is true, and truth in one's beliefs does seem to be valuable. If truth in one's beliefs is valuable, and knowledge demands truth, then we may be at least halfway towards answering our question of why knowledge is valuable.

Truth in one's beliefs is at least minimally valuable in the sense that, *all other things being equal at any rate*, true beliefs are better than false ones because having true beliefs enables us to fulfil our goals. This sort of value – a value which accrues to something in virtue of some further valuable purpose that it serves – is known as **instrumental value**. Think, for example, of the value of a thermometer. Its value consists in the fact that it enables us to find out something of importance to us (i.e., what the temperature is).

In order to see the instrumental value of true belief, think about any subject matter that is of consequence to you, such as the time of your crucial job interview. It is clearly preferable to have a true belief in this respect rather than a false belief, since without a true belief you'll have difficulty making this important meeting. That is, your goal of making this meeting is best served by having a true belief about when it takes place rather than a false one.

The problem, however, lies with the 'all other things being equal' clause which we put on the instrumental value of true belief. We have to impose this qualification because sometimes having a true belief could be unhelpful and actually impede one's goals, and in such cases true belief would lack instrumental value. For example, if one's life depended upon it, could one really summon the courage to jump a ravine and thereby get to safety if one knew (or at least truly believed) that there was a serious possibility that one would fail to reach the other side? Here, it seems, a false belief in one's abilities would be better than a true belief if the goal in question (jumping the ravine) is to be achieved. So while true belief might *generally* be instrumentally valuable, it isn't *always* instrumentally valuable.

Moreover, some true beliefs are beliefs in trivial matters and in this case it isn't at all clear why we should value such beliefs at all. Imagine someone who, for no good reason, concerns herself with measuring each grain of sand on a beach, or someone who, even while being unable to operate a telephone, concerns herself with remembering every entry in a foreign phonebook. In each case, such a person would thereby gain lots of true beliefs but, crucially, one would regard such truth-gaining activity as rather pointless. After all, these true beliefs do not obviously serve any valuable purpose, and so do not seem to have any instrumental value (or, at the very least, what instrumental value these beliefs have is vanishingly small). It would, perhaps, be better – and thus of more value – to have fewer true beliefs, and possibly more false ones, if this meant that the true beliefs that one had were regarding matters of real consequence.

At most, then, we only seem able to marshal the conclusion that *some* true beliefs have instrumental value, not all of them. As a result, if we are to show that knowledge is valuable then we need to do more than merely note that knowledge entails truth and that true belief is instrumentally valuable. Nevertheless, this conclusion need not be that dispiriting once we remember that while knowledge requires truth, not every instance of a true belief is an instance of knowledge (as we saw in the previous chapter, for example, some true beliefs are just lucky guesses, and so not knowledge at all). Accordingly, it could just be that those true beliefs that are clearly of instrumental value are the ones that are also instances of knowledge.

The problem with this line of thought ought to be obvious, since didn't our 'sand-measuring' agent *know* what the measurements of the sand were? Moreover, didn't our agent who was unable to jump the ravine because she was paralysed by fear fail to meet her goals because of what she *knew*? The problems that afflict the claim that all true beliefs are instrumentally valuable therefore similarly undermine the idea that all knowledge is instrumentally valuable. There is thus no easy way of defending the thesis that *all* knowledge must be valuable.

There is also a second problem lurking in the background here, which is that even if this project of understanding the value of knowledge in terms of the value of true belief were to be successful, it would still be problematic because it would entail that knowledge is no more valuable than mere true belief. But if that's right, then why do we value knowledge more than mere true belief?

• THE VALUE OF KNOWLEDGE

So we cannot straightforwardly argue from the instrumental value of true belief that *all* knowledge must therefore be instrumentally valuable. That said, we can perhaps say something about the specific value of knowledge that is a little less ambitious and which simply accounts for why, in general and all other things being equal, we desire to be knowers as opposed to being agents who have mostly true beliefs but lack knowledge (or, worse, have mostly false beliefs). After all, if we want to achieve our goals in life then it would be preferable if we had knowledge which was relevant to these goals since knowledge is very useful in this respect. The idea is, therefore, that while not all knowledge is instrumentally valuable, in general it is instrumentally valuable and, what is more, it is of *greater* instrumental value, typically at least, than mere true belief alone (thus explaining our intuition that knowledge is of more value than mere true belief).

Consider the following case. Suppose I want to find my way to the nearest restaurant in an unfamiliar city. Having mostly false beliefs about the locale will almost certainly lead to this goal being frustrated. If I think, for example, that all the restaurants are in the east of the city, when in fact they are in the west, then I'm going to spend a rather dispiriting evening trudging around this town without success.

True beliefs are better than false beliefs (i.e., are of more instrumental value), but not as good as knowledge. Imagine, for instance, that you found out where the nearest restaurant was by reading a map of the town which is, unbeknownst to you, entirely fake and designed to mislead those unfamiliar with the area. Suppose further, however, that, as it happens, this map inadvertently shows you the right route to the nearest restaurant. You therefore have a true belief about where the nearest restaurant is, but you clearly lack knowledge of this fact. After all, your belief is only luckily true, and as we saw in Chapter 1, you can't gain knowledge by luck in this way.

Now one might think that it is neither here nor there to the value of your true belief whether it is also an instance of knowledge. So long as I find the nearest restaurant, what does it matter that I don't know where it is but merely have a true belief about where it is? The problem with mere true belief, however, is that, unlike knowledge, it is very *unstable*. Suppose, for example, that as you were walking to this restaurant you noticed that none of the landmarks corresponded to where they ought to be on the fake map in front you. You pass the town hall, for instance, and yet according to the map this building is on the other side of town. You'd quickly realise that the map you're using is unreliable, and in all likelihood you'd abandon your belief about where the nearest restaurant was, thereby preventing you from getting there.

In contrast, imagine that you form your belief about where the nearest restaurant is by looking at a reliable map, and thereby *know* where the nearest restaurant is. Since this is genuine knowledge, it would not be undermined in the way that the mere true belief was undermined, and thus you'd retain your true belief. This would mean that you would make it to the restaurant after all, and thereby achieve your goal. Having knowledge can thus be of greater instrumental value than mere true belief since having knowledge rather than mere true belief can make it more likely that one achieves one's goals.

Plato (*c.* 427–*c.* 347 BC)

> Bodily exercise, when compulsory, does no harm to the body; but knowledge which is acquired under compulsion obtains no hold on the mind.
>
> Plato, *The Republic*

Plato is one of the most famous of all philosophers. He lived for most of his life in Athens, in Greece, which is also where he came under the influence of Socrates (470–399 BC). After Socrates' death – an account of which is offered in Plato's book, *The Apology* – Plato founded 'The Academy', a kind of early university in which philosophy, among other subjects, was taught.

Plato's writing was often in the style of a dialogue between Socrates, the mouthpiece of Plato, and an imagined adversary (or adversaries) on topics of vital philosophical importance. In *The Republic*, for example (perhaps his most famous work), he examines the question, central to political philosophy, of what the ideal political state is. Of more interest for our purposes, however, is his book *The Theaetetus*, in which he discusses the nature of knowledge.

• THE STATUES OF DAEDALUS

The previous point picks up on a famous claim made by the ancient Greek philosopher, Plato (*c.* 427–*c.* 347 BC), regarding knowledge. In his book, *The Meno* (see §§96d–100b), Plato compares knowledge to the statues of the ancient Greek sculptor Daedalus which, it is said, were so realistic that if one did not tether them to the ground they would run away. Plato's point is that mere true belief is like one of the untethered statues of Daedalus, in that one could very easily lose it. Knowledge, in contrast, is akin to a tethered statue, one that is therefore not easily lost.

The analogy to our previous discussion should be obvious. Mere true belief, like an untethered statue of Daedalus, is more likely to be lost (i.e., run away) than knowledge, which is far more stable. Put another way, the true belief one holds when one has knowledge is far more likely to remain fast in response to changes in circumstances (e.g., new information that comes to light) than mere true belief, as we saw in the case just described of the person who finds out where the nearest restaurant is by looking at a reliable map, as opposed to one who finds out where it is by looking at a fake map.

Of course, knowledge isn't *completely* stable either, since one could always acquire a false, but plausible piece of information that seems to call one's previous true information into question; but this is less likely to happen when it comes to knowledge than when it comes to true belief. In the example given earlier, suppose that the map is indeed reliable, and thus that you do know where the nearest restaurant is. Nevertheless, there might still be further misleading counter-evidence that you could come across which would undermine this knowledge, such as the testimony of a friend you bump into who tells you (out of mischief) that the map is a fake. In the light of this new information, you'll probably change your belief and so fail to get to the restaurant after all.

Even so, however, the fact remains that knowledge is more stable than mere true belief. In the case just described, for example, the fact that the map had been working so far would give you good grounds to continue trusting it, and so you might naturally be suspicious of any testimony you receive to the contrary. Suppose a perfect stranger told you that the map was a compete fake. Would that lead you to change your belief given that it has been reliable so far? Probably not. A friend's testimony carries more weight than a stranger's, but even this testimony might be ignored if you had reason to think your friend might be playing a trick on you.

If you merely had a true belief about where the nearest restaurant was, in contrast, and had no good reason in support of that true belief, then all kinds of conflicting information would undermine that belief. As we saw, as soon as you start walking on your journey and you notice that none of the landmarks correspond to their locations on the map, then you would be liable to tear the map up in despair, even though the map is, in the one respect that is important to you (how to get to the nearest restaurant), entirely reliable.

There is a good reason why knowledge is more stable than mere true belief, and this is because knowledge, unlike mere true belief, could not easily be mistaken. Imagine, for instance, a doctor diagnoses a patient by (secretly) tossing a coin, thus leading the patient to form a particular belief about what is wrong with her. Suppose further that this diagnosis is, as it happens, correct. Clearly the doctor does not know what is wrong with the patient, even though she happened to get it right on this occasion, and neither does the patient know what is wrong with her given that she acquired her belief by listening to the doctor. The problem here is that it was just a matter of luck that the doctor chanced upon the right answer, and thus it is also a matter of luck that the patient formed a true belief about what was wrong with her. In both cases they could so easily have been wrong.

Compare this scenario, however, with that in which a doctor forms her diagnosis of the patient's illness in a diligent fashion by using the appropriate medical procedures. This doctor will (in most cases at least) end up with the same correct diagnosis as our irresponsible doctor, and thus the patient will again acquire a true belief about the nature of her condition. This time, though, the doctor and the patient will *know* what the correct diagnosis is. Moreover, there is no worry in this case that this verdict could so easily have been mistaken; given that the doctor followed the correct procedures, it is in fact very *unlikely* that this diagnosis is wrong. Here we clearly have a case in which our goal of correctly determining the source of someone's illness is better served by the possession of knowledge rather than the possession of mere true belief because of the instability of mere true belief relative to knowledge (i.e., the fact that mere true belief, unlike knowledge, could so easily be wrong). In this sense, then, knowledge is more valuable to us than true belief alone.

For the most part, then, if one wishes to achieve one's goals it is essential that one has, at the bare minimum, true beliefs about the subject matter concerned. True belief is thus mostly of instrumental value, even if it is not always of instrumental value. Ideally, however, it is better to have knowledge, since mere true belief has an instability that is not always conducive to success in one's projects. Since knowledge entails true belief, we can therefore draw two conclusions. First, that most knowledge, like most mere true belief, is of instrumental value. Second, and crucially, that knowledge is of greater instrumental value than mere true belief.

● IS SOME KNOWLEDGE INTRINSICALLY VALUABLE?

At this point we might wonder whether the value of knowledge is only ever instrumental. That is, we might wonder whether the value of knowledge is *always* dependent upon what further goods, such as gaining relief from your illness, which knowledge (in this case of the correct diagnosis of your illness) can help you attain. Intuitively, this claim is too strong in that there do seem to be certain kinds of knowledge that have a value which is not purely instrumental. Put another way, some kinds of knowledge seem to have an **intrinsic value**.

If something has intrinsic value, then it is valuable *in itself*, regardless of what, for instance, it enables one to do. Friendship is intrinsically valuable, for example. We don't value our friends *because* they are useful to us (though having friends is undoubtedly useful), but simply because they are our friends. If you valued someone just for what they can do for you (help you to make more money, for example), then you wouldn't count as their friend. Put another way, although there is clearly an instrumental value to having friends (they improve our quality of life, for example), the true value of friendship is not instrumental at all, but intrinsic to the friendship itself.

In order to see how knowledge could be intrinsically valuable, think of those types of knowledge which are very refined, such as *wisdom* – the sort of knowledge that wise people have. Wisdom is clearly at least instrumentally valuable since it can enable one to lead a productive and fulfilled life. Crucially, however, it seems that knowledge of this sort would still be valuable even if, as it happens, it *didn't* lead to a life that was good in this way. Suppose, for instance, that nature conspires against you at every turn so that, like the biblical character Job, you are subject to just about every dismal fate that can befall a person. In such a case one's knowledge of most matters may well have no instrumental value at all because one's goals will be frustrated by forces beyond your control regardless of what you know.

Nevertheless, it would surely be preferable to confront such misfortune as a wise person, and not because such wisdom would necessarily make you feel any better or enable you to avoid these disasters (whether wise or not, your life is still wretched). Instead, it seems, being wise is just a good thing, regardless of what further goods it might lead to. That is, it is something that is good *in itself*; something which has intrinsic value. And notice that this claim marks a further difference between knowledge and mere true belief, since it is hard to see how mere true belief could ever be of intrinsic value.

There may be stronger claims that we can make about the value of knowledge, but the minimal claims advanced here suffice to make the study of knowledge important. Recall that we have seen that knowledge is at least for the most part instrumentally valuable in that it enables us to achieve our goals, and that it is more instrumentally valuable in this respect than true belief alone. Moreover, we have also noted that some varieties of knowledge, such as wisdom, seem to be intrinsically valuable. Clearly, then, knowledge is something that we should care about. Given that this is so, it is incumbent upon us as philosophers to be able to say more about what knowledge is and the various ways in which we might acquire it. These are the goals of epistemology.

• CHAPTER SUMMARY

- One of the central tasks of epistemology is to explain the value of knowledge. But while it is obvious that we do value knowledge, it is not obvious why this is the case, nor what the nature of this value is.

- One way of accounting for the value of knowledge is to note that if you know a proposition, then you have a true belief in that proposition, and true beliefs are clearly useful, and therefore valuable. In particular, true belief has instrumental value in that it enables you to achieve your goals.
- One problem with this proposal is that it is not obvious that *all* true beliefs are instrumentally valuable. For one thing, some true beliefs are so trivial that it seems that they have no value at all. For another, sometimes it is more useful to have a false belief than a true belief.
- Moreover, even if one could evade this problem, another difficulty would remain, which is that, intuitively, knowledge is *more* valuable than mere true belief. If this intuition is right, then we need to say more than simply that knowledge entails true belief and that true belief is instrumentally valuable.
- One option is to say that knowledge is of greater instrumental value than mere true belief, since it is more useful to us (it enables us to achieve more of our goals than mere true belief alone). Part of the explanation one might offer for this could be that there is a 'stability' to knowledge which is lacking in mere true belief in that in knowing that something is the case one couldn't have easily been wrong.
- We also explored another suggestion, which was that *some* knowledge is of intrinsic value – i.e., is valuable in its own right. The example we gave here was that of *wisdom*. The idea, then, is that while knowledge is generally of greater instrumental value than mere true belief, some knowledge is also, in addition, intrinsically valuable (unlike mere true belief, which is never intrinsically valuable).

● STUDY QUESTIONS

1 What does it mean to say that something has instrumental value? Explain your answer by offering two examples of your own of something that is instrumentally valuable.
2 Is true belief always instrumentally valuable? Evaluate the arguments for and against this claim, paying attention to such issues as the fact that sometimes false beliefs can be useful (as in the case of the person trying to jump a ravine), and that true beliefs can sometimes be entirely trivial (as in the case of the person who measures grains of sand).
3 Is knowledge of *greater* instrumental value than mere true belief, insofar as the latter is indeed generally instrumentally valuable? Consider some cases in which one person has a mere true belief while someone else in a relevantly similar situation has knowledge. Is it true to say that the latter person's knowledge is of more instrumental value than the former person's mere true belief?
4 What does it mean to say that something has intrinsic value? Explain your answer by offering two examples of your own of things that are intrinsically valuable.
5 Is knowledge *ever* intrinsically valuable? Evaluate this question by considering some plausible candidates for intrinsically valuable knowledge, such as the knowledge possessed by the wise person.

• INTRODUCTORY FURTHER READING

Annas, Julia (2002) *Plato: A Very Short Introduction* (Oxford: Oxford University Press). This is a succinct and very readable introduction to Plato's philosophy.

Greco, John (2009) 'Epistemic Value', *The Routledge Companion to Epistemology*, (eds.) S. Bernecker & D. H. Pritchard, (New York: Routledge). An accessible and completely up-to-date survey of the main issues as regards epistemic value.

Schofield, Malcolm (2002) 'Plato (427–347 BC)', *Routledge Encyclopedia of Philosophy*, (ed.) E. Craig, (London: Routledge), <http://www.rep.routledge.com/article/A088?ssid=873935527&n=1#>. A comprehensive and readable overview of Plato's life and philosophical works.

Thomas, Alan (1998) 'Values', *Routledge Encyclopedia of Philosophy*, (ed.) E. Craig, (London: Routledge), <http://www.rep.routledge.com/article/L110?ssid=798722269&n=4#>. A very neat overview of some of the main views in the philosophy of value. Quite hard going in places, but just accessible enough to count as 'introductory' further reading.

• ADVANCED FURTHER READING

Haddock, Adrian, Millar, Alan & Pritchard, Duncan (2009) *The Nature and Value of Knowledge: Three Investigations* (Oxford: Oxford University Press). The most up-to-date contribution to the debate about the value of knowledge. Note that it is quite demanding.

Kvanvig, Jonathan (2003) *The Value of Knowledge and Pursuit of Understanding* (Cambridge: Cambridge University Press). This is the most recent, and comprehensive, discussion of the value of knowledge.

Zagzebski, Linda (1996) *Virtues of the Mind: An Inquiry into the Nature of Virtue and the Ethical Foundations of Knowledge* (Cambridge: Cambridge University Press). A clear, challenging and historically orientated account of knowledge which pays particular attention to the issue of the value of knowledge, including those types of knowledge, like wisdom, that might plausibly be regarded as intrinsically valuable.

• FREE INTERNET RESOURCES

Chappell, Tim (2005) 'Plato on Knowledge in *The Theaetetus*', *Stanford Encyclopedia of Philosophy*, <http://www.seop.leeds.ac.uk/entries/plato-theaetetus/>. An excellent overview of Plato's view of knowledge, as expressed in his book, *The Theaetetus*.

Epistemic Value <http://epistemicvaluestirling.blogspot.com/>. This is a weblog devoted entirely to discussion of issues associated with the value of knowledge.

Kraut, Richard (2004) 'Plato', *Stanford Encyclopedia of Philosophy*, <http://www.seop.leeds.ac.uk/entries/plato/>. A very good overview of the life and works of Plato.

Perseus Archive (Tufts University) <http://www.perseus.tufts.edu/cache/perscoll_Greco-Roman.html#text1>. This is a fairly comprehensive archive of ancient Greek and Roman texts, including the works of Plato.

Pritchard, Duncan (2007) 'The Value of Knowledge', *Stanford Encyclopedia of Philosophy*, <http://plato.stanford.edu/entries/knowledge-value/>. A very up-to-date and thorough overview of the debate regarding the value of knowledge.

Schroeder, Mark (2008) 'Value Theory', *Stanford Encyclopedia of Philosophy*, <http://plato.stanford.edu/entries/value-theory/>. A comprehensive and completely up-to-date survey of the main philosophical issues as regards value.

Zimmerman, Michael (2004) 'Intrinsic Versus Extrinsic Value', *Stanford Encyclopedia of Philosophy*, <http://plato.stanford.edu/entries/value-intrinsic-extrinsic/>. A great survey of the literature on intrinsic and non-intrinsic (e.g., instrumental) value.

3
defining knowledge

- The problem of the criterion
- Methodism and particularism
- Knowledge as justified true belief
- Gettier cases
- Responding to the Gettier cases
- Back to the problem of the criterion

THE PROBLEM OF THE CRITERION

Anyone who wishes to offer a definition of knowledge – who wishes to say what knowledge *is* – faces an immediate problem, which is how to begin. Now it might seem as if the answer here is obvious, in that one should start simply by looking at the cases in which one has knowledge and considering what is common to each case. So, for example, one might think of such paradigm cases of knowledge acquisition as the scientist who, upon conducting her experiments, correctly determines the chemical structure of the substance before her, or the 'star' witness in the murder trial who knows that the defendant is guilty of the murder because she saw him do it in clear daylight. The thought is that all one needs to do is determine what is common to each of these paradigm cases and one will be well on one's way to discerning what knowledge is.

The problem with this suggestion, however, is that if one doesn't already know what knowledge is (i.e., what the defining characteristics, or *criteria*, of knowledge are), how can one correctly identify cases of knowledge in the first place? After all, one cannot simply assume that one knows what the criteria for knowledge are without thereby taking a definition of knowledge for granted from the outset. But, equally, neither is it plausible to suppose that we can correctly identify instances of knowledge without assuming knowledge of such criteria, since without a prior grasp of these criteria how are we supposed to tell what is a genuine case of knowledge and what isn't?

This difficulty regarding defining knowledge is known as the **problem of the criterion**, and it dates right back to antiquity. We can roughly summarise the problem in terms of the following two claims:

1 I can only identify instances of knowledge provided I already know what the criteria for knowledge are.

2 I can only know what the criteria for knowledge are provided I am already able to identify instances of knowledge.

We thus seem to be trapped inside a very small circle of unpleasant options. I must either assume that I can independently know what the criteria for knowledge are in order to identify instances of knowledge, or else I must assume that I can identify instances of knowledge in order to determine what the criteria for knowledge are. Either way, the dubious nature of the assumption in question appears to call the legitimacy of the epistemological project of defining knowledge into dispute.

Roderick Chisholm (1916–99)

We start with particular cases of knowledge and then from those we generalise and formulate criteria [which tell] us what it is for a belief to be epistemologically respectable.

Chisholm, *The Foundations of Knowing*

The American philosopher Roderick Chisholm was without doubt the most influential epistemologist of the second half of the twentieth century. A good deal of his influence is due to his best-selling textbook on epistemology, *Theory of Knowledge*, which was first published in 1966 (a third edition came out in 1989) and which quickly became a standard text in this area throughout the world. His influence is also felt through his students – such as Keith Lehrer and Ernest Sosa – who have gone on to become very prominent philosophers in their own right.

Central to Chisholm's contribution to epistemology is a commitment to epistemic internalism and a version of classical foundationalism. In addition, he published important work in epistemology on such areas as the problem of the criterion and the epistemology of perception. Chisholm also made significant contributions to other areas of philosophy, such as metaphysics and ethics.

● METHODISM AND PARTICULARISM

Although the problem of the criterion dates right back to antiquity, the contemporary focus on it is due almost entirely to the work done on this problem by the American philosopher **Roderick Chisholm** (1916–99). As he noted, historically, philosophers have tended to begin by assuming that they already know – or at least are able to identify through philosophical reflection alone – what the criteria for knowledge are, and have proceeded on this basis to examine the issue of whether or not we have any knowledge. Chisholm calls such a stance **methodism**, and cites as a famous example of a methodist the French philosopher **René Descartes** (1596–1650), whom we will hear more about in the next chapter.

In contrast to methodism, Chisholm argues that we should grip the other horn of the dilemma and adopt a position that he calls **particularism**. According to particularism, rather than assuming that one can identify the criteria for knowledge independently of examining any particular instances of knowledge, one should instead assume that one can correctly identify particular instances of knowledge and proceed on this basis to determine what the criteria for knowledge are.

There is much to be said both for and against these two positions. One of the main advantages of methodism is that it doesn't begin by assuming the falsity of **scepticism** (i.e., the worry that we might not know anything much at all), since it leaves it an open question whether there is anything that meets the criteria for knowledge. The big problem facing the view, however, is that it just seems plain mysterious how we are to get a grip on the criteria for knowledge without appealing to particular instances of knowledge.

Persuaded by this sort of objection to methodism, most epistemologists have followed Chisholm in opting for particularism instead. In favour of particularism is the thought that if one has to assume anything in this regard (as seemingly we must, given the problem of the criterion), it is far less extravagant to suppose that we can correctly identify particular cases of knowledge independently of any prior awareness of what the criteria for knowledge are than to suppose that we can identify what the criteria for knowledge are without prior appeal to cases of knowledge. Unsurprisingly, those sympathetic to scepticism will baulk at the particularist methodology since they will argue that the claim that we do indeed possess knowledge is something that has to be *shown*, not assumed.

Notice that the problem of the criterion might not be so pressing if the criteria for knowledge were entirely obvious, since if they were, then the assumption – key to methodism – that we can know what the criteria for knowledge are independently of examining any particular instances of knowledge (by simply reflecting on the concept of knowledge, say), would not be nearly so implausible. The difficulty, however, is that reflection itself indicates that there is no simple account of the criteria for knowledge available.

For example, we saw in Chapter 1 that it is certainly the case that if one is to know a proposition, then one had better have a true belief in that proposition. If knowledge required only true belief, then we might be entitled to think that so obvious a set of criteria for knowledge could be determined without making use of any putative instances of knowledge (though note that we have already begun to illicitly bring examples into our discussion, so this claim is far from uncontentious). In this way, we might be able to weaken the force of the problem of the criterion.

The problem, however, as we also saw in Chapter 1, is that knowledge demands much more than mere true belief. Moreover, as we will now see, specifying just what it demands in this regard is notoriously difficult. Accordingly, even if this strategy of claiming that the criteria for knowledge are manifest could work in principle (which is far from obvious), it won't work in practice for the simple reason that the criteria for knowledge are manifestly *not* manifest at all.

KNOWLEDGE AS JUSTIFIED TRUE BELIEF

We noted in Chapter 1 that knowledge cannot just be true belief since one can, for example, gain a true belief in all manner of bizarre and inappropriate ways, and in such cases one would not think that one had knowledge. Think again about our gambler from Chapter 1, Harry, who forms his belief about which horse will win the race by considering which horse's name most appeals to him. Even if the horse does go on to win the race, so that Harry's belief is true, he clearly did not know that this would happen.

So it seems that there must be more to knowledge than just true belief. But what could this additional component be? The natural answer to this question, one that is often ascribed to Plato, is that what is needed is a *justification* for one's belief, some good reasons or grounds for believing what one does. Back in Chapter 1, we contrasted Harry with a 'Mr Big' who bases his belief that Lucky Lass will win on excellent grounds, for he has fixed the race by drugging the other horses. That justification is the missing ingredient in our account of knowledge certainly seems to accord with the cases of Harry and Mr Big, since what the former lacks, but the latter possesses, is the ability to offer good reasons in favour of his belief, and this is just what being justified intuitively involves. It is thus plausible to contend that knowledge is simply justified true belief and, whilst this isn't as straightforward an analysis as one which held that knowledge is merely true belief, it is fairly simple. Perhaps we could determine that these were the criteria for knowledge by reflection alone without difficulty.

GETTIER CASES

Unfortunately, matters are not nearly so straightforward. The reason for this is that this three-part, or *tripartite*, theory of knowledge has itself been shown to be completely untenable. The person who illustrated this was a philosopher named Edmund Gettier who, in a three-page article, offered a devastating set of counter-examples to the tripartite account: what are now known as **Gettier cases**. In essence, what Gettier showed was that you could have a justified true belief and yet still lack knowledge of what you believe because your true belief was ultimately gained via luck in much the same way as Harry's belief was gained by luck.

Gettier's amazing article

The tale behind Edmund Gettier's famous article on why the classical three-part, or *tripartite*, account of knowledge is unsustainable is now part of philosophical folklore. So the story goes, Edmund Gettier was a young American philosopher who knew that he needed to get some publications under his belt if he was to get tenure in his job (in the US, junior academic appointments are usually provisional on the person publishing their research in suitably high-profile journals). Spurred on by this consideration, he looked around for something to write about, something which was interesting, publishable, and, most of all, something which could be written-up very quickly.

While it is said that he had no real interest in epistemology at that time (and, as we will see, he has shown little interest since), he was struck by the prevalence of the justified-true-belief account of knowledge in the literature, and believed it to be fatally defective. In a quick spurt of activity, he wrote a short three-page article outlining his objection to the view, and sent it to the highly regarded philosophy journal *Analysis*, which specialises in short papers of this sort. It was duly published in 1963 and created quite a storm.

Initially, there was a number of responses from philosophers who felt that the problem that Gettier had highlighted for the tripartite account could be easily resolved with a mere tweak of the view. Very soon, however, it became apparent that such easy 'fixes' did not work, and quickly a whole industry of papers on the 'Gettier problem', as it was now known, came into being.

The most incredible part of this story, however, is that Gettier, having written one of the most famous articles in contemporary philosophy, never engaged at all with the vast literature that his short paper prompted. Indeed, he never published anything else in epistemology. The paper he'd written had gained him the tenure that he wanted, and that, it seems, was enough for him as far as publishing in epistemology was concerned.

Gettier is presently Professor Emeritus in Philosophy at the University of Massachusetts, USA.

We will use a different example from the ones cited by Gettier, though one that has the same general structure. Imagine a man, let's call him John, who comes downstairs one morning and sees that the time on the grandfather clock in the hall says '8.20'. On this basis John comes to believe that it is 8.20 a.m., and this belief is true, since it *is* 8.20 a.m. Moreover, John's belief is justified in that it is based on excellent grounds. For example, John usually comes downstairs in the morning about this time, so he knows that the time is about right. Moreover, this clock has been very reliable at telling the time for many years and John has no reason to think that it is faulty now. He thus has good reasons for thinking that the time on the clock is correct.

Suppose, however, that the clock had, unbeknownst to him, stopped 24 hours earlier, so that John is now forming his justified true belief by looking at a stopped clock. Intuitively, if this were so then John would lack knowledge even though he has met the conditions laid down by the tripartite account. After all, that John has a true belief in this case is, ultimately, a matter of luck, just like Harry's belief that Lucky Lass would win the 4.20 at Kempton.

If John had come downstairs a moment earlier or a moment later – or if the clock had stopped at a slightly different time – then he would have formed a false belief about the time by looking at this clock. Thus we can conclude that knowledge is not simply justified true belief.

There is a general form to all Gettier cases, and once we know this we can use it to construct an unlimited number of them. To begin with, we need to note that you can have a justified false belief, since this is crucial to the Gettier cases. For example, suppose you formed a false belief by looking at a clock that you had no reason for thinking wasn't working properly but which was, in fact, and unbeknownst to you, not working properly. This belief would clearly be justified, even though it is false. With this point in mind, there are three stages to constructing your own Gettier case.

First, you take an agent who forms her belief in a way that would usually lead her to have a false belief. In the example above, we took the case of someone looking at a stopped clock in order to find out the time. Clearly, using a stopped clock to find out the time would usually result in a false belief.

Second, you add some detail to the example to ensure that the agent's belief is justified nonetheless. In the example above, the detail we added was that the agent had no reason for thinking that the clock wasn't working properly (the clock is normally reliable, is showing what appears to be the right time, and so on), thus ensuring that her belief is entirely justified.

Finally, you make the case such that while the way in which the agent formed her belief would normally have resulted in a justified false belief, in this case it so happened that the belief was true. In the stopped clock case, this is done by stipulating that the stopped clock just happens to be 'telling' the right time.

Putting all this together, we can construct an entirely new Gettier case from scratch. As an example of someone forming a belief in a way that would normally result in a false belief, let's take someone who forms her belief that Madonna is across the street by looking at a life-sized cardboard cut-out of Madonna which is advertising her forthcoming tour, and which is posted just across the street. Forming one's belief about whether someone is across the street by looking at a life-sized cut-out of that person would not normally result in a true belief. Next, we add some detail to the example to ensure that the belief is justified. In this case we can just stipulate that the cut-out is very authentic-looking, and that there is nothing about it which would obviously give away the fact that it is a cardboard cut-out – it does not depict Madonna in an outrageous costume that she wouldn't plausibly wear on a normal street, for example. The agent's belief is thus justified. Finally, we make the scenario such that the belief is true. In this case, for instance, all we need to do is stipulate that, as it happens, Madonna *is* across the street, doing some window shopping out of view of our agent. *Voilà*, we have constructed our very own Gettier case!

• RESPONDING TO THE GETTIER CASES

There is no easy way to respond to the Gettier cases, and since Gettier's article back in 1963, a plethora of different theories of knowledge have been developed in order to offer an account of knowledge that is Gettier-proof. Initially, it was thought that all one needed to do to deal with these cases is simply tweak the tripartite account of knowledge. For example, one proposal was that in order to have knowledge, one's true belief must be justified and also not in any way based on false presuppositions, such as, in the case of John just described, the false presupposition that the clock is working and not stopped. There is a pretty devastating problem with this sort of proposal, however, which is that it is difficult to spell out this idea of a 'presupposition' such that it is strong enough to deal with Gettier cases and yet not so strong that it prevents us from having most of the knowledge that we think we have.

For example, suppose that John has a sister across town – let's call her Sally – who is in fact at this moment finding out what the time is by looking at a working clock. Intuitively, Sally *does* gain knowledge of what the time is by looking at the time on the clock. Notice, however, that Sally may believe all sorts of other related propositions, some of which may be false – for example, she may believe that the clock is regularly maintained, when in fact no one is taking care of it. Is this belief a presupposition of her belief in what the time is? If it is (i.e., if we understand the notion of a 'presupposition' liberally) then this false presupposition will prevent her from having knowledge of the time, even though we would normally think that looking at a reliable working clock is a great way of coming to know what the time is.

Alternatively, suppose we understand the notion of a 'presupposition' in a more restrictive way such that this belief isn't a presupposition of Sally's belief in the time. The problem now is to explain why John's false belief that he's looking at a working clock counts as a presupposition of his belief in the time (and so prevents him from counting as knowing what the time is) if Sally's false belief that the clock is regularly maintained is not also treated as a presupposition. Why don't they *both* lack knowledge of what the time is?

If this problem weren't bad enough, there is also a second objection to this line of response to the Gettier cases, which is that it is not clear that the agent in a Gettier case need presuppose *anything* at all. Consider a different Gettier case in this regard, due to Chisholm. In this example, we have a farmer – let's call her Gayle – who forms her belief that there is a sheep in the field by looking at a shaggy dog which happens to look just like a sheep. As it turns out, however, there *is* a sheep in the field (standing behind the dog), and hence Gayle's belief is true. Moreover, her belief is also justified because she has great evidence for thinking that there is a sheep in the field (she can see what looks to be a sheep in the field, for example).

Given the immediacy of Gayle's belief in this case, however, it is hard to see that it really presupposes any further beliefs at all, at least unless we are to understand the notion of a presupposition *very* liberally. And notice that if we do understand the notion of a presupposition so liberally that Gayle counts as illicitly making a presupposition, the problem then re-emerges of how to account for apparently genuine cases of knowledge, such as that intuitively possessed by Sally.

The dilemma for proponents of this sort of response to the Gettier cases is thus to explain how we should understand the notion of a presupposition broadly enough so that it applies to the Gettier cases while at the same time understanding it narrowly enough so that it doesn't apply to other non-Gettier cases in which, intuitively, we would regard the agent concerned as having knowledge. In short, we want a response to the problem which explains why John lacks knowledge in such a way that it doesn't thereby deprive Sally of knowledge.

Once it was recognised that there was no easy answer to the problem posed to the tripartite account of knowledge by the Gettier cases, the race was on to find a radically new way of analysing knowledge which was Gettier-proof. We will consider some of these proposals below. One feature that they all share is that they understand the conditions for knowledge such that they demand more in the way of co-operation from the world than simply that the belief in question is true. That is, on the traditional tripartite account of knowledge there is one condition which relates to the world – the truth condition – and two conditions that relate to us as agents – the belief and justification conditions. These last two conditions, at least as they are usually under-stood in any case, don't demand anything from the world in the sense that they could obtain regardless of how the world is. If I were the victim of an hallucination, for example, then I might have a whole range of wholly deceptive experiences, experi-ences which, nonetheless, lead me to believe something and, moreover, to justifiably believe it. (For example, if I seem to see that, say, there is a glass in front of me, then this is surely a good, and thus justifying, reason for believing that there is a glass in front of me, even if the appearance of the glass is an illusion.) The moral of the Gettier cases is, however, that you need to demand more from the world than simply that one's justified belief is true if you are to have knowledge.

In the stopped-clock Gettier case, for example, the problem came about because, although John had excellent grounds for believing what he did, it nevertheless remained that he did not know what he believed because of some oddity in the world – in this case that the normally reliable clock had not only stopped but had stopped in such a way that John still formed a true belief. It thus appears that we need an account of knowledge which imposes a further requirement on the world over and above the truth of the target belief – that, for example, the agent is, *in fact*, forming his belief in the right kind of way. We will return to this issue later on (see especially Chapter 6).

BACK TO THE PROBLEM OF THE CRITERION

So where does this leave us as regards the problem of the criterion that we started with? One thing that is certain is that the criteria for knowledge are far from obvious, and this calls into question the idea that we could determine such criteria without making reference to actual cases of knowledge. This conclusion is, however, double-edged in that if it really is the case that knowledge is such a complicated notion, then how can it be that we are able to identify cases of knowledge correctly even whilst lacking a prior grasp of what the criteria for knowledge are? Right from the start of the epistemological project, then, we are faced with a deep and seemingly intractable puzzle, one that appears to undermine our prospects for making any progress in this area.

CHAPTER SUMMARY

- One of the central tasks in epistemology is to offer a definition of knowledge. The problem of the criterion, however, shows us that this task is in fact very difficult, if not impossible.
- Here, in a nutshell, is the problem of the criterion. Suppose we begin the task of defining knowledge by pointing to cases in which we have knowledge and trying to identify what is common to each case. The problem with this suggestion is that it assumes that we can already identify cases of knowledge, and thus that we already know what the marks, or *criteria*, of knowledge are. Alternatively, we might begin the task of defining knowledge by simply reflecting on the nature of knowledge, and determine its essence that way. That is, through reflection we might determine what the criteria for knowledge are. The problem with this suggestion, however, is that it is difficult to see how we could possibly identify the criteria for knowledge without first being able to identify particular cases of knowledge. It seems, then, that either one must assume that one has (at least some of) the knowledge that one thinks one has, or else one must assume that one knows, independently of considering any particular instance of knowledge, what the criteria for knowledge are. Neither assumption is particularly plausible.
- But perhaps the criteria for knowledge are very simple, so simple that we can plausibly tell by reflection that they obtain without considering particular cases of knowledge? It's not clear that the simplicity of the criteria could help us to resolve this problem, but even granting that it does, we saw that there were a number of problems with this suggestion. We considered two proposals in this respect. First, that knowledge is just true belief, a proposal which is undermined by cases of lucky true belief which clearly aren't knowledge. Second, that knowledge is justified true

belief, a proposal which we saw is undermined by Gettier cases. Either way, there is no plausible and yet simple analysis of knowledge.

- Gettier cases are cases in which one forms a true justified belief and yet lacks knowledge because the truth of the belief is largely a matter of luck. (The example we gave of this was that of someone forming a true belief about what the time is by looking at a stopped clock which just so happens to be displaying the right time.) Gettier cases show that the three-part, or tripartite, account of knowledge in terms of justified true belief is unsustainable.
- There is no easy answer to the Gettier cases; no simple way of supplementing the tripartite account of knowledge so that it can deal with these cases. Instead, a radically new way of understanding knowledge is required, one that demands greater co-operation on the part of the world than simply that the belief in question be true.

● STUDY QUESTIONS

1 Check that you understand the problem of the criterion. In order to get clear in your own mind exactly what the problem is, try to formulate this problem in your own words – have a go at offering a definition of knowledge without appealing either to instances of knowledge or to the presupposition that you already know what the criteria for knowledge are.

2 Explain in your own words the distinction between methodism and particularism. For each position, offer one reason in favour of the view and one against.

3 Explain, in your own words, why the criteria for knowledge are not obvious.

4 What is a Gettier case, and what do such cases show? Try to formulate a Gettier case of your own.

5 In what way might it be said that the problem with Gettier cases is that they involve a justified true belief which is based on a false presupposition? Explain, with an example, why one cannot straightforwardly deal with the Gettier cases by advancing a theory of knowledge which demands justified true belief that does not rest on any false presuppositions.

● INTRODUCTORY FURTHER READING

Gettier, Edmund (1963) 'Is Justified True Belief Knowledge?', *Analysis* 23, 121–3. The article which started the contemporary debate about how best to define knowledge and which contains, by definition, the first official Gettier cases. Very easy to read.

Hetherington, Stephen (2009) 'The Gettier Problem', *The Routledge Companion to Epistemology*, (eds.) S. Bernecker & D. H. Pritchard, (New York: Routledge). A very useful and completely up-to-date survey of the main issues raised by Gettier-style examples.

Shope, Robert K. (2002) 'Conditions and Analyses of Knowing', *The Oxford Handbook to Epistemology*, (ed.) P. K. Moser, pp. 25–70, (Oxford: Oxford University Press). A comprehensive treatment of the problem posed by Gettier cases and the various contemporary responses to that problem in the literature. The discussion that starts on page 29 is most relevant to this chapter. Note that as this chapter develops it becomes increasingly more demanding.

• ADVANCED FURTHER READING

Chisholm, Roderick (1973) *The Problem of the Criterion* (Milwaukee, Wis.: Marquette University Press). This is the classic discussion of the problem of the criterion of (relatively) recent times.

Shope, Robert K. (1983) *The Analysis of Knowing A Decade of Research* (Princeton, N.J.: Princeton University Press). A comprehensive survey of the initial wave of responses that were offered to the Gettier cases. Not for beginners.

Zagzebski, Linda (1999) 'What is Knowledge?', *The Blackwell Companion to Epistemology*, (eds.) J. Greco and E. Sosa, pp. 92–116 (Oxford: Blackwell). A very thorough overview of the issues surrounding the project of defining knowledge, especially in the light of the Gettier cases.

• FREE INTERNET RESOURCES

'Edmund Gettier', *Wikipedia*, <http://en.wikipedia.org/wiki/Edmund_Gettier>. A short biographical sketch of the man who formulated the famous Gettier cases. This entry also includes a short (and, be warned, not altogether reliable) overview of the Gettier problem, as it is known, and some of the post-Gettier literature.

'Epistemology', *Wikipedia*, <http://en.wikipedia.org/wiki/Epistemology>. A very good introduction to the main topics in epistemology which also covers issues to do with the definition of knowledge. It also has an excellent list of further internet resources.

Hetherington, Stephen (2005) 'Gettier Problems', *Internet Encyclopedia of Philosophy*, <http://www.iep.utm.edu/g/gettier.htm>. An excellent overview of the Gettier problem, and the main responses to it, by one of the leading epistemologists.

'Roderick Chisholm', *Wikipedia*, <http://en.wikipedia.org/wiki/Roderick_Chisholm>. A nice short biographical sketch of the philosopher Roderick Chisholm.

Steup, Matthias (2005) 'The Analysis of Knowledge', *Stanford Encyclopedia of Philosophy*, <http://plato.stanford.edu/entries/knowledge-analysis/>. An excellent and comprehensive overview of the issues regarding the project of defining knowledge.

Truncellito, David (2007) 'Epistemology', *Internet Encyclopedia of Philosophy*, <http://www.iep.utm.edu/e/epistemo.htm>. Read up to the end of §2.b for more on the basic requirements for knowledge.

4
the structure of knowledge

- Knowledge and justification
- The enigmatic nature of justification
- Agrippa's trilemma
- Infinitism
- Coherentism
- Foundationalism

KNOWLEDGE AND JUSTIFICATION

Pick a belief that you hold, a belief the truth of which you are about as certain of as anything else you believe. Take, for example, your belief that the earth orbits the sun, rather than vice versa. If you are certain about this matter then, intuitively, you must regard this belief as being rightly held, as being *justified*. Now ask yourself the following question: what is it that justifies this belief?

This question is vital to the theory of knowledge since, as we saw in Chapter 3, even though Gettier cases show that justification is not sufficient (with true belief) for knowledge, it is at least plausible to suppose that justification is *necessary* for knowledge. Accordingly, understanding what constitutes justification is essential to understanding what constitutes knowledge. As we will see, however, it is very hard to specify the nature of justification.

THE ENIGMATIC NATURE OF JUSTIFICATION

One possible answer to this question of what justifies your belief that the earth orbits the sun could be that *nothing* justifies it; that this belief does not need further support in order to be rightly held. However, as far as most beliefs are concerned (if not all of them), this possibility is not very plausible.

Think of one's belief as being like a house. If a house lacks foundations, then it falls down. The same applies to a belief. If it lacks a solid foundation – if there is nothing that is justifying this belief – then the belief is not properly held, and so 'falls down'. After all, if one can rightly hold a belief without that belief being supported by good grounds of any sort, then that seems to preclude us from making any epistemic distinction between the beliefs of rational and irrational agents.

For example, one could imagine a child forming a belief that the moon is a balloon on no particular basis whatsoever. If we are to regard our belief that the earth orbits the sun as unsupported by further grounds, then this puts it on par with this child's belief about the earth. Surely, however, our belief is justified in a way that the child's belief is not. And note that the difference here cannot be simply that our belief that the earth orbits the sun is true since, as we noted in Chapter 3, a belief does not have to be true to be justified. Those living a thousand years ago, before it was widely known that the earth went around the sun, were surely justified in believing that the sun orbited the earth.

So it seems that, at least in the vast majority of cases, there must be some sort of support that can be offered in favour of one's belief; some sort of supporting ground or reason. In the case of one's belief that the earth goes around the sun, one possible supporting reason that might be offered in favour of this belief could be that one read that this is so in a science textbook, one that was written by an expert in the field. In effect, what one is doing here is supporting one's belief that the earth goes around the sun by offering one's further belief that this claim can be found in a reliable textbook.

The problem with supporting one's beliefs by offering further beliefs, however, is that it invites the question of what grounds these 'supporting' beliefs. Since we have already rejected the possibility that our beliefs can, in the main at least, be justified whilst being groundless, this means that we must offer further support for the supporting beliefs. Moreover, insofar as we grant that it is these supporting beliefs that are in some way justifying the original belief, then if we are unable to offer adequate grounds to back up the supporting beliefs then neither the supporting beliefs *nor* the original belief are justified. If I believe that the earth goes around the sun because that's what science textbooks tell me, but I have no good reason for believing what science textbooks tell me, then I can hardly consider my belief that the earth goes around the sun to be adequately supported. The trouble is, of course, whatever grounds I offer in favour of my belief that I can trust what science textbooks tell me will be itself a further belief that stands in need of support, and so a regress looms. Once one starts offering grounds in favour of one's belief, one seems doomed to continue offering further grounds endlessly on pain of failing to offer any adequate support for the original belief.

In order to see this point more clearly, think again of the analogy with the house. We noted above that a house that lacks any foundations will fall down. But a house that has a foundation which is supported by a further foundation, and a further foundation, and a further foundation, and so on indefinitely, will be no better off. Unless there is something holding the whole structure up, then having a limitless series of foundations will do nothing to stop the building tumbling to the floor.

In real life, of course, we will be unable to offer new grounds in favour of our beliefs beyond a certain point. Instead, we will start to return to claims that have already been entered. What justifies you in believing that the earth orbits the sun? Because that's what science textbooks tell you. What justifies you in believing what science textbooks tell you? Because, back in school, your science teacher assured you that they were good sources of information of this sort. What justifies you in trusting what your science teacher told you? Because what she said tallied with what is printed in science textbooks. Here we have a chain of justification that has eventually come full circle in that a supporting reason – regarding the reliability of science textbooks – offered earlier is reappearing further down the chain of justification. But a circular justification is hardly much of a justification.

Think again of the analogy with the house. If the foundations for that house rest on further foundations which ultimately rest in turn on the original foundations, then the house won't have a chance of standing for long. *Something* needs to be holding everything up, and as matters stand nothing is doing this job at all!

• AGRIPPA'S TRILEMMA

We thus seem to be faced with three unpalatable alternatives regarding how we answer the question of what justifies our beliefs. These alternatives are as follows:

1 our beliefs are unsupported; or
2 our beliefs are supported by an infinite chain of justification (i.e., one in which no supporting ground appears more than once); or
3 our beliefs are supported by a circular chain of justification (i.e., one in which a supporting ground appears more than once).

All of these alternatives are unpalatable since they all seem to imply that we aren't really justified in holding our original belief. Just as a house with no foundations, or with an unending chain of foundations, or with circular foundations, would not be well-supported – it would simply fall down – so a belief with no foundations (i.e., option 1), or with an unending chain of foundations (i.e., option 2), or with circular foundations (i.e., option 3), would not be well-supported, and thus, intuitively, would not be justified.

This problem regarding the structure of justification is known as **Agrippa's trilemma**, named after the ancient Greek philosopher **Agrippa**. A *trilemma* is like a dilemma except that it forces you to choose from *three* unpalatable options rather than just two. What is useful about this puzzle is that it enables us to focus our attentions on the different ways in which knowledge might be structured if it is to avoid the trilemma. Three particular kinds of epistemological theory suggest themselves.

• INFINITISM

The least plausible (and thus historically less popular) response to Agrippa's trilemma involves embracing option 2 and holding that an infinite chain of justification *can* justify a belief. This position is known as **infinitism**. On the face of it, the view is unsustainable because it is unclear how an infinite chain of grounds could ever justify a belief any more than an infinite series of foundations could ever support a house. Nevertheless, this view does have some defenders, and those who advance this thesis argue that aside from brute counter-intuition, it isn't obvious why an infinite chain of grounds can't justify.

Agrippa (*c.* AD 100)

> The [Pyrrhonian] sceptic, being a lover of his kind, desires to cure by speech, as best he can, the self-conceit and rashness of the dogmatists.
> Sextus Empiricus, *Outlines of Pyrrhonism*

Agrippa belongs to a group of ancient Greek philosophers who are known as Pyrrhonian sceptics. Very little is known about him because, in common with other Pyrrhonian sceptics, he doesn't seem to have written anything himself. In essence, the reason for this is that such philosophers don't think that you should ever assert anything, and so they certainly don't think that you should write down what your philosophical views are for posterity. Indeed, all we really know about Agrippa relates to the trilemma that was attributed to him by the ancient Greek historian Diogenes Laertius (*c.* AD 250) in his history of Greek philosophy. In this work, as in the other main source for our knowledge of the Pyrrhonian sceptics – *Outlines of Pyrrhonism*, by Sextus Empiricus (*c.* AD 200) – the Agrippan sceptical strategy was actually expressed in terms of *five* sceptical strategies which are designed to induce doubt. Since it is three of these strategies which pose the main sceptical threat, however, Agrippa's sceptical challenge was soon understood in terms of them alone, and thus we get Agrippa's trilemma as it is described here.

For reasons of space, we won't dwell on this view here, however, but focus instead on the two theories about the structure of justification, and thus knowledge, which have been historically more popular (see the further readings at the end of this chapter for a recent defence of infinitism).

• COHERENTISM

A more plausible (and more popular) response to Agrippa's trilemma takes on option 3 and holds that a circular chain of supporting grounds *can* justify a belief. This view, known as **coherentism**, is usually supplemented with the proviso that the circle of justification needs to be sufficiently large if it is to play this supporting role, so the position accepts that small circles of justification won't do. Still, it is hard to reconcile coherentism with the simple-minded thought that a circular chain of justification, no matter how large, offers no support to a belief at all.

W. V. O. Quine (1908–2000)

No statement is immune to revision.

Quine, 'Two Dogmas of Empiricism'

The American philosopher, **Willard Van Orman Quine**, was without doubt one of the towering figures of twentieth-century philosophy. One of the guiding themes of Quine's work was a rejection of what is known as 'first' philosophy (*see* **Descartes**), where this is understood as a standpoint which is prior to, and completely independent of, scientific investigation and from which science can be evaluated. In this spirit, Quine argued against there being claims – such as philosophical claims – which cannot be, even in principle, revised by future science.

Such a view naturally goes hand-in-hand with coherentism, where the epistemic standing of any belief depends on one's network of beliefs as a whole, with no one belief standing apart, epistemically, from the others.

Aside from his coherentism, Quine also made significant contributions to such areas of philosophy as logic, the philosophy of language, metaphysics, and the philosophy of truth.

Part of the motivation for coherentism tends to be somewhat practical in that coherentists claim that we do in fact justify our beliefs in the way that they describe, in that our grounds for believing any particular proposition often implicitly involve a general network, or 'web', of other beliefs that we hold. One way of expressing this idea is by saying that the particular beliefs that we hold reflect a general world-view that we have. That I experience the world in the way that I do – such that I spontaneously form beliefs about that world – is a product of this world-view.

Consider, for example, the difference between myself and someone who lived several hundred years ago and who still thinks that the sun orbits the earth rather than vice versa. Given his world-view, his seeing the sun rising in the morning lends support to his belief that the earth is the centre of the sun's orbit. In contrast, someone like myself who lives in the present day, and who therefore knows full well that the earth in fact orbits the sun, treats the sun's 'rising' in the morning as indicating nothing of the sort. We each have different world-views which inform the beliefs that we spontaneously form. Notice, however, that while the person who lives prior to the Copernican revolution is wrong in his beliefs, it is plausible to suppose that his belief is justified by virtue of the background of beliefs that he holds. Given the way his belief is supported by the general world-view that he holds, and the mesh of beliefs that make up this world-view, it is entirely reasonable for him to believe that the sun's rising in the morning is further confirmation of his belief that the sun orbits the earth.

Still, even if this is in fact the way in which we ordinarily form our beliefs – by implicit appeal to a network of beliefs which make up our general world-view – that fact by itself doesn't ensure that we are right to do so. Perhaps we are just not careful enough in how we form our beliefs, and this lack of care is reflected in how we simply take a certain world-view for granted. After all, it took quite some time before people abandoned the old pre-Copernican picture of how the earth and the sun interacted, which prompts the question of whether if people had been more critical of their world-view and the beliefs that make up this world-view, then this would have resulted in this false picture of how the earth relates to the sun being overturned far quicker. In short, the point is that the mere fact that we all have a tendency to form beliefs in a certain way does not by itself show that we *ought* to form our beliefs in this way.

The motivation for coherentism isn't just practical, however, since part of the story involves pointing out that given the implausibility of alternative theories, it is essential that we understand justification in this way. We have already looked at infinitism, which is clearly an unintuitive view (though note that this is not to say that it is false), so it remains to consider the third option – and certainly the most popular option, historically – that is available.

• FOUNDATIONALISM

This option is known as **foundationalism**, and it responds to Agrippa's trilemma by accepting, in line with option 1, that sometimes a belief can be justified without being supported by any further beliefs. On the face of it this view might seem problematic for the reason mentioned above regarding how beliefs that are not properly grounded – such as the child's belief that the moon is a balloon – do not appear to be likely candidates to be counted as justified. What the dominant form of foundationalism argues, however, is that some beliefs do not require further justification because they are, in a sense, *self-justifying*. This type of foundationalism is known as **classical foundationalism** and it argues that knowledge is structured in such a way that chains of justification end with special self-justifying foundational beliefs which do not stand in need of any further support.

René Descartes (1596–1650)

I think, therefore I am. (Cogito ergo sum)

Descartes, *Discourse on Method*

The French philosopher and mathematician René Descartes is one of the founding fathers of modern philosophy. His most famous work is his *Meditations on First Philosophy* in which, amongst other things, he offers a radically new way of approaching epistemology.

Descartes' idea is that in order to put our knowledge on a secure foundation, it is necessary to first subject it to what he called the 'method of doubt'. This involves doubting as much as can be doubted amongst one's beliefs until one finds the indubitable, and thus epistemologically secure, foundation on which one's knowledge can be built. In the service of this end, Descartes put forward a number of radical **sceptical hypotheses** – scenarios which are indistinguishable from normal experience, but in which one is radically in error, such as that one's experiences are a product of a dream – in order to discover which of his beliefs were immune to doubt. By applying the method of doubt, Descartes was led to the conclusion that the indubitable foundation of our knowledge is our belief in our own existence, since in doubting our existence we thereby prove that we exist (since how else could we be able to doubt?). Hence the famous claim, 'I think, therefore I am'.

Ironically, the powerful sceptical arguments that Descartes invented have held more sway than his subsequent anti-sceptical arguments. Accordingly, although it was not his aim to make us sceptical about the possibility of knowledge, this is in fact what his epistemological investigations seem to have achieved.

Aside from his work in epistemology, Descartes made important contributions to just about every other area of philosophy as well. In addition, he also conducted research on scientific and mathematical questions, making a long-standing contribution to, for example, geometry.

Perhaps the most famous exponent of classical foundationalism is Descartes, whom we first saw in Chapter 3. Descartes argued that the foundations for our knowledge were those beliefs that were immune to doubt and which were therefore certain and self-evidently true. The example he gave of such a belief was one's belief in one's own existence. As Descartes argued, such a belief is indubitable because in doubting it one proves that one is alive to doubt it, and therefore proves that it is true. Such a belief is therefore by its nature self-justifying, and so does not stand in need of further grounds in order to be justifiably held. In a sense, one's belief in this proposition is, plausibly, infallible, in that one could not possibly be in error in this regard. If this is right, then any chain of justification which ended with this belief could thus properly stop at this juncture.

The main problem facing classical foundationalism has always been to identify those self-justifying beliefs that can serve as foundations; or at least offer an account of the foundational beliefs that is not unduly restrictive. The difficulty is that it seems there must be some fairly strict constraint put on foundational beliefs if we are to allow them to serve as the basis for our non-foundational beliefs. But if the constraints on foundational beliefs are too strict, then we risk having a set of foundational beliefs which is problematically small.

For example, suppose one argues, plausibly, that the foundational beliefs had better be those beliefs that one is infallible about – that is, beliefs which just could not be wrong – since only an immunity to error of this sort would ensure that these beliefs could be justified without reliance on any further beliefs. The idea would thus be that the epistemic status of one's everyday **fallible** beliefs which could be in error is traced back to infallible foundational beliefs where the regress of justification comes to an end.

The problem, however, is that there are very few (if any) beliefs that we are infallible about, and the candidate beliefs in this regard do not seem to be able to perform the function of supporting most of our everyday beliefs. Take my belief that two plus two makes four, for example, something which I might plausibly take myself to be infallible about, since it is far from obvious how I could be wrong about this (though with a little ingenuity we can think of cases in which even this belief might be rationally in doubt). Even if this is right, it is far from clear how this belief is supposed to support the numerous beliefs about the world that I currently hold – such as that I am currently sitting at my desk – since this mathematical belief bears no obvious relation to my beliefs about the world.

The same goes for the belief in one's existence that we looked at above in our discussion of Descartes' classical foundationalism. How could the great mass of beliefs that I have about the world be dependent upon a very narrow and specific belief of this sort? The only way to deal with this problem is, it seems, to weaken the requirements one sets on foundational beliefs, perhaps allowing that they could be fallible beliefs after all. For example, maybe one's beliefs about one's immediate experience – about how the world seems to you, for instance – should be regarded as foundational beliefs. The problem with this approach, however, is that it faces the problem of explaining why such beliefs deserve to be treated as foundational in the first place (such beliefs are not obviously infallible). That is, we are stuck between two unpalatable options here. Either we set the requirements on foundational beliefs quite high so that they are plausible, but then face the problem of explaining how such a narrow set of foundational beliefs can serve as a foundation for all the non-foundational beliefs; or else we set the requirements on foundational beliefs quite low, but then face the problem of explaining just why such beliefs should be treated as foundational at all.

It is thus not clear that we get any more comfort from the threat posed by Agrippa's trilemma by appealing to a form of foundationalism than we do by appealing to one of the other standard responses to this problem, such as coherentism or infinitism.

• CHAPTER SUMMARY

- We began by noting that, intuitively, if we are to have knowledge then we must be justified in what we believe. We therefore asked the question of what justification is.
- According to Agrippa's trilemma, there are only three alternatives in this regard, and none of them are particularly appealing on the face of it. The first alternative is to regard one's belief as being justified by nothing at all; no further grounds. The problem with this option is obvious, since if there is nothing supporting the belief, then in what sense can it be justified? (We used the analogy with a house to illustrate this. A house with no foundations will not stand.) The second alternative is to regard one's belief as justified by a further ground which, presumably, will be itself another belief. The problem with this suggestion is that this further belief will also need to be justified, since if the original belief is based on an unjustified second belief then it is hard to see how the second belief can offer any support to the first belief. But if the second belief needs to be justified, then that belief will itself need to be supported by a further belief, and so on indefinitely. We thus have an infinite regress looming. (Consider the analogy with the house again. A house with an unending series of foundations will not stand.) Finally, there is the third option of allowing the supporting beliefs, at some point in the chain of justification, to be beliefs that have appeared elsewhere in the chain. This option thus allows circular justifications. This third option is not appealing either, however, since a circular chain of justification seems little better than no justification at all. (To return to the analogy, a house with a circular set of foundations, with no foundations holding all the other foundations up, will not stand.) It thus seems hard to fathom how any belief could be justified.
- We considered three responses to Agrippa's trilemma, where each of them took one of the unpalatable options just mentioned. The first option was infinitism, which holds that an infinite chain of grounds *can* justify a belief.
- The second response was coherentism, as defended by Quine, which holds that a circular chain of grounds, so long as it has the right sort of properties at any rate (e.g., being large enough), *can* justify a belief.
- Finally, we looked at foundationalism, and classical foundationalism in particular – as defended by Descartes – which holds that there are some grounds which do not require any further support, and which can thus act as foundations for the beliefs that rest upon them. We noted that what is specific to classical foundationalism is that it regards these 'foundational' beliefs as having properties which ensure that they are self-justifying – such as the property of being indubitable or infallibly held. The problem facing this view, however, is that it is difficult to find an account of

these foundational beliefs that is plausible while at the same time counting a sufficient number of our beliefs as foundational so that they can support the other beliefs we hold.

• STUDY QUESTIONS

1 Describe, in your own words, Agrippa's trilemma. Consider a belief that you hold and then try to use Agrippa's trilemma to call into question this belief (you may find it helpful to try this with a friend).
2 What is infinitism, and how does it respond to Agrippa's trilemma? What, if anything, is wrong with it?
3 What is coherentism, and how does it respond to Agrippa's trilemma? What do you think of the claim made by some defenders of coherentism that it offers the best description of how we in fact go about justifying our beliefs? Do you agree? Assuming that it is true, do you think this fact is relevant to whether or not coherentism is true?
4 What is foundationalism, and how does it respond to Agrippa's trilemma? Explain, in your own words, what properties foundational beliefs must have according to classical foundationalism, and give three examples of your own of beliefs which might be said to have these properties.
5 Why did Descartes think that his belief in his own existence was a foundational belief? Could foundational beliefs of this sort provide support for your beliefs about the world? If so, then explain how. If not, then say why.

• INTRODUCTORY FURTHER READING

Bett, Richard (2009) 'Pyrrhonian Skepticism', *The Routledge Companion to Epistemology*, (eds.) S. Bernecker & D. H. Pritchard, (New York: Routledge). A helpful overview of Pyrrhonian scepticism, and its import for the contemporary epistemological debate.

Chisholm, Roderick (1989) *The Theory of Knowledge* (Englewood Cliffs, N.J.: Prentice-Hall). A classic textbook in epistemology which also contains an influential defence of a version of classical foundationalism.

Williams, Bernard (1978) *Descartes: The Project of Pure Inquiry* (Harmondsworth: Penguin). A classic introduction to the philosophy of Descartes, paying particular attention to his epistemology.

Williams, Michael (2001) *Problems of Knowledge* (Oxford: Oxford University Press). See Chapter 5 for an excellent introduction to Agrippa's trilemma, and some of the issues that it raises.

• ADVANCED FURTHER READING

Bailey, Alan (2002) *Sextus Empiricus and Pyrrhonian Scepticism* (Oxford: Oxford University Press). A recent and lively treatment of Pyrrhonian scepticism.

Bonjour, Laurence (1985) *The Structure of Empirical Knowledge* (Cambridge, Mass.: Harvard University Press). Perhaps the most famous and comprehensive defence of coherentism in recent times. Note, however, that Bonjour has since recanted and now advances a form of foundationalism.

Hookway, Christopher (1988) *Quine: Language, Experience and Reality* (Oxford: Polity Press). A classic book introducing the philosophy of W. V. O. Quine.

Klein, Peter (1998) 'Foundationalism and the Infinite Regress of Reasons', *Philosophy and Phenomenological Research* 58, 919–25. A recent defence of infinitism. Not for beginners.

• FREE INTERNET RESOURCES

Groake, Leo (2003) 'Ancient Skepticism', *Stanford Encyclopedia of Philosophy*, <http://plato.stanford.edu/entries/skepticism-ancient/>. An excellent overview of ancient scepticism, including discussion of the style of scepticism, known as Pyrrhonian scepticism, which was advocated by Agrippa, and discussion of Agrippa's trilemma. Marginally better than the internet entry written by Thorsrud (see below).

Klein, Peter (2005) 'Skepticism', *Stanford Encyclopedia of Philosophy*, <http://plato. stanford.edu/entries/skepticism/>. See §§7–11 for an excellent overview of Pyrrhonian scepticism – and of Agrippa's trilemma in particular – and some of the main responses.

Newman, Lex (2005) 'Descartes' Epistemology', *Stanford Encyclopedia of Philosophy*, <http://plato.stanford.edu/entries/descartes-epistemology/>. A helpful introduction to the epistemological ramifications of Descartes' epistemology.

Thorsrud, Harold (2004) 'Ancient Greek Skepticism', *Internet Encyclopedia of Philosophy*, <http://www.iep.utm.edu/s/skepanci.htm>. An excellent overview of ancient scepticism, including discussion of the style of scepticism, known as Pyrrhonian scepticism, which was advocated by Agrippa, and discussion of Agrippa's trilemma. See especially §3. Note that the internet entry written by Groake (see above) is marginally better.

5

rationality

- Rationality, justification, and knowledge
- Epistemic rationality and the goal of truth
- The goal(s) of epistemic rationality
- The (un)importance of epistemic rationality
- Rationality and responsibility
- Epistemic internalism/externalism

RATIONALITY, JUSTIFICATION, AND KNOWLEDGE

We often praise people for their rationality and, conversely, criticise others for their irrationality. For example, a judge who is clear-headed and conscientious in her reasoning when forming a judgement in the light of the evidence put before her might well be commended for her rationality. In contrast, we would no doubt chastise a judge who reached her verdict simply by tossing a coin on the grounds that such activity is irrational. A crucial question for epistemologists, however, has been how to explain the distinction that is being made here.

The importance of this question for those who wish to theorise about knowledge is that intuitively it is only rational beliefs that are candidates for knowledge, with irrational beliefs by their nature not being instances of knowledge. Think again of the rational judge, for example, and one of the beliefs that she forms in reaching a verdict, such as regarding the defendant's guilt. Such a well-founded belief, if true, seems an obvious candidate for knowledge. If the belief had been formed irrationally, however – such as if it had been formed as part of a judgement that was reached in the light of prejudice against the defendant's race or religion, rather than in terms of the facts of the case – then intuitively it wouldn't count as a case of knowledge. If you believe that a defendant is guilty because of the colour of her skin, rather than because of the evidence, then even if this belief is true it won't count as a case of knowledge, and one natural explanation for this is that the belief in question is irrational and irrational beliefs don't count as knowledge.

Another reason for those who theorise about knowledge to be interested in rationality is that there seems to be a close connection between rationality and justification. In particular, it is plausible to suppose that, in most cases at least, a justified belief is a rational one, and vice versa. Think again of the rational judge's belief in the defendant's guilt. Wouldn't we also say that it was justified? In contrast, consider the irrational judge's belief in the defendant's guilt based on prejudice. Wouldn't we say that it was unjustified? Moreover, given that (as we noted in Chapter 4) justification is plausibly necessary for knowledge, this close connection between justification and rationality would explain why we also tend to regard rationality as necessary for knowledge as well. For now, we will focus on rationality independently of justification, but there are prima-facie grounds for thinking that the two notions are closely associated, and we will return at the end of the chapter to look at the relation between the two notions in more detail.

• EPISTEMIC RATIONALITY AND THE GOAL OF TRUTH

Before we begin our examination of rationality we need to notice that as theorists of knowledge we are interested in a specific sort of rationality, what is known as **epistemic rationality**, since it is only this sort of rationality that is relevant to the theory of knowledge. Very simply, epistemic rationality is a form of rationality which is aimed at the goal of true belief.

In order to see this distinction between types of rationality that are epistemic and those that aren't, consider the following case (one that we have seen before, as it happens, in Chapter 2). Suppose that you need to jump a ravine in order to save your life (you are being pursued by an angry mob, perhaps, and this is the only escape route). Knowing what you do about your psychology, you may be entirely aware that if you reflect on the dangers involved in this jump, then you won't be able to summon the necessary commitment and concentration to make the required leap. In such circumstances, where your aim is to save your skin, the best course of action is to ignore the dangers as best as you can – to set them from your mind – and focus solely on the leap. Moreover, insofar as one can 'manufacture' one's beliefs, it would also be wise to do what you can to convince yourself that you can indeed make this jump, since it is only if one is convinced that one will succeed (and failure doesn't bear thinking about).

In a sense, what you are doing here is entirely rational, since the course of action that you are undertaking is indeed the best way to achieve your goals. The kind of rationality here, however, is not epistemic rationality, since it is not a rationality that is aimed at truth at all. Indeed, if anything, this sort of rationality is aimed at a sort of self-deception. If, in contrast, one were focused solely on gaining true beliefs, then that would actually *mitigate* against you attaining the goal in question since it would lead you to recognise the dangers involved in the jump and so undermine your attempt to successfully make that jump.

Because the rationality in this case is not aimed at the truth, even if the belief that resulted from this course of action was indeed true (i.e., you could make this jump), it wouldn't be a case of knowledge since you can't come to know that you can make a leap by reflecting on how you must make the leap in order to survive. Compare this case with that of the belief formed by the rational judge, who forms her belief by judiciously weighing up the evidence involved. Clearly this belief, if true, can count as an instance of knowledge, thus again indicating that the rationality in question is epistemic rationality.

Moreover, notice that although the non-epistemic form of rationality in play in the 'self-deception' case does result in you holding a belief as a result of undertaking a course of action, we could just as well talk about the rationality of your *action* as your belief. It is rational, for example, for you to confidently make that leap given that your goal is to save your life. As epistemologists, however, we are primarily interested in belief rather than action, since it is only beliefs that can be cases of knowledge, as we saw in Chapter 1.

Pascal's wager

> If God does not exist, one will lose nothing by believing in him, while if he does exist, one will lose everything by not believing.
>
> Blaise Pascal, *Pensees*

A good way of highlighting the distinction between a rational belief and a specifically epistemically rational belief is by considering **Pascal's wager**, named after the French philosopher, scientist, and mathematician Blaise Pascal (1623–62). The devoutly religious Pascal wanted to show that belief in God is rational. To this end he offered the argument that one has nothing to lose and everything to gain by believing in God, and thus that belief in God is the rational thing to do.

After all, if one believes in God and this belief is false, then one has lost very little, while if the belief is true, then the reward of eternal life in Heaven will more than compensate for whatever minor inconvenience belief in God's existence brought you during your life. In contrast, if you don't believe in God, then you run the risk of spending an eternity in Hell, which is clearly a heavy price to pay. Moreover, you have to do one or the other (believe or not believe), so there is no way of avoiding this choice.

Put another way, we can imagine the issue of whether we should believe in God as being like a bet (or *wager*) that we all must take. Either we bet on God's existence (and so believe in God), or we bet on God's non-existence (and so don't believe in God). Pascal is saying that given the fantastic possible benefits that can accrue from having a true belief in God (i.e., eternal life), the tremendous costs involved in failing to believe in God if God does exist (i.e., eternal damnation), and the absence of any substantial costs in falsely believing in God's existence, the best thing to do is bet on God's existence: it is rational to believe in God.

There has been much philosophical debate over the effectiveness of this argument, but note that even if the argument works, it does not show that belief in God is epistemically rational, as Pascal fully recognised. Pascal is not, for example, saying that this argument gives you a reason for thinking that God does in fact exist (i.e., for thinking that a belief in God's existence would be *true*), only that it is *prudent* (and thus in this sense rational) for you to believe in God, which is not the same thing. Pascal thus gives us a neat illustration of how a belief can be (in some sense) rational without thereby being epistemically rational.

The kind of rationality that we are particularly interested in as theorists of knowledge is thus epistemic rationality. Note that that's not to say that there aren't close connections between epistemic and non-epistemic forms of rationality – indeed, we would expect there to be many overlaps and similarities – it is just that our primary focus as theorists of knowledge is epistemic rationality. With this point in mind, we will proceed.

• THE GOAL(S) OF EPISTEMIC RATIONALITY

One problem facing the notion of epistemic rationality is that to say that this form of rationality is concerned with true belief doesn't tell us all that much since we still need to know exactly *how* it is concerned with true belief. As we will see, explaining how epistemic rationality is concerned with true belief is harder to do than it might initially appear.

Let's start with perhaps the most natural way of understanding epistemic rationality. If true belief is the goal of an epistemic rationality, then the obvious way of understanding this claim is to demand that one should *maximise* one's true beliefs (i.e., try to believe as many truths as possible). With this account of epistemic rationality in mind, we could explain the rationality of the non-coin-tossing judge in terms of the way in which she formed her judgement on the grounds that evaluating all the evidence in a careful and objective manner (i.e., without allowing oneself to be swayed by the emotion of the case) is a good way of getting to the truth in this regard. In contrast, whilst the coin-tossing judge may well end up delivering the same verdict as our rational judge, we would not count her as rational because the method she is using to form her belief is not likely to lead to the truth.

There are problems with the *maximising* conception of epistemic rationality, however. For example, if this account of epistemic rationality just means that we should try to have as many true beliefs as possible, then it is open to some fairly straightforward counter-examples. After all, memorising names and addresses from the phone book may well lead me to have thousands of true beliefs, but the beliefs in question wouldn't be of any consequence. Indeed, we would usually regard this sort of truth-seeking behaviour as very *irrational*. Even setting this problem to one side, however, there remains the fundamental difficulty that the best way to maximise the number of one's true beliefs might well be to believe just about anything, since this would ensure that one has the most chance of believing the truth. Crucially, of course, this sort of truth-seeking strategy would lead one to form lots of *false* beliefs as well, and that is hardly desirable.

One way of dealing with this latter problem (we will come back to the former problem in a moment) might be to modify our conception of epistemic rationality so that it demands not that one maximises truth in one's beliefs, but rather that one *minimises* falsehood. That way we would be able to treat any agent who simply believes as many things as possible as irrational on the grounds that this will not be the best way of minimising falsehood. The problem with this suggestion, however, is that the best way of minimising falsehood in one's beliefs is surely not to believe anything (or at least believe as little as possible), but this would mean that one would have very few true beliefs either, if any.

What is needed then is some way of balancing the goal of maximising truth in one's beliefs with the related goal of minimising falsehood. We want agents to take some risks regarding the falsity of their beliefs, and so we don't want them to be overly cautious and not believe anything; but equally neither do we want agents to go 'all out' for the truth at the expense of widespread falsity in their beliefs. Specifying just how we should understand this 'balanced' conception of rationality is, however, quite hard to do.

• THE (UN)IMPORTANCE OF EPISTEMIC RATIONALITY

Moreover, don't forget that we still have the outstanding problem of specifying epistemic rationality such that it doesn't count someone who merely aims to believe lots of trivial truths (such as names in a phone book) as epistemically rational.

One way of responding to this problem is to deny that there is any challenge here to respond to. In this view, such beliefs are entirely epistemically rational, and that's the end of the matter. Proponents of this line of thought will concede, of course, that there is *something* irrational about this way of forming one's beliefs, but will claim that the irrationality in question is not epistemic (recall that we noted above that there may be other types of rationality besides epistemic rationality). That is, they will argue that this person has rather trivial goals, and that this is to be deplored, but that, from a purely epistemic point of view, there is nothing wrong with forming one's beliefs in this way.

The problem with this line of thought is that it has the unfortunate consequence of trivialising the importance of epistemology, since the specifically epistemic rationality that we are interested in as epistemologists does not turn out to be all that rational, generally speaking. I'm not sure that we should be persuaded all that much by considerations such as this, however, since, after all, there is a lot more to life than gaining true beliefs, and one could well argue that this way of dealing with the problem in hand simply recognises this fact. Put another way, we are interested in gaining knowledge, and thus true beliefs, because we have all sorts of other goals that this knowledge can be utilised in the service of, such as furthering our relationships, our career, and our interests. A life purely devoted to gaining true beliefs might not be a life that we are interested in leading.

Others are not so sanguine in the face of this objection, however, and I'm inclined, on balance, to agree with them. One way of resisting the pessimistic line of argument just sketched is to claim that, contrary to first appearances, the agent in the 'phone book' case, and others like her, are not **epistemically rational** after all. This way of responding to the problem is not nearly as hopeless as it might at first sound. After all, the thing about important truths is that they beget lots of other truths. If I come to have true beliefs about the ultimate physics of the universe, for example, then I will thereby acquire many other true beliefs about related matters. Learning names from the phone book is not like that, since these truths are pretty much self-standing – in acquiring these true beliefs you are unlikely to acquire many others. Thus, if your goal is to maximise true belief, while minimising false beliefs, then you would be wise to aim at those true beliefs of substance and set such trivial goals as memorising names in a phone book to one side. If this is right, then epistemic rationality is rescued from the grip of this objection.

There is thus some room for manoeuvre when it comes to this objection to epistemic rationality: one can either accept it while maintaining that its importance can be easily overestimated, or else one can resist it and claim that the cases offered for thinking that being epistemically rational can result in trivial true beliefs are based on a mistake.

• RATIONALITY AND RESPONSIBILITY

Even if we have a suitable conception of what the goals of epistemic rationality are, problems still remain. In the examples given above of the rational and irrational judges we implicitly took it for granted that the agents were in some sense responsible for the truth-seeking procedures that they were employing. There is a good reason for this, since, typically at least, we only praise or blame agents for doing things where they can reasonably be thought to be responsible for their actions. The rational judge is thus responsible, and so praiseworthy, for her conscientious behaviour because she could have been biased or careless in passing her judgement if she'd been so inclined. Equally, the irrational coin-tossing judge is responsible, and so blameworthy, for her epistemically reckless behaviour because she could have used proper procedures if she'd wanted to.

It isn't always obvious, however, that agents can be held responsible for the way in which they form their beliefs. One consideration in this respect is that some beliefs, such as basic perceptual beliefs, are both *spontaneous* and *involuntary*, and so just don't seem to be the sort of thing that agents can have any control over. If, in good lighting conditions and so forth, I see my father come into the hallway, then I will *immediately* form a belief that he is in the hallway – there is no room here for a prior rational deliberation. In this regard, beliefs are very unlike actions (most actions at any rate), since the latter do tend to be in our control.

Even setting this issue to one side, there remains the problem that sometimes agents are simply taught the wrong **epistemic norms** to follow, where an epistemic norm is a rule which one follows in order to gain true beliefs. That one should take care when weighing up evidence, and be as impartial as possible as one does so, is an example of an epistemic norm, since it enables one to have a better chance of getting to the truth. We are usually taught these kinds of norms – often tacitly – as we grow up (our teacher might, for example, criticise us for guessing an answer to a question rather than working it out properly).

Imagine, however, someone who has been raised by being taught all the *wrong* epistemic norms (she has been isolated from the world at large, say, and has been systematically misled by all those that she has come into contact with in her secluded community). Suppose, for example, that she has been taught that one ought to find out the truth about certain subject matters (such as whether or not a defendant is guilty) by simply tossing a coin. Is this person forming her beliefs in an epistemically rational way?

One possibility here is that we might regard this agent as being entirely epistemically rational, at least in one sense of that notion, since, *by her lights* at least, she is forming her beliefs in the right kind of way. There is, one might argue, a very big difference between someone who forms her belief by tossing a coin who *should know better* – who has, that is, been taught the correct epistemic norms – and someone who forms her belief by tossing a coin and who, *to the best of her knowledge*, believes that this is the right way to proceed. In the former case the agent is responsible for the way in which she is forming her belief, and so blameworthy, in a way that is not applicable in the latter case.

The kind of epistemic rationality that is at issue here is called a **deontic epistemic rationality**. It holds that an agent's belief is epistemically rational just so long as the agent does not contravene any epistemic norm in coming to form that belief *by her own lights*. That is, an agent can be epistemically rational *and* employ the wrong epistemic norms, just so long as she is not to blame for her employment of the wrong epistemic norms. Since even those who form their beliefs by tossing a coin can sometimes count as epistemically rational on this view, deontic epistemic rationality is a very weak conception of what epistemic rationality demands.

In contrast, a stronger, non-deontic, conception of epistemic rationality would demand that agents not only do not blamelessly contravene any epistemic norm, but that the epistemic norms in question should be, as a matter of fact, the *right* ones (i.e., the truth-conducive ones). In this non-deontic view, even the agent who blamelessly forms her belief by tossing a coin does not count as epistemically rational, and this might be thought to be an advantage of the thesis. The problem with this stance, however, is that it appears to break the very intuitive connection between epistemic rationality and responsibility. We don't hold the hapless agent who forms her belief by tossing a coin responsible for her epistemic failings since it isn't her fault that she was taught the wrong epistemic norms. And yet in this view we should count her as not being epistemically rational nonetheless. In short, in this view, one can be responsible and yet not at the same time be epistemically rational.

• EPISTEMIC INTERNALISM/EXTERNALISM

It thus seems that we are caught between two opposing conceptions of epistemic rationality. The first has the advantage of directly connecting the notion of epistemic rationality with that of responsibility, but has the drawback that the demands it imposes are very weak. The second imposes a stronger constraint on epistemic rationality, but does so at the expense of breaking the link between epistemic rationality and responsibility. We might call the former deontic notion of epistemic rationality an **epistemic internalist** conception of epistemic rationality in that it ties epistemic rationality to what the agent can be held accountable for. In contrast, we might call the latter notion of rationality an **epistemic externalist** conception of epistemic rationality in that it breaks the connection between epistemic rationality and what the agent can be held accountable for. Roughly speaking, epistemic internalism makes one's epistemic standing something that one has control over; while epistemic externalism allows that one's epistemic standing can sometimes depend on factors outside one's control (e.g., whether one has been taught the right epistemic norms).

There is a general philosophical issue here which has ramifications for epistemology as a whole. The problem is that the best way in which to get to the truth (i.e., the most reliable way) need not be discernible to the agent herself. The question we therefore need to ask is whether our epistemology should be *egocentric*, and therefore focused on what the agent is able to discern (i.e., what the agent has good reason to believe are the correct epistemic norms, whether or not they really are the correct epistemic norms); or whether it should be *non-egocentric* in the sense that it allows that other considerations can play role in determining whether or not an agent's belief is epistemically rationally held (e.g., whether the epistemic norms that the agent is using are, in fact, the right ones).

In order to see how this issue relates to epistemology as a whole, it is worthwhile considering how the notion of epistemic rationality relates to concepts like justification and knowledge, which are central to epistemological theorising. On the face of it, there ought to be a close connection between justification and epistemic rationality, since we often use terms like 'rational' and 'justified' as if they were roughly synonymous. With this in mind we might argue that justification is just epistemic rationality. Accordingly, if one held that epistemic rationality is just deontic epistemic rationality, then one would end up with an *epistemic internalist egocentric* conception of justification. The problem with this proposal is that it would have the consequence that justified true belief and knowledge could come *radically* apart. After all, our coin-tossing agent, who is only deontically epistemically rational, could hardly be said to *know* anything on this basis, since even if she does end up with a true belief by employing the wrong epistemic norm, it would merely be a matter of luck that her belief is true, and we don't normally treat agents who get to the truth via luck as knowers. In this view of the relationship between justification and epistemic rationality, however, the agent concerned would be entirely justified in forming her belief this way.

On the face of it, this might look like just another Gettier case in which one has a justified true belief which is not thereby knowledge, and so one might think that the problem at hand here is just a variant on the familiar problem posed by Gettier cases more generally. Notice, however, that the case just described is in fact importantly different from the normal Gettier case since in Gettier cases the agent typically forms her belief via the correct epistemic norm, it is just that the truth of the belief is nevertheless lucky. In this case, in contrast, the agent is employing the wrong epistemic norm, albeit blamelessly. Given this difference between the two sorts of cases, the divorce between justified true belief and knowledge opened up by this conception of the relationship between deontic epistemic rationality and justification may remain even if we found a way to deal with the Gettier cases – the two problems are thus importantly different.

Another reason to think that a conception of justification in terms of deontic epistemic rationality pulls justification apart from knowledge is that we often ascribe knowledge to agents even when they don't form their beliefs responsibly, just so long as they form their beliefs in the right kind of way (i.e., they don't contravene the right epistemic norms). Accordingly, it seems that deontic epistemic rationality cannot be necessary for knowledge, since this form of rationality entails that the belief in question was responsibly formed, and yet knowledge, it seems, does not require this.

For example, consider the way that a small child may go about forming a perceptual belief by simply believing what she seems to see (e.g., she sees a toy in front of her, and so believes that there's a toy in front of her). Suppose that circumstances are otherwise normal and there is nothing specific to indicate that her senses should be doubted in this case (e.g., no one has (falsely) told her that Daddy has left some of the prototypes around which look like her toys but which in fact aren't). Wouldn't we say that such a belief is an instance of knowledge – that the child *knows* that there is a toy in front of her? The problem is, of course, that we would hardly regard the child as believing responsibly, since she isn't in fact paying any attention to how she forms her belief at all – she's simply doing what comes naturally to her, entirely unreflectively (notice that this is not necessarily to say that she's being irresponsible in her believing). Nevertheless, forming your beliefs in this way (i.e., in response to what your senses tell you in normal circumstances and where there are no specific reasons for doubt) is a generally reliable way to form one's beliefs about the world, and, indeed, a good way of gaining knowledge in this regard. Moreover, it doesn't seem to contravene any epistemic norms. So even while not believing responsibly, one can, intuitively, gain knowledge, and this seems to suggest that knowing does not require deontic epistemic rationality.

If we want to have a conception of justification which is understood in terms of epistemic rationality but which also bears a more direct relationship to knowledge, then we might therefore be attracted to the idea of characterising justification in terms of non-deontic epistemic rationality. The difficulty facing this proposal, however, is that our everyday notion of epistemic rationality does seem to be closely associated with the notion of responsibility, and thus with the deontic conception of epistemic rationality. After all, we *would* normally regard an agent as epistemically rational if she responsibly formed her belief via the blameless use of the wrong epistemic norms. Moreover, consider those cases – like that of the child's perceptual belief just outlined – in which the agent concerned does not form her beliefs in a responsible manner. Would we really say that such a belief, even while being (let's agree) a case of knowledge, is epistemically rational? (Of course, we wouldn't say that it was epistemically *irrational*, but that's not the same thing.)

There is thus no straightforward way of reconciling these conflicting intuitions about the relationship between such notions as epistemic rationality, responsibility, justification, and knowledge, and much of contemporary epistemological theorising has been concerned with offering different pictures of how these concepts relate to one another. Indeed, this conflict of intuitions has prompted some to argue that perhaps we should treat epistemic rationality and knowledge as very different types of notions. The thought is that perhaps justification is, essentially, epistemic rationality, and that epistemic rationality is just deontic epistemic rationality, and thus that we should simply accept that there is no direct connection between knowledge and justification. In this view we replace the traditional conception of epistemology which seeks an integrated account of these three notions with one that regards epistemology as concerned with *two* distinct projects. The first is to analyse those epistemic concepts that are closely tied to responsibility: epistemic rationality and justification. The second is to analyse knowledge. At the very least, the problems that we have explored here should give us pause to take this suggestion very seriously indeed.

• CHAPTER SUMMARY

- Rationality is important to epistemologists since there seems to be a close connection between having a rational belief and having knowledge (and, conversely, between having an irrational belief and lacking knowledge). Moreover, as we have seen in a previous chapter, knowledge is closely connected with justification, and there seems to be a tight connection between rationally held beliefs and justified beliefs. Understanding rationality could thus cast light on the theory of knowledge, whether indirectly (via the light it casts on justification) or directly.
- The type of rationality that we are interested in as epistemologists is epistemic rationality. Epistemic rationality is specifically aimed at true belief.

- One way of understanding epistemic rationality is that it demands that one should try to maximise one's true beliefs (i.e., have as many true beliefs as possible).
- We noted two problems with the proposal. The first was that one could achieve this goal by acquiring lots of trivial true beliefs (e.g., by learning all the names in a phone directory). Intuitively, however, this is not a very rational thing to do at all. The second problem that we noted with this proposal was that one could maximise one's true beliefs by believing as much as possible, but this would also result in lots of false beliefs. Intuitively, however, having truth as a goal means not just having lots of true beliefs, but also avoiding having false beliefs.
- Reflection on the second problem led us to consider a different conception of epistemic rationality, one that demanded not that we maximise true beliefs but that we minimise false ones. The key problem with this proposal, however, is that the best way to go about meeting this requirement is by believing *nothing*, and this is hardly what we would regard as epistemically rational behaviour.
- We thus concluded that what was required of epistemic rationality was to achieve a balance between the two goals of maximising true beliefs and minimising false beliefs.
- There still remained the problem of apparently epistemically rational agents who devote themselves to gaining trivial true beliefs (e.g., by learning all the names in a phone book). We saw two ways of responding to this problem. The first response embraced the problem and argued that all that it showed is that there is nothing irrational, from a purely epistemic point of view, with such behaviour. The second response argued that the problem was illusory because such cases do not stand up to close scrutiny: the agent in these cases is not, in fact, epistemically rational after all.
- We then distinguished between two conceptions of epistemic rationality: deontic and non-deontic conceptions. According to a deontic epistemic rationality, one is epistemically rational just so long as one forms one's beliefs responsibly. In this view, one can form one's beliefs by using the wrong epistemic norms just so long as one does so blamelessly. In contrast, a non-deontic epistemic rationality demands that one employs the right epistemic norms.
- The deontic conception of epistemic rationality is a form of epistemic internalism in that it draws a close connection between epistemic standing and what the agent can be held responsible for. In contrast, the non-deontic conception of epistemic rationality is a form of epistemic externalism in that it allows that one can responsibly form one's beliefs and yet, because one blamelessly employs the wrong epistemic norms, one's belief is not epistemically rational. Roughly speaking, epistemic internalism makes one's epistemic standing something the agent has control over; while epistemic externalism allows that one's epistemic standing can sometimes depend on factors outside one's control (e.g, whether one has been taught the right epistemic norms).
- We noted that the deontic conception of epistemic rationality seems closest to our ordinary use of the term 'rational' and our ordinary understanding of 'justification'. Nevertheless, this type of epistemic rationality does not seem to bear such a close relation to knowledge; or at least not as close as a non-deontic conception of

epistemic rationality. We thus considered the possibility that there are two distinct epistemological projects: one which examines knowledge and another which examines justification and deontic epistemic rationality. In this picture, while there may be important connections between the two projects, they are not as closely related as we might at first suppose.

• STUDY QUESTIONS

1 What is epistemic rationality? Try to give a description of it in your own words and offer one example of each of the following:
   • an epistemically rational belief;
   • a belief which is not epistemically rational but which might plausibly be considered rational in some other respect;
   • a belief which is not rational in *any* sense, epistemic or otherwise.
   Make sure to explain your examples fully and also explain why they fit the relevant description.
2 Why can't we simply understand epistemic rationality as demanding that we *maximise* the number of our true beliefs?
3 Why can't we understand epistemic rationality as demanding that we *minimise* the number of our false beliefs?
4 Explain, in your own words, why the fact that many true beliefs are entirely trivial might be thought to pose a problem for epistemic rationality. How should one respond to this problem, do you think?
5 What is an epistemic norm? Give an example of your own of a possible epistemic norm.
6 What does it mean to call a conception of epistemic rationality *deontic*? In what sense is a deontic conception of epistemic rationality a form of epistemic internalism? Give examples to illustrate your answers.
7 Is it essential for possessing knowledge that one forms one's belief in an epistemically rational way? Why might it be thought problematic to think that it is essential? Is justification and epistemic rationality the same thing, do you think? As best as you can, try to answer these questions with the distinction between a deontic and non-deontic conception of epistemic rationality explicitly in mind.

• INTRODUCTORY FURTHER READING

Alston, William P. (1998) 'Internalism and Externalism in Epistemology', *Routledge Encyclopedia of Philosophy*, (London: Routledge) <www.rep.routledge.com/article/P028?ssid=168779753 andn=1#>. A useful overview of the issues as regards the epistemic externalism/internalism distinction.
Foley, Richard (2009) 'Epistemic Rationality', *The Routledge Companion to Epistemology*, (eds.) S. Bernecker & D. H. Pritchard (New York: Routledge). An

excellent overview of the topic of epistemic rationality, written by one of the leading figures in the field.

Lehrer, Keith (1999) 'Rationality', *The Blackwell Guide to Epistemology*, (eds.) J. Greco and E. Sosa, pp. 206–19 (Oxford: Blackwell). This is a rather involved discussion of the topic by one of the main experts in the field, but certainly worth reading.

Steup, Mathias and Sosa, Ernest (eds.) (2005) *Contemporary Debates in Epistemology* (Oxford: Blackwell). This edited collection contains two excellent symposia that are relevant to this chapter. The first (§10) is a debate between Jonathan Kvanvig and Marian David on whether truth is the primary epistemic goal. The second (§11) is a debate between Richard Foley and Nicholas Wolterstorff on whether justified belief is responsible belief.

• ADVANCED FURTHER READING

Foley, Richard (1987) *The Theory of Epistemic Rationality* (Cambridge, Mass.: Harvard University Press). The classic account of epistemic rationality in the recent literature.

Kornblith, Hilary (ed.) (2001) *Epistemology: Internalism and Externalism* (Oxford: Blackwell). Collects many of the classic papers on the epistemic externalism/internalism distinction together in one place. Note that some of these papers are not for beginners.

Lehrer, Keith (1999) 'Rationality', *The Blackwell Guide to Epistemology*, (eds.) J. Greco and E. Sosa, pp. 206–19 (Oxford: Blackwell). This is a rather involved discussion of the topic by one of the main experts in the field, but certainly worth reading.

Pollock, John (1986) 'Epistemic Norms', *Contemporary Theories of Knowledge*, Chapter 5 (Totowa, N.J.: Rowman and Littlefield). This is quite difficult, but a good place to look to get a more comprehensive discussion of epistemic norms.

• FREE INTERNET RESOURCES

Hajek, Alan (2004) 'Pascal's Wager', *Stanford Encyclopedia of Philosophy*, <http://plato.stanford.edu/entries/pascal-wager/>. A neat little overview of Pascal's wager and some of the issues that it raises.

Pappas, George (2005) 'Internalist vs. Externalist Conceptions of Epistemic Justication', *Stanford Encyclopedia of Philosophy*, <http://plato.stanford.edu/entries/justep-intext/>. A comprehensive overview of the externalism/internalism distinction as it applies to epistemic justification.

Poston, Ted (2008) 'Internalism and Externalism in Epistemology', *Internet Encyclopedia of Philosophy*, <http://www.iep.utm.edu/i/int-ext.htm>. An excellent discussion of the externalism/internalism debate in epistemology.

6
virtues and faculties

- Reliabilism
- A 'Gettier' problem for reliabilism
- Virtue epistemology
- Virtue epistemology and the externalism/internalism distinction

• RELIABILISM

Whatever else we might want to say about knowledge, one thing that is clear is that knowledge involves a cognitive success which is creditable to the agent. This is why (or at least part of the reason why) we don't count someone as having knowledge if she merely gets to the truth by luck. For example, if I form my belief about what the weather will be like tomorrow simply by tossing a coin, then, even if this belief happens to turn out to be true, I won't count as a knower since I gained this true belief only by luck. After all, it wasn't a cognitive success of mine that I gained this true belief, but it was instead just due to serendipity. What we want from an epistemological theory is thus some account of knowledge which accommodates this intuition that knowledge involves creditable cognitive success, where this means that if one knows what one truly believes then one has gained this true belief in a non-lucky fashion.

As so often in philosophy, the devil lies in the detail, since there are a number of different and incompatible ways in which we can spell out this idea of knowledge as creditable non-lucky true belief. As we saw in Chapter 3, one obvious way of doing this – by defining knowledge as justified true belief – was found to be susceptible to devastating counter-examples (the Gettier cases), and so unsustainable. We therefore need to look elsewhere for an account of knowledge. One thought that one might have in this regard is that knowledge must be true belief that is gained in a reliable way, where 'reliable' here means that, at the very least, the method used was more likely to get you to the truth than not. This sort of view is known as **reliabilism**.

One can see the attractions of the position. After all, the problem with my belief in the 'coin-tossing' case is simply that coin-tossing is not a very reliable way of finding out the truth about what the weather will be tomorrow (indeed, it is not a very reliable way of finding out the truth about *anything*), since more often than not this method will lead me to form false beliefs about tomorrow's weather. Compare coin-tossing in this respect with consulting an authoritative weather news source. This way of finding out what the weather will be like tomorrow *is* reliable (though not, note, infallible as it is sometimes wrong). Relatedly, were you to gain a true belief via this method then we would be unlikely to regard you as lucky. Instead, we would treat you as a knower since you found out the truth in the right kind of way. This case thus lends support to the thesis that knowledge requires reliability, in that it supports the idea that a reliably formed true belief will be a cognitive success that is creditable to the agent rather than to luck.

A 'GETTIER' PROBLEM FOR RELIABILISM

So there does seem to be a certain plausibility in the reliabilist idea that knowledge is basically true belief that is reliably formed. The problem of this view, however, is that if it is understood simply as the thesis that knowledge is reliable true belief then it is susceptible to a number of rather serious problems. In particular, it seems that sometimes one can form a true belief in a reliable fashion and yet it still be a matter of luck that your belief is true. If this is right, then reliability does not exclude knowledge-undermining luck and so cannot serve to demarcate bona fide knowledge, which involves a cognitive success that is creditable to the agent, from mere lucky cognitive success, which does not.

Imagine, for example, that you find out what the temperature of the room is by looking at the thermometer on the wall. Furthermore, let us grant that this thermometer is very reliable in this respect in that it will enable you to form accurate beliefs about what the temperature is. Suppose, however, that unbeknownst to you someone is playing a trick on you. The thermometer is, in fact, broken and is fluctuating randomly. Crucially, however, this isn't making the thermometer an unreliable indicator of what the temperature in the room is for the simple reason that someone is hidden in the room and adjusting the temperature of the room to match whatever reading is on the thermometer whenever she sees you look at the thermometer (we won't concern ourselves with why). Accordingly, in this case you are forming true beliefs about what the temperature of the room is via a method (i.e., looking at the thermometer) that is entirely reliable, since every time you form a belief about what the temperature in the room is by looking at the thermometer that belief will be true. Intuitively, however, you don't *know* what the temperature of the room is because the thermometer is broken and you can't find out the temperature by looking at a broken thermometer.

Indeed, this is also a case in which one's cognitive success is not creditable to one but is rather due to luck. After all, it is not as if your beliefs are adapting themselves to the way the world is (as would be the case if you were forming your beliefs by looking at a working thermometer). Instead, the world is, as it were, adapting itself to your beliefs (in that there is someone who is changing the temperature so that it matches with your beliefs about what the temperature is). In a sense, then, it is just a matter of luck that you happen to have true beliefs in this regard, since if someone wasn't playing a trick on you in this way then you'd form false beliefs about what the temperature of the room is by looking at this broken thermometer.

In fact, this sort of case should be familiar to you from our previous discussion of Gettier cases, since it shares many of the essential features of Gettier cases. Recall that in the Gettier cases we had a belief which met two conditions. First, it was justified and yet formed in such a way that a belief so formed would normally have been false (such as a belief formed by looking at a broken clock which the agent had every reason to think was working). So far, the belief is infected with 'bad' epistemic luck which would normally have prevented the agent from having knowledge. The second condition needed for Gettier cases, however, is that this 'bad' epistemic luck is cancelled out by the 'good' epistemic luck so that despite the problematic way in which the belief was formed, it is true nonetheless (such as would happen if the agent happened to look at the clock at the two times in the day when it was showing the right time). We thus have a case of justified true belief which is not knowledge because it is just too lucky that the agent's belief is true. As a result, the agent's cognitive success is not creditable to her, but is rather just down to good fortune.

The counter-example to a simple form of reliabilism that we just offered has the same structure to the Gettier cases, except that instead of a case of justified true belief, we have a case of reliable true belief. As with a Gettier case, we have 'good' epistemic luck cancelling out 'bad' epistemic luck, as when a process that would not normally lead to a true belief (e.g., gaining one's belief about the temperature by looking at a broken thermometer) in fact leads to a true belief because of some further fact about the case (in this example, that there is someone playing a trick on the agent). Moreover, the way the trick is being played ensures that the belief is nonetheless reliably formed. Just as Gettier cases show that the traditional account of knowledge in terms of justified true belief is unsustainable, so examples like this show that a simple reliabilist theory of knowledge in terms of reliable true belief is unsustainable.

What is interesting about the parallel between this counter-example to reliabilism and the Gettier cases is that one might have thought that reliabilism would be in a good position to respond to the Gettier cases. After all, what is characteristic of most of the standard Gettier cases – such as, indeed, the 'stopped clock' case just noted – is that they involve the agent forming a justified belief via an unreliable process (normally, forming one's belief by looking at a stopped clock is an unreliable way of forming a belief about what the time is). The trouble is, however, as we have just seen, we can manipulate the case so that the reliability of the way in which the belief was formed is preserved.

• VIRTUE EPISTEMOLOGY

Nevertheless, there is *something* right about the reliabilist idea that knowledge must be gained by a process which tends towards the truth. After all, the feature of the standard construal of justification that Gettier cases trade upon is that one could form one's justified true belief in ways that in no way tend towards the truth (e.g., by looking at a stopped clock). As we saw in Chapter 1, however, gaining knowledge is like having a skill at getting at the truth. Think again of the example of a skilled archer hitting the bull's-eye that we gave there. Insofar as this archer genuinely is skilled, then it is not merely a matter of happenstance that she hits the target this time. Instead, we would expect her to hit the target across a range of relevantly similar conditions (such as if she were standing two inches to her left, or if the light was oh so slightly darker, or the wind oh so slightly stronger, and so on); this is just what it means to hit the target because of one's skill, rather than just because one got lucky.

The same goes for the knower. This ought not to be someone who just happened to form a true belief, but rather someone who would have got a true belief in a range of relevantly similar circumstances. In the 'stopped clock' Gettier case, for example, the problem is that the agent only happened to have a true belief, since if she'd have looked at the clock a minute later or earlier, then she would have formed a false belief. Contrast this with someone looking at a working – and thus *reliable* – clock. This person will tend to have true beliefs across a range of relevantly similar scenarios, such as if the time were slightly different, and so the way in which she is forming her belief is more akin to the skill of the archer in hitting the bull's-eye.

So although we cannot understand knowledge as simply reliable true belief, we ought to be careful about completely dismissing the reliabilist proposal. Perhaps, for example, there is some way of modifying the view so that it can evade the Gettier-style problem that we have raised?

One way in which one might modify the position could be to demand that knowledge is true belief that is gained as a result of the operation of reliable *epistemic virtues* or *cognitive faculties*. An **epistemic virtue** (sometimes called an *intellectual virtue*) is a character trait which makes you better suited to gaining the truth. An example of such a trait might be *conscientiousness*. An agent who is conscientious in the way in which she forms her beliefs (i.e., she is careful to avoid error and takes all available evidence into account), will be more likely to form true beliefs than someone who is uncon-scientious. A **cognitive faculty** is also a character trait of sorts, though it tends to be natural and innate, rather than acquired like an epistemic virtue, and doesn't usually demand any reflection on the part of the agent as an epistemic virtue often does. Like an epistemic virtue, a cognitive faculty also enables you to reliably form true beliefs. One's perceptual faculties, such as one's eyesight, are cognitive faculties, in that, when working properly in an environment for which they are suited at least, they enable you to reliably gain true beliefs, in this case about the world around you.

The idea behind this adaptation to the general reliabilist thesis is that what is important when we talk about reliability is not the reliability of the process by which the belief was formed *simpliciter*, but rather the specific reliability of the *agent* (and thus the agent's cognitive traits, such as her epistemic virtues and cognitive faculties) in gaining beliefs of this sort. Because this view essentially defines knowledge in terms of the epistemic virtues and cognitive faculties, it is a version of what is known as *virtue epistemology*. **Virtue epistemology** is one of the oldest views in the theory of knowledge – a version of virtue epistemology was advanced by the ancient Greek philosopher, **Aristotle** (384–322 BC).

In order to see what this reliabilist version of virtue epistemology involves, consider again the case in which you are forming your beliefs via the broken but, as it happens, reliable thermometer. Proponents of this type of virtue epistemology try to deal with examples like this by contending that the reason why you lack knowledge is that your true belief is not the result of you appropriately employing your cognitive faculties and epistemic virtues, but is instead the product of the interference of the person hidden in the room who is altering the temperature to suit. In contrast, if you had formed your true belief by looking at a working thermometer with no 'funny business' going on in the room, then your true belief *would* have been brought about by you employing your cognitive faculties and epistemic virtues (e.g., your faculty of sight in looking at the reading on the thermometer), and thus it would have been a genuine case of knowledge.

Aristotle (384–322 BC)

All men by nature desire to know.

Aristotle, *Metaphysics*

Aristotle (384–322 BC) is, with Plato (*c.* 427–*c.* 347 BC), one of the two towering figures of ancient Greek philosophy. Many of the philosophical disputes engaged in today were discussed by Aristotle, and the views that he presented all those years ago are still common currency in the contemporary debate.

Aristotle spent most of his life in Athens. He studied under Plato at Plato's Academy, and then went on to teach there. Later, he founded his own school of philosophy, The Lyceum. Of the many interesting events of Aristotle's life – and perhaps the most significant in terms of world history – was his tutelage of Alexander the Great, over whom he exercised a considerable degree of influence (perhaps as much influence as one can exercise over a strong-headed military leader). Aside from contributing to just about every area of philosophy (indeed, he could rightly be said to have single-handedly created certain sub-branches of philosophy), he also did work in areas that we would today classify as biology, anthropology, psychology, physics, cosmology, chemistry and literary criticism.

The range of Aristotle's work is such that to attempt a brief summary of it would be pointless. One general feature of his work that does stand out, however, is the plainness of his rhetorical style and the direct way in which he approached philosophical problems. Aristotle was clearly a practical man who wished in his philosophy to offer words that could help others more usefully live their lives. For him, philosophy was not an abstract affair at all, but an essential part of a good life.

Reliabilism, suitably understood as a kind of virtue epistemology, can thus go some way to capturing the idea that knowledge involves a cognitive success that is creditable to the agent. The point behind this version of reliabilism is that one should reliably get to the truth because of some trait that you possess, rather than merely because you form your belief in a reliable fashion (where the reliability may have nothing to do with any cognitive trait that you possess, as happened in the case of the broken thermometer).

• VIRTUE EPISTEMOLOGY AND THE EXTERNALISM/INTERNALISM DISTINCTION

Nevertheless, there are other problems with reliabilism, and these afflict even this modified version of the thesis. The most pressing of these is that reliabilism seems to allow that it is sometimes very easy to have knowledge.

Consider the following example that is often discussed in epistemology, that of the chicken-sexer. A **chicken-sexer** is, so the story goes at any rate, someone who, by being raised around chickens, has acquired a highly reliable trait which enables them to distinguish between male and female chicks. Crucially, however, chicken-sexers tend to have false beliefs about how they are doing what they do because they tend to suppose that they are distinguishing the chicks on the basis of what they can see and touch. Tests have shown, however, that there is nothing distinctive for them to see and touch in this regard, and that they are actually discriminating between the chicks on the basis of their smell. Furthermore, imagine a chicken-sexer who not only has false beliefs about how she is distinguishing between the chicks, but who also hasn't yet determined whether she is reliable in this respect (e.g., she hasn't sought an independent verification of this fact). Would we really say that such a person *knows* that the two chicks before her are of a different sex?

If one is persuaded by the general reliabilist thesis, at least in its modified guise as a type of virtue epistemology, then one will be inclined to answer 'yes' to this question. After all, the agent is gaining a true belief in this regard by employing her reliable cognitive faculties – in this case her reliable 'chicken-sexing' faculty. Moreover, her cognitive success does seem to be creditable to her, in that she is gaining a true belief by properly employing one of her own reliable cognitive traits. It is not, for example, a matter of luck that her belief is true.

Nevertheless, some epistemologists feel uneasy about allowing ascriptions of knowledge to chicken-sexers. Imagine, for example, that the chicken-sexer claimed to know that the chicks before her were of a different sex. Wouldn't this sound like an improper assertion to make? After all, from her point of view, she has no good reason at all for thinking that this belief is true.

The strange case of the chicken-sexer

Philosophers often use rather strange examples in order to illustrate their points, and epistemologists are no exception. One of the stranger cases they discuss is that of the chicken-sexer. As we have seen, the idea is that there are agents who can reliably determine the sex of a chick via their sense of smell, but who tend to think that they are doing this not via their sense of smell at all but via some of their other senses, such as sight and touch. Typically, the chicken-sexer case is also supplemented with the additional piece of information that the agent concerned doesn't know that her ability works.

What is interesting about the chicken-sexer case is that it tests some of our intuitions about the importance of reliability in gaining knowledge. If reliability is all important, as reliabilism (a form of epistemic externalism) claims, then the mere fact that these agents don't know how they are doing what they are doing (nor even how reliable they are) ought not to bar them from gaining knowledge. In contrast, one might think that in order to know it is not enough that one is reliable, one must also have good reason to think that one is reliable. This is the standard line taken by epistemic internalists.

You might be surprised to learn that there is actually some debate as to whether there really are chicken-sexers as we have just described them. Some claim, for example, that chicken-sexers are not reliable, or that they are indeed reliable but gain their beliefs in exactly the way that they think they are gaining their beliefs (i.e., via their sense of touch and sight). Given that there is this controversy about chicken-sexers, one might naturally hold that epistemologists should abstain from using the example until the matter is settled.

This way of thinking is based on a mistake, however, since it really doesn't matter whether the chicken-sexer example is true in the way it is usually described. What is important is only that it *could* very well be true, where its possible truth highlights an important difference between those theories that hold that reliability is all-important, and those which maintain that mere reliability by itself can never suffice for knowledge (i.e., unless it is supplemented with adequate grounds for thinking that one is reliable).

The conflict of intuitions in play here relates to whether you think that it is always essential that 'internal' factors are involved in the acquisition of bona fide knowledge, such as the agent being in the possession of good reasons for believing what she does. In this case, for instance, if the agent is credited with knowledge, then this will be because purely 'external' factors have obtained, such as the trait in question being reliable. This factor is 'external' because the agent has no good reason for believing that she is reliable in this respect, and so the fact that she is reliable is in this sense 'external' to her. Those who are inclined towards the view that 'internal' factors are essential to knowledge are called *epistemic internalists*, while those who think that 'external' factors alone can at least sometimes suffice for knowledge are called *epistemic externalists*.

We saw this distinction for the first time at the end of Chapter 5 when we were discussing epistemic rationality. The issue then was whether there was a close link between being epistemically rational and being epistemically responsible for one's beliefs (i.e., making sure one had adequate supporting evidence for thinking that one's beliefs were true), and we noted that epistemic internalists tended to demand a closer connection between epistemic rationality and epistemic responsibility than epistemic externalists.

We can see this point re-emerging here with our discussion of chicken-sexers. After all, the epistemic externalist (of a reliabilist stripe at any rate) would count such a person as having knowledge, and yet we would hardly regard her beliefs as being responsibly formed – she has not, for example, acquired any evidence in support of her chicken-sexing beliefs but simply formed them 'blindly'. In contrast, the epistemic internalist would be inclined to deny knowledge to this agent because she lacks adequate evidence in favour of her beliefs. For the epistemic internalist, it is not enough to be reliable, one must also have good grounds for thinking that one is reliable. In doing so, though, one will tend to be epistemically responsible for one's beliefs; hence the close tie between epistemic responsibility and epistemic internalism.

Typically, the epistemic virtues like conscientiousness are understood in such a way that to be virtuous in this sense demands of the agent that she always has good grounds available to her in support of what she believes. Accordingly, one way of staying within the epistemic internalist model while still offering a virtue epistemology is to hold that in order to know, it is not enough merely to form one's belief via a reliable cognitive faculty, such as a chicken-sexing faculty. Instead, one must also have formed one's belief in a way that is epistemically virtuous (i.e., via an epistemic virtue), and thus in a way that is supported by adequate grounds. In this view, the chicken-sexer lacks knowledge because, although she is forming her belief via one of her reliable cognitive faculties, she is not exercising her epistemic virtues – she is not, for example, being conscientious in the way that she forms her belief, since she has no good reason at all for believing what she does.

We thus have a distinction emerging between epistemic externalist (and, usually at least, reliabilist) versions of virtue epistemology and epistemic internalist versions of virtue epistemology. While the former claim that sometimes one can have knowledge merely by exercising one's reliable cognitive faculties, as the chicken-sexer does, the latter demand that one can only gain knowledge by employing one's epistemic virtues, and thereby gaining adequate supporting grounds in favour of one's beliefs.

This is an important difference, but it is also important not to exaggerate it. After all, while these two sorts of views take a very different stance when it comes to cases like the chicken-sexer – as regards most instances of knowledge where both cognitive faculties and epistemic virtues are involved – they will tend to produce the same verdict.

• CHAPTER SUMMARY

- We began by looking at a view known as reliabilism, which, in its simplest form, holds that knowledge is reliably formed true belief. The idea behind such a position was to use the reliability requirement to capture the intuition that when one has knowledge one does not merely happen upon the truth, but rather one gets to the truth in a way that would normally ensure that one has a true belief (i.e., one uses a *reliable* process).
- We saw, however, that there was a Gettier-style problem for this view in its simplest form, in that one could reliably form true beliefs in a way that the true beliefs formed are still essentially due to luck, and hence not genuine cases of knowledge at all.
- One way around this sort of counter-example is to restrict the kinds of reliable processes that are relevant to whether or not an agent has knowledge. In particular, the suggestion we looked at held that to gain knowledge one must gain one's true belief via one's epistemic virtues or cognitive faculties, where these are understood so that they by their nature are reliable. Such a view is called a virtue epistemology.
- A different problem facing reliabilism, even in this modified form, is that it allows knowledge in some controversial cases. The case we looked at was that of the chicken-sexer, an agent who is reliably forming her beliefs about the sex of chicks, but who is doing so even though she has false beliefs about how she is doing what she's doing, and even though she has no good reason for thinking that she is reliable in this regard. Reliabilists tend to allow knowledge in such cases, but some think that one cannot gain knowledge simply by being reliable – instead, one must further have grounds for thinking that one is reliable.
- This dispute over the chicken-sexer example is a manifestation of the debate between epistemic externalists and epistemic internalists. While epistemic internalists insist that knowers must always be in possession of supporting grounds for their beliefs, epistemic externalists allow that sometimes one might have knowledge even while lacking such grounds – just so long as one meets other relevant conditions, such as a reliability condition. Reliabilists, and those virtue epistemologists who regard their view as a variant on reliabilism, thus tend to be

epistemic externalists. Since employing an epistemic virtue, unlike employing a cognitive faculty, tends to always result in an agent having supporting grounds for her beliefs, one way of advancing a virtue epistemology which is allied to epistemic internalism is to insist that the employment of an epistemic virtue is essential to gaining knowledge.

● STUDY QUESTIONS

1 What does it mean to say that one has formed one's belief in a *reliable* way? Could a belief so formed be false, do you think? Give an example of a reliable and an unreliable way of forming a belief about the following subject matters (try to avoid repetition in your answers):
   - the time;
   - the capital of France;
   - the solution to a crossword puzzle clue.
2 In your own words, try to say how the 'thermometer' example described on p. 56 creates severe problems for a simple form of reliabilism. Formulate your own counter-example to simple reliabilism that is structured in the same way as the thermometer case. How are cases of this sort similar to Gettier cases?
3 What is an epistemic virtue? What is a cognitive faculty? Give two examples of each.
4 What is a virtue epistemology? As best as you can, try to explain what it means to cast reliabilism as a form of virtue epistemology, and how understanding reliabilism in this way enables it to evade the thermometer example.
5 What is the chicken-sexer case? How does this example highlight the differences between epistemic externalists and epistemic internalists? (In answering the second question, try to state, in your own words, what the epistemic externalism/ internalism distinction is.)

● INTRODUCTORY FURTHER READING

Barnes, Jonathan (2000) *Aristotle: A Very Short Introduction* (Oxford: Oxford University Press). A readable and (as the title suggests) short book on Aristotle's work by an international expert on ancient philosophy.

Battaly, Heather (2008) 'Virtue Epistemology', *Philosophy Compass* (Oxford: Blackwell). An excellent and very up-to-date survey of the recent literature on virtue epistemology.

Bonjour, Laurence & Sosa, Ernest (2003) *Epistemic Justification: Internalism vs. Externalism, Foundations vs. Virtues* (Oxford: Blackwell). See especially Part Two, which offers an accessible defence of virtue epistemology by one of its most famous proponents.

Irwin, T. H. (2003) 'Aristotle', *Routledge Encyclopedia of Philosophy*, (ed.) E. Craig, (London: Routledge), <http://www.rep.routledge.com/article/A022?ssid=30358

9753andn=2#>. An excellent overview of Aristotle's philosophy, written by an expert on ancient philosophy.

• ADVANCED FURTHER READING

Greco, John (1999) 'Agent Reliabilism', *Philosophical Perspectives* (volume 13), (ed.) J. Tomberlin, (Atascadero, Calif.: Ridgeview). An excellent overview of a popular form of reliabilism – what Greco refers to as 'agent reliabilism' – which is allied to virtue epistemology.

Kornblith, Hilary (ed.) (2001) *Epistemology: Internalism and Externalism* (Oxford: Blackwell). A great collection of classic and recent papers on the epistemic externalism/internalism distinction, including specific papers devoted to reliabilism. Note that some of the papers are not for beginners.

Zagzebski, Linda (1996) *Virtues of the Mind: An Inquiry into the Nature of Virtue and the Ethical Foundations of Knowledge* (Cambridge: Cambridge University Press). A very readable, and influential, statement of an epistemically internalist version of virtue epistemology.

• FREE INTERNET RESOURCES

'Aristotle: A General Introduction', *The Internet Encyclopedia of Philosophy*, <http://www.iep.utm.edu/a/aristotl.htm>. This is a reasonable overview of Aristotle's work. See also the related articles on specific themes in Aristotle's thought that are posted in this internet encyclopedia.

Baehr, Jason (2006) 'Virtue Epistemology', *Internet Encyclopedia of Philosophy*, <http://www.iep.utm.edu/v/VirtueEp.htm>. A first-rate survey of the main issues regarding virtue epistemology.

Greco, John (2004) 'Virtue Epistemology', *Stanford Encyclopedia of Philosophy*, <http://plato.stanford.edu/entries/epistemology-virtue/>. An excellent overview of the topic from one of the main proponents of such a view.

Part II

where does knowledge come from?

7

perception

- The problem of perceptual knowledge
- Indirect realism
- Idealism
- Transcendental idealism
- Direct realism

THE PROBLEM OF PERCEPTUAL KNOWLEDGE

A great deal of our knowledge of the world is gained via perception – that is, via our sensory faculties such as our sense of sight, hearing, touch, and so forth. My knowledge, if that's what it is, that I am presently at my desk writing these words is itself largely perceptually gained. I can see the computer before me, and I can feel the hard touch of the computer keyboard on my fingers as I type. If we know much of what we think we know, then we must have a great deal of perceptual knowledge. As we will see, however, it is far from obvious that we do have widespread perceptual knowledge of the world around us, at least as that knowledge is usually understood.

Part of the problem is that the way things look isn't always the way things are; appearances can be deceptive. There are familiar examples of this sort of deception, such as the way a straight stick will look bent when placed underwater, or the mirages that result from wandering dehydrated through a barren desert. In these cases, if one were not suitably refining one's responses to one's sensory experiences, then one would be led into forming a false belief. If one did not know about light refraction, for example, then one would think that the stick really is bending as it enters the water; if one did not know that one was experiencing a mirage, then one would really believe that there was an unexpected oasis on the horizon.

There are also less mundane cases of perceptual error where the illusion is more widespread. One could imagine, for example, an environment in which one's sensory experiences are a completely unreliable guide as to the nature of the environment. This could be achieved by hiding the real colours of the objects in the environment by employing fluorescent lights, or by using visual tricks to distort one's sense of perspective in order to give the impression that objects are closer or farther away than they really are. The existence of perceptual error of this sort reminds us that, whilst we must depend upon our perceptual faculties for much of our knowledge of the world, the possibility always remains that these faculties can lead us into forming false beliefs if left unchecked.

Given that we can usually correct for misleading perceptual impressions when they occur – as when we make use of our knowledge of light refraction to account for why straight sticks appear bent when placed in water – the mere possibility of perceptual error is not that worrying. The problem posed by perception is not, then, that it is a fallible way of gaining knowledge of the world; instead, it is its apparent *indirectness*.

Consider the visual impression caused by a genuine sighting of an oasis on the horizon, and contrast it with the corresponding visual impression of an illusory sighting of an oasis on the horizon formed by one who is hallucinating. Here is the crux: *these two visual impressions could be exactly the same.* The problem, however, is that it seems that if this is the case then what we experience in perception is not the world itself, but something that falls short of the world, something that is common to both the 'good' case in which one's senses are not being deceived (and one is actually looking at an oasis) and the 'bad' case in which one's senses are being deceived (and one is the victim of an hallucination). This line of reasoning which makes use of undetectable error in perception in order to highlight the indirectness of perceptual experience is known as the *argument from illusion*.

The **argument from illusion** suggests an 'indirect' model of perceptual knowledge, such that what we are immediately aware of when we gain such knowledge is a sensory impression – a *seeming* – on the basis of which we then make an inference regarding how the world is. That is, in both the deceived and non-deceived 'oasis' case just considered, what is common is a sensory impression of an oasis on the horizon which leads one to infer something about the world: that there really is an oasis on the horizon. The difference between the two cases is that whilst the inference generates a true belief in the non-deceived case, it generates a false belief in the deceived case. In the former case, one is thus in a position, all other things being equal at least, to have perceptual knowledge that there is an oasis before one; whilst in the latter case perceptual knowledge is out of the question because one's visual impressions are deceiving oneself.

But why is the indirectness, in this sense, of perceptual knowledge a problem? Well, the worry is that on this model of our perceptual interactions with the world, it seems that we are never actually perceiving a world external to our senses at all, strictly speaking, since our experiences are forever falling short of the world and requiring supplementation from reason. But isn't this conclusion more than just a little odd? Think of your perceptual experiences just now as you read this book. Aren't you *directly* experiencing the book in your hands?

Moreover, notice that this picture of the way we perceive the world, and thus gain perceptual knowledge, seems to have the result that our perceptual knowledge is far less secure than we might have otherwise thought. We normally regard our perceptual knowledge as the most secure of all. We often say, for example, that seeing is believing, and if we do indeed see something in clear daylight with our own two eyes, then this will tend to trump any counter-evidence we might have. For example, suppose that those around you assure you that your brother is out of town, and yet you see him walking towards you in the high street. Surely the testimony of your peers would be quickly disregarded and you would immediately believe that he is in town. According to our ordinary conception of perceptual knowledge, then, it is *privileged* relative to (at least some) other types of knowledge. But if perceptual experience does not put us in direct contact with the world, as the argument from illusion suggests – such that perceptual knowledge rests in part on an inference – then it appears that our perceptual knowledge is no more privileged than other 'indirect' knowledge that we have of the world. In short, our knowledge of the world when we see that things are so is no better than it is when, say, we are merely told that things are so. But why, then, are we so confident in our perception-based judgements about the world?

● INDIRECT REALISM

The way of understanding perceptual knowledge which embraces the apparent indirectness of perceptual experience that we just noted is known as *indirect realism*. It holds that we gain knowledge of an objective world indirectly by making inferences from our sense impressions. The main argument for **indirect realism** is, in essence, the *argument from illusion* just given. The general idea is that the phenomenon of perceptual illusion highlights that what is presented to us in perceptual experience is not the world itself but merely an impression of the world from which we must draw inferences about how the world really is.

There is also another type of consideration in favour of indirect realism which concerns the distinction between *primary qualities* and *secondary qualities* that was drawn (in modern times) by the philosopher **John Locke** (1632–1704), himself a proponent of a version of indirect realism. A **primary quality** is a feature of an object that the object has independently of anyone perceiving the object; the **secondary quality** of an object is dependent upon the perception of an agent.

A good example of a primary quality is shape, in that the shape of an object is not in any way dependent upon anyone perceiving that object. Compare shape in this respect with colour. The colour of an object is a secondary quality in that it depends upon a perceiver. If human beings were kitted-out with different perceptual faculties, then colours would be discriminated very differently. Indeed, think of the animal kingdom in this respect, where there are creatures who can see colours that we can't see, and also creatures who are unable to see colours that we can see.

Note that this is not to suggest that colour is in some way an unreal or illusory feature of an object, since it is certainly a stable fact about, say, the UK's Royal Mail postboxes that they will generate a visual impression of redness to any person with the standard visual faculties who is looking at the postbox in normal lighting conditions. It is thus a real feature of the world that there are objects that generate visual impressions in this way. The point is rather that the colour of an object is not intrinsic to the object in the way that its shape is, but instead depends upon there being perceivers who respond to the object with the appropriate visual impressions.

***

John Locke (1632–1704)

No man's knowledge [. . .] can go beyond his experience.
                    Locke, *An Essay Concerning Human Understanding*

The English philosopher John Locke is perhaps most noted for his work on political theory, especially regarding the limits of the power of the state. Indeed, Locke's broadly liberal conception of the role of the state was very influential on the establishment of the US constitution.

In his philosophy more generally, Locke belongs to a school of thought known as **empiricism**, which traces all knowledge of any substance back to sensory experience. Along with **George Berkeley** (1685–1753) and **David Hume** (1711–76), Locke is often referred to as one of the British empiricists. This commitment to empiricism is reflected in his famous claim that the mind at birth is like a *tabula rasa* – that is, like a 'blank slate' on which nothing is written. What Locke means by this is that there are no innate ideas. Instead, all our ideas, and thus our knowledge, are derived via experience of the world.

***

The indirect realist is clearly in a good position to accommodate the primary/secondary quality distinction. After all, there is, in this view, a distinction between the world as it is perceived and the world as it really is, independently of being perceived. This distinction maps neatly onto the primary/secondary quality distinction, with the secondary qualities of an object belonging to the former realm, and the primary qualities of an object belonging to the latter realm.

The chief problem with indirect realism is that by making our perceptual knowledge of the world inferential, it threatens to dislocate us from the world altogether. Intuitively, what I am aware of when I open my eyes is the world itself, not a sensory impression of the world from which I infer specific beliefs about the world. Indeed, once one has departed down the road of indirect realism, it is not difficult to see the attraction of a widespread scepticism about our knowledge of the world (i.e., the view that it is impossible to know anything about the world). After all, if what I am immediately aware of when I perceive is only an impression of the world from which I must then make an inference about the way the world is that could be either right or wrong, then why should I think that I have *any* knowledge at all of how the world really is?

This point is exacerbated once one considers the possibility that the way the world appears and the way that it really is could be drastically different in this view. Suppose, for example, that I am being radically deceived in my sensory impressions by some mischievous super-being who is 'feeding' me sensory impressions that are entirely misleading. If all that I am directly aware of in perceptual experience is the way the world appears, then it seems that I could never be in a position to detect that this deception was going on. If it were taking place, however, then the way the world appeared would be no guide at all to how the world is, and thus the inferences I would be making about the nature of the world on the basis of my visual impressions would be dubious at best. Given this problem, it seems that all that I am entitled to take myself to know on this view is how the world appears, not how it really is.

This difficulty is known as the **problem of the external world**, and whilst this problem is one that must be dealt with, in some form, by all theories of perceptual knowledge, it does seem as if indirect realism aggravates this difficulty by offering an account of perceptual knowledge which makes our knowledge of the external world shakily inferential rather than direct. Indeed, some have responded to indirect realism by arguing that, if this is how we are to understand perceptual knowledge, then we lose any grounds for thinking that there is a world that is independent of our experience of it (i.e., a world which is 'external' in the relevant sense).

• IDEALISM

The view which denies that there is an external world in this sense – that is, which denies that there is a world that is independent of our experience of it – is known as **idealism**. Perhaps the most famous exponent of a version of this position is George Berkeley (1685–1753). Idealists respond to the problem of the external world by claiming that perceptual knowledge is not knowledge of a world that is independent of our perception of it, but rather knowledge of a world that is *constituted* by our perception of it. In this view the world is, so to speak, 'constructed' out of appearances rather than being that which gives rise to such appearances, and thus it is not 'external' in the relevant sense at all. (Another way of putting the point is that for the idealist there are only secondary qualities.) As Berkeley famously put it in his book, *A Treatise Concerning the Principles of Human Knowledge*, 'To be is to be perceived'. This is a very dramatic conclusion to draw, and appears to call much of our ordinary conception of the world and our relation to it into question.

George Berkeley (1685–1753)

To be is to be perceived.
Berkeley, *A Treatise Concerning the Principles of Human Knowledge*

George Berkeley, otherwise known as Bishop Berkeley (he was the Bishop of Cloyne in what is now the Republic of Ireland), was, like John Locke (1632–1704) and David Hume (1711–76), an empiricist. An empiricist is someone who believes that all knowledge of substance is ultimately derivable from experience. (Locke, Berkeley and Hume are collectively known as the British empiricists.) Unlike Locke and Hume, however, he famously saw in empiricism a motivation for idealism – the view that there is no mind-independent world.

Berkeley led a very interesting life, including a spell living in Bermuda. He also has the unusual distinction of having a city (and a university) named after him, the city of Berkeley in California.

If the view is not qualified in some way, then it will end up maintaining that the world ceases to exist when no one is perceiving it. For example, one can't say that a tree fell in the forest if there was no one around to see or hear (or otherwise sense) it fall; if no one experienced the falling of the tree, then in the idealist view the event didn't happen. This is clearly a very radical claim to make! Indeed, it is hard to distinguish a simple-minded idealism of this sort from plain scepticism about our perceptual knowledge. Although, unlike the sceptic, the idealist claims that we do know a great deal about the world. The idealist does this by making what we mean by the 'world' so different from what we usually take it to mean that it feels as if the idealist is agreeing with the sceptic after all.

Berkeley's way of lessening some of the more outlandish consequences of a simple idealism was to introduce the idea of an ever-present God. With God in the picture, we now no longer need to worry about what to make of unobserved events, since all events will be observed by an all-seeing God. Accordingly, we aren't forced to say that events which aren't observed by us mere mortals therefore don't happen. Berkeley was a Christian – a bishop, in fact – so this appeal to God is unsurprising. This sort of refinement to idealism would clearly offer little comfort to an idealist who was also an atheist though!

● TRANSCENDENTAL IDEALISM

Others have tried to lessen the more counterintuitive aspects of idealism while retaining the guiding thought behind it in different ways. One prominent version of idealism which is modified to make it more appealing is the **transcendental idealism** proposed by **Immanuel Kant** (1724–1804).

Kant agrees with the simple idealist that what we are immediately aware of in sensory experience is not the world itself. Nevertheless, unlike the idealist, he argues that we are required to suppose that there is an external world that gives rise to this sensory experience since, without this supposition, we would not be able to make any sense of such experience. Very roughly, the idea is that we can only make sense of our perceptual experiences as responses to an external world, even if we are not directly acquainted with this world in perceptual experience.

Immanuel Kant (1724–1804)

All our knowledge begins with the senses, proceeds then to the under-standing, and ends with reason. There is nothing higher than reason.

Kant, *Critique of Pure Reason*

Immanuel Kant is quite possibly the most important and influential philosopher of the modern era.

Although he contributed to just about every area of philosophy, he is most known for his transcendental idealism and his contribution to ethics. As regards the former, the leading idea was that much of the structure that we ascribe to the world – such as the temporal or casual order – is in fact a product of our minds. In ethics, he is mostly known for arguing that the source of the moral good lies in the good will. A morally good action is thus one that is done with a good will (though note that Kant imposes some rather austere demands on what counts as a good will, so good acts are not as easy to come by as this short précis might suggest!).

Aside from philosophy, Kant also taught and wrote on such subjects as anthropology, physics, and mathematics. Famously, Kant spent his entire life in the city of Königsberg in what was then East Prussia (the city is now called Kaliningrad, and is part of Russia).

On the face of it, such a view might look like a version of indirect realism, and hence not a type of idealism at all, since doesn't it just make our knowledge of the world indirect? What is key to the view, however, is that we cannot gain knowledge of a world that is independent of experience through experience at all, directly or otherwise. In this sense, then, transcendental idealism *is* a form of idealism. Unlike simple idealism, however, Kant claims that reason shows us that, given the nature of our experiences, there must be a mind-independent world beyond experience which gives rise to these experiences. So although we have no experiential knowledge of a world that is independent of experience, we do have knowledge of its existence through reason.

• DIRECT REALISM

All this talk of idealism can make one wonder whether something didn't simply go wrong in our reasoning right at the start of our thinking about this topic. How could it be that reflecting on the nature of our perceptual experience of the world has led us to think that perhaps there is no external world to have knowledge of in the first place (or at least no external world that we can know through experience)? With this in mind, it is worth considering the prospects for the simple-minded *direct realism* that we set aside earlier in order to opt for the indirect realism that appeared to be able to resolve the difficulties posed by the argument from illusion whilst also accounting for our intuitive distinction between primary and secondary qualities.

In its simplest form, **direct realism** takes our perceptual experiences at face value and argues that, at least in non-deceived cases, what we are aware of in perceptual experience is the external world itself. That is, if I am genuinely looking at an oasis on the horizon right now, then I am directly aware of the oasis itself, and thus I can have perceptual knowledge that there is an oasis before me without needing to make an inference from the way the world seems to how it is.

The motivation behind direct realism, besides the obvious attraction that of all the views it most accords with common sense, is that other theories of perceptual knowledge, such as indirect realism and idealism, are far too quick to infer from the fact that our perceptual experience could be undetectably misleading that we are only directly aware of the way the world seems to us rather than the way the world is. The idea is that although it is true that in deceived cases, such as the scenario in which I am visually presented with a mirage of an oasis, I am not directly aware of the world but only with the way the world appears, this should not be thought to entail that in non-deceived cases, such as where I am actually looking at an oasis in the distance, I am not directly acquainted with objects in the world. In this view, the fact that I am not always able to distinguish between deceived and non-deceived cases is neither here nor there, since it is not held to be a precondition of perceptual knowledge that one can tell the genuine cases of perceptual knowledge apart from the merely apparent cases.

Of course, the direct realist cannot leave matters there, since she needs to go on to explain how such a view is to function. For one thing, she needs to develop a theory of knowledge which can allow us to have perceptual knowledge directly via perceptual experience even in cases where one is unable to distinguish genuine from apparent perception. Moreover, she also needs to offer an explanation of the primary/

secondary quality distinction. Nevertheless, given the unattractiveness of indirect realism and the versions of idealism that are suggested by the move to indirect realism, direct realism needs to be taken very seriously indeed.

• CHAPTER SUMMARY

- A great deal of our knowledge of the world is gained via perception (i.e., via our senses). Our senses are sometimes prone to deceive us, though, as we noted, this is not a problem in itself, since we can often tell when they are not to be trusted (as when we see a stick 'bend' as it enters water). What is problematic about perceptual experience is brought out via the argument from illusion. In essence, this states that since a situation in which we are deceived about the world could be one in which we have, it seems, exactly the same experiences as we would have in a corresponding undeceived case, we don't directly experience the world at all.

- The conception of perceptual knowledge suggested by the argument from illusion is that of indirect realism. This holds that there is an objective world out there, one that is independent of our experience of it – this is the 'realism' part – but that we can only know this world indirectly through experience. In particular, what we directly experience is only how the world appears to us, and not how it is. On this basis, we can then make inferences to how the world really is.

- Indirect realism can also easily account for the primary/secondary quality distinction – the distinction between those (primary) properties or qualities of an object that are inherent in the object, such as its shape, and those (secondary) properties or qualities of an object that are dependent upon the perceiver, such as its colour.

- On the indirect realist view, we don't have any direct experience of the external world, and this has prompted some to argue for a view known as idealism, which maintains that there is no external world. In particular, idealism maintains that the world is constructed out of appearances and does not extend beyond it – that is, there is no mind-independent world.

- We also looked at a more refined form of idealism, known as transcendental idealism. Transcendental idealism maintains that, while we are unable to have any experiential knowledge of the external world (i.e., a world that is independent of experience), nevertheless, given the nature of our experience, we can use reason to show that there must be an external world that gives rise to our experiences.

- Finally, we considered a common-sense view of perceptual experience called direct realism. This view holds that we *can* directly experience the world, and so rejects the conclusion usually derived from the argument from illusion that direct experience of the world is impossible.

• STUDY QUESTIONS

1 Think of two examples of when your experiences have been a misleading guide as to the way the world is.
2 What is the argument from illusion? What is indirect realism? Explain, in your own words, why the argument from illusion offers support for indirect realism.
3 Explain, in your own words, what the primary/secondary quality distinction is. Pick an object, and give an example of a primary quality that this object has and a secondary quality that this object has.
4 Explain, in your own words, what idealism is. Do you find this position plausible? If not, say why. If so, then try to think why others might find it implausible, and try to see if you can offer any considerations in defence of the view in light of these concerns.
5 What is transcendental idealism? How does it differ from idealism? How does it differ from indirect realism?
6 What is direct realism? Do you find this position plausible? If not, say why. If so, then try to think why others might find it implausible, and try to see if you can offer any considerations in defence of the view in light of these concerns.

• INTRODUCTORY FURTHER READING

Dancy, Jonathan (1987) *Berkeley: An Introduction* (Oxford: Blackwell). The best introduction to Berkeley's philosophy in recent years.
Dunn, John (2003) *Locke: A Very Short Introduction* (Oxford: Oxford University Press). A nice introduction to Locke's philosophy.
Guyer, Paul (2004) 'Kant', *Routledge Encyclopaedia of Philosophy*, (ed.) E. Craig, (London: Routledge), <http://www.rep.routledge.com/article/DB047>. A superb introduction to Kant's philosophy by one of the world's leading Kant scholars.
Scruton, Roger (2001) *Kant: A Very Short Introduction* (Oxford: Oxford University Press). A very readable introduction to Kant's philosophy.
Sosa, David (2009) 'Perceptual Knowledge', *The Routledge Companion to Epistemology*, (eds.) S. Bernecker & D. H. Pritchard, (New York: Routledge). A sophisticated, yet accessible, overview of the epistemological issues raised by perception.

• ADVANCED FURTHER READING

Robinson, Howard (1994) *Perception* (London: Routledge). A good recent discussion of the central issues in this area. Not for the beginner.
Shwartz, Robert (ed.) (2003) *Perception* (Oxford: Blackwell). A nice collection of articles on the philosophy of perception, including both historical texts and contemporary readings.

● FREE INTERNET RESOURCES

Bonjour, Laurence (2001) 'Epistemological Problems of Perception', *Stanford Encyclopedia of Philosophy*, <http://plato.stanford.edu/entries/perception-episprob/>. An excellent overview of the central issues by one the leading figures in the field.

Downing, Lisa (2004) 'Berkeley', *Stanford Encyclopedia of Philosophy*, <http://plato. stanford.edu/entries/berkeley/>. A good introduction to the work of Berkeley.

O'Brien, Daniel (2004) 'The Epistemology of Perception', *Internet Encyclopedia of Philosophy*, <http://www.iep.utm.edu/e/epis-per.htm>. A first-rate introduction to the main issues regarding the epistemology of perception.

Uzgalis, William (2005) 'Locke', *Stanford Encyclopedia of Philosophy*, <http://plato. stanford.edu/entries/locke/>. An excellent overview of the life and works of Locke.

8

testimony
and memory

- The problem of testimonial knowledge
- Reductionism
- Credulism
- The problem of memorial knowledge

THE PROBLEM OF TESTIMONIAL KNOWLEDGE

Think of all the things that you think you know right now – such as that the earth is round, or that the Nile flows through Egypt. Most of these beliefs will have been gained not by finding out the truth of the claim in question yourself, but by being *told* that this claim was true by others. Indeed, often we do not even remember exactly how we come by most of our beliefs. I don't recall who it was who first told me that the earth was shaped as it is (or whether I was 'told' it at all, as opposed to reading it in a book, or seeing the image on a TV screen), but I do know that this isn't the kind of claim that I could verify for myself with my own eyes, since this would involve an investigation that is well beyond my present means (e.g., a space mission). This might not seem particularly worrying, given that others have seen that this is the way things are and have passed this information on to the rest of the world (with pictures and so forth). Still, one might be troubled by the extent to which what we believe is dependent upon the word of others. What is our justification for forming our beliefs via the word of others?

The issue here is that of the status of **testimony**, where this means not only the formal verbal transmission of information that one finds taking place in a courtroom, but also the intentional transmission of information in general, whether verbally or through books, pictures, videos, and so forth. A great deal of what you learn you learn via the testimony of others rather than by finding out the truths in question for yourself. It is actually quite important that you find out the truth of most of what you believe in this way since if what you believed was restricted to only those claims that you could verify yourself (i.e., without any assistance from others), then you wouldn't be able to know all that much about the world. Someone like myself, who has never visited northern Africa, for example, would be unable to know which country the Nile flows through, and much else besides. Much of our knowledge is thus *social* in the sense that it involves a process of co-operation between lots of different people, including people in different parts of the world and even people who have long since passed away but who transmitted their knowledge on to subsequent generations.

Sometimes, of course, the testimony we receive is false or misleading. For example, someone with a political agenda might try to make us think that a certain problem, such as immigration, is much worse than it actually is in order to further their own political ends. In itself, this kind of testimonial deceit is not all that troubling since we have a number of checks and balances which we can use to evaluate the testimony of others. If, for example, we know that someone has something to gain by making us believe a certain claim (as in the political case just mentioned), then we instinctively put this claim under greater scrutiny than we would have done otherwise.

The same goes for testimony that, on the face of it, must be false (i.e., testimony that conflicts with other beliefs that we currently hold). If someone told me that the Nile does not flow through Egypt, I wouldn't simply accept this claim at face value but would rather test its credibility. Is the person making the assertion authoritative in this regard (is she, for example, a geography teacher)? Does this testimony accord with what is in my atlas and, if not, why not? This is not to say that we never accept testimony that conflicts with our other beliefs, since even our most ingrained beliefs can change over time; look at how human beings have adjusted their beliefs to accommodate the fact that the earth goes around the sun rather than vice versa. Rather, the point is that we are more suspicious when it comes to surprising testimony than when it comes to testimony that accords with what we already believe, and in this way we avoid being radically misled.

These policies for dealing with problematic testimony do not, however, wholly justify our practice of relying on testimony. After all, we often check suspect testimony by comparing it with other testimony we have received. For example, I evaluate the politician's claim about immigration by considering it in the light of the newspaper articles I've read on the subject from reliable news sources, but these too are instances of testimony. One might wonder, then, whether there is any way of justifying our reliance on testimony as a whole.

Suppose, for example, that all, or nearly all, of the testimony that we receive is false or misleading. How would we tell? Perhaps everyone is out to trick us, as in the film *The Truman Show* in which the protagonist, Truman, is, unbeknownst to him, the main character in a TV show whose world is in fact nothing more than a TV production set. Just about everything that he has been told is false. If the majority of the testimony that we received were misleading in this way, how would we find out? Typically, one might try to detect deception by asking someone reliable, but clearly this option is of little use in this case!

The Truman Show

The Truman Show is a 1998 movie starring Jim Carrey as Truman Burbank. On the face of it, Truman is a normal man: married, working in insurance, and living in a small American town. In reality, however, Truman's life is being controlled by Christof (played by Ed Harris), a TV producer whom he has never met, who is broadcasting Truman's life live to the nation in a reality TV show called *The Truman Show*. Everyone around poor Truman is thus an actor, and a great deal of what he is told on a day-to-day basis is false. Slowly, though, Truman starts to realise that something fishy is going on, and he tries to escape.

In short, the problem of testimonial knowledge is that we are unable to offer any *independent* grounds for a wide range of the testimony-based beliefs that we hold (i.e., grounds which are not themselves simply other testimony-based beliefs). Unless we have some general entitlement to trust testimony, it seems to follow that much of our knowledge is on a rather insecure footing.

• REDUCTIONISM

If one is troubled by this sort of problem then one solution could be to claim that the justification for a testimony-based belief will always ultimately rest on non-testimonial evidence. That is, if one's testimony-based belief is to be rightly held, then it is not enough that one's evidence for this belief is itself merely gained via testimony. Instead, one needs further non-testimonial grounds, such as personal experience of the fact that this informant is reliable (e.g., one might have observed on a number of occasions in the past that this person's testimony has turned out to be true).

This way of understanding testimony is often known as **reductionism**, since it tries to trace testimonial justification back to the non-testimonial evidence that we have, thereby 'reducing' testimonial justification to non-testimonial justification. Historically, this position is often associated with the Scottish Enlightenment philosopher David Hume (1711–76).

If we take the reductionist thesis entirely at face value, then it is susceptible to some fairly immediate problems. Think again of the protagonist in *The Truman Show*. In this model, Truman is justified in believing all those things which he can vouch for himself or which he has gained via a testimonial source which he knows is reliable because he has verified its reliability for himself in the past.

When it comes to Truman's 'local' beliefs about his immediate environment, such as whether the newspaper shop is presently open, this seems fine because he can independently verify what is being asserted. Moreover, where he can't verify these 'local' claims, he can at least usually be sure that the informant in question is generally reliable about 'local' matters like this. Furthermore, most of Truman's beliefs in this respect will be true, since, although his world is in one sense make-believe, it is true that there are shops and buildings and people inhabiting this TV production set (i.e., it is not a dream or an illusion). Truman's 'local' beliefs thus appear, on the whole at least, to be entirely in order by reductionist lights, even though Truman is the victim of a widespread conspiracy to deceive him.

David Hume (1711–76)

> Reason is, and ought to be, the slave of the passions, and can never pretend to any other office than to serve and obey them.
>
> Hume, *A Treatise on Human Nature*

David Hume is one of Scotland's most important philosophers. Born in Edinburgh, he led an interesting and varied life, writing a celebrated history of England as well as a number of central works in philosophy. Possibly his greatest work, *A Treatise on Human Nature*, was completed by the time he was 26. Hume's intellectual achievements made him a key figure in the period of Scottish history known as the *Scottish Enlightenment*, a time of great intellectual ferment.

Hume's philosophy is characterised by his empiricism, which is the belief that all knowledge is ultimately traceable back to the senses. Hume's empiricism led him to be sceptical (*see* **scepticism**) about a lot of things that his contemporaries took for granted, particularly when it came to religious belief. Because of his ardent empiricism, Hume is often described, along with George Berkeley (1685–1753) and John Locke (1632–1704), as one of the British empiricists.

The problem with Truman's beliefs, however, does not reside in his 'local' beliefs about shop opening hours or which building is where on the town square, but rather concerns his 'non-local' beliefs, such as that the earth is round. After all, Truman has only vouched for the reliability of his informants when it comes to local matters about which he can verify, yet the problem here is their reliability about *non-local* matters. There is no inherent reason why reliability in the one case should extend to the other. My doctor is a reliable informant about medical conditions, but that doesn't mean that she is thereby a reliable informant regarding whether or not I need the electrics in my house rewired. The same goes for the people in Truman's world. That they are reliable informants when it comes to local matters, such as whether the shops are open on the high street, does not mean that they are going to be reliable informants when it comes to non-local matters, such as the shape of the earth.

The trouble is, of course, that Truman is unable to verify their reliability about non-local matters of this sort. So while lots of Truman's testimony-based beliefs are in order, there is an important class of testimony-based beliefs that he holds – those that concern non-local matters – which are problematic by reductionist lights since he has no independent grounds for them. Herein lies the rub, however; we are all in pretty much the same situation as Truman in this regard, since we are no more able to independently verify our non-local beliefs than Truman. Epistemically, therefore, by reductionist lights we are no better off than Truman on this score. In this view, then, it turns out that we know a lot less than we thought we knew.

● CREDULISM

Some have reacted to this conclusion by rejecting reductionism altogether and arguing instead that we don't always need to have further grounds in favour of a testimony-based belief in order to justifiably hold it. Instead, there is, they claim, a default presumption in favour of testimony-based beliefs such that they are justifiably held unless there is a special reason for doubt. Accordingly, we don't need to worry about the problem of offering independent support for our ('non-local') testimony-based beliefs on this view, since such beliefs can be justified in the absence of *any* independent grounds.

In this view, then, Truman was entirely justified in holding his non-local beliefs until counter-evidence which called these beliefs into question emerged. (In the film this consisted of lighting rigs falling onto the ground near where he stood, and people coming up to him in the street to tell him that he was part of a TV show.)

This position is often known, somewhat pejoratively, as **credulism**. Historically, this kind of thesis is usually associated with the work of another Scottish Enlightenment philosopher, and a contemporary of Hume's, **Thomas Reid** (1710–96).

This sort of approach to the justification of testimonial belief may be more in accord with common sense, since it would allow us to have the widespread testimonial knowledge that we typically credit to ourselves. But this common-sense element to the view also highlights one of its least appealing features, which is that it appears to simply turn our naturally trusting nature into a virtue. The key point is this: perhaps we *should* be more suspicious about the information we receive, even though this would place a lot of restrictions on what we may justifiably believe.

Thomas Reid (1710–96)

It is evident that, in the matter of testimony, the balance of human judgement is by nature inclined to the side of belief.

Reid, *An Inquiry into the Human Mind*

Like his contemporary, David Hume (1711–76), Thomas Reid was one of the main figures in a period of Scottish history known as the Scottish Enlightenment, in which radical new ideas came to the fore. Unlike Hume, however, who was notoriously prone to take a sceptical attitude towards the beliefs held by most of those around him (*see* **scepticism**), Reid was a defender of what is known as a 'common-sense' philosophy, which put the claims of common sense above the conclusions of abstract philosophical reasoning.

Just as in his treatment of testimony, Reid favoured trusting our common-sense judgements, so in his treatment of perception he favoured a view known as direct realism, which maintains that we are able to experience the world directly.

Perhaps, however, there is a way of understanding the credulist thesis so that it is not quite so permissive. Recall the epistemic externalism/internalism distinction that we first drew in Chapter 5. In particular, recall that epistemic externalists allowed that one could be justified in believing a certain proposition – and hence potentially know that proposition – even though one lacked grounds in support of that belief, just so long as some further relevant facts about the belief were true (e.g., it was formed by a reliable process). One way of developing the credulist position could be along epistemic externalist lines. On this reading, while it is true that one's testimony-based beliefs can be justified, and hence possible cases of knowledge, even though one is unable to offer any independent grounds in their favour, it is not that the justification for these beliefs isn't based on *anything*. Instead, the justification is in virtue of some further relevant fact about the belief. In this case, for example, it could be that trusting testimony is, as a matter of fact, a reliable way of forming belief. One could thus allow that the agent can be justified in forming a testimony-based belief even while lacking supporting grounds for that belief, while not at the same time conceding that the belief is not being epistemically supported by anything, since it *is* being epistemically supported, just not by grounds that the agent can offer in the belief's favour.

As we saw in Chapter 6, however, epistemic externalism is a controversial thesis, and it may seem particularly controversial when applied to this case. If we are not already persuaded by the credulist idea that a testimony-based belief could be justified even though the agent is unable to offer adequate supporting grounds, then it is not obvious why adding that the belief is, as it happens, reliably formed would make a difference. After all, remember that the agent has no reason for thinking that the belief is reliably formed. Still, if one finds epistemic externalism independently plausible, then modifying the credulist thesis along epistemic externalist lines might look like an attractive way of making the view more palatable.

• THE PROBLEM OF MEMORIAL KNOWLEDGE

So far in this chapter we have talked about the epistemology of testimony without saying anything about memory. Notice, however, that the same sort of problem faces the justification of our reliance on memory as we saw above facing our reliance on testimony. After all, just as we depend upon testimony in a great deal of the beliefs that we form, we also depend upon memory. (Many of the examples that we have cited of testimony-based belief are also beliefs that are based on memory.) Furthermore, just as there seems no obvious reason why testimony should necessarily be thought trustworthy, so there seems no obvious reason why memory should necessarily be thought trustworthy; whether or not we can trust our memory depends, intuitively, on what independent grounds we can offer for thinking that memory is reliable (i.e., grounds which are not themselves dependent upon the use of one's memory).

It seems, then, that in common with a reductionist view about the epistemology of testimony, we similarly ought to advance a parallel reductionist view about the epistemology of memory. That is, that a memory-based belief is only justified, and thus a case of knowledge, if it can be given adequate *independent* (i.e., non-memorial) epistemic support.

The problem is, of course, that, just as with testimony-based beliefs, when one thinks of the grounds one can offer in favour of one's memory-based beliefs, one will usually think of further memory-based beliefs, and so the required independent epistemic support is lacking. For example, suppose I think I recall being told by a geography teacher that the Arctic is not in fact a land mass at all, but merely a block of ice, and so believe on this basis that the Arctic is a block of ice. If this recollection is true, then I would have grounds to trust this belief, since geography teachers are good sources of information about matters such as this. But what further grounds can I cite in support of this memory-based belief? Note that the obvious grounds that would naturally spring to mind in such a case would tend to be themselves memory-based beliefs. For example, one might say in support of this memory-based belief that one recalls putting this answer down in a class test and having the answer marked correctly, which would indeed support the original memory that one was told by a geography teacher that the Arctic is a block of ice. But this further belief is itself gained by memory, so unless one is already presupposing the epistemic legitimacy of using one's memory to gain knowledge, then this further belief wouldn't obviously be of any use.

The reductionist demand as regards memorial justification and knowledge, just like the parallel demand as regards testimonial justification and knowledge, thus seems to lead to a kind of scepticism in that it turns out that we lack a lot of the knowledge that we would ordinarily attribute to ourselves. One way around this problem is to opt for a version of credulism as regards memorial justification and knowledge, and therefore argue that we should grant memory-based beliefs a default epistemic status, such that beliefs so formed are justified, and hence candidates for knowledge, just so long as we have no special grounds for doubt. As with the credulist position as regards testimony, however, the problem with the view is that it merely seems to make a virtue out of necessity. Absent a general ground for trusting memory, it is just not clear why we should be willing to grant such a default status to memory-based belief.

Just as we saw above that credulism as regards testimony can be understood along epistemic externalist lines, one could try to turn the same trick here. Accordingly, one would hold that one's memory-based beliefs for which one lacks adequate grounds can still be justified, and hence potential cases of knowledge, just so long as further relevant facts about the beliefs obtain, such as that the beliefs were reliably formed (i.e., trusting one's memory is a reliable way to form one's beliefs). As with credulism about testimony that is cast along epistemic externalist lines, whether you find this sort of rendering of credulism about memory plausible will depend on whether you find epistemic externalism plausible (and even then you might not think that epistemic externalism, while generally plausible, is applicable in this case).

So just as there is no easy answer to the question of how one justifies one's reliance on testimony, it is equally difficult to say what justifies one's reliance on memory.

• CHAPTER SUMMARY

- Testimonial knowledge is knowledge that we gain via the testimony of others. In the usual case, this will simply involve someone telling us what they know, but we can also gain testimonial knowledge in other more indirect ways, such as by *reading* the testimony of others (in a textbook like this one, say).
- A lot of what we believe is dependent upon the testimony of others. Moreover, it is hard to see how we could verify for ourselves much of what we are told via testimony since such verification would itself involve making appeal to further testimony-based beliefs that we hold, and so would simply be circular.
- One response to this problem is reductionism, which claims that we need to be able to offer non-testimonial support for our testimony-based beliefs if they are to be rightly held. In doing so, we would offer non-circular justification for our testimony-based beliefs. The problem is, however, that for a large number of our testimony-based beliefs this is practically impossible, and so reductionism seems to entail that we know very little of what we usually think we know.
- We also looked at a very different response to the problem of testimonial knowledge, which is known as credulism. This view maintains that we can rightly hold a testimony-based belief even if we are unable to offer independent support (non-testimonial or otherwise) for it, at least provided there are no special reasons for doubt. Thus, since we don't need to offer independent support for a testimony-based belief in order for it to be rightly held, we don't need to worry about whether such independent support would be circular. The chief worry about credulism, however, is that it might be thought simply to license gullibility.

- We did consider, however, the possibility that credulism could be understood as an epistemic externalist thesis, such that while one could have justified testimony-based beliefs even whilst being unable to offer adequate supporting grounds for those beliefs, nevertheless one's beliefs should meet a further relevant condition, such as that they were formed in a reliable way (i.e., that testimony should be in fact reliable, even if we lack good reason for thinking that it is). Such an epistemic externalist rendering of credulism inherits the problems of epistemic externalism more generally, however.
- Finally, we turned to the issue of the epistemology of memory, and found that it raises much of the same issues that testimony does. In particular, there seems no obvious reason to think that our memory is trustworthy by its nature. Absent such a reason, it seems that for a memory-based belief to be justified, and hence a case of knowledge, is for that belief to be given adequate epistemic support from *independent* grounds (i.e., non-memorial grounds). We thus seem led to a form of reductionism about memorial justification and knowledge. The trouble is, as with testimony, such independent grounds are usually lacking. Accordingly, again as with testimony, there is a similar move in the debate concerning the epistemology of memory towards a kind of credulism about memory-based beliefs which accords them a default epistemic standing (with the credulist thesis possibly supplemented by an appeal to some version of epistemic externalism). Such a view (even in its epistemic externalist guise) faces the same kinds of problems that afflict the parallel credulist position regarding testimony.

• STUDY QUESTIONS

1 Try to briefly state in your own words what testimony is. Classify the following cases in terms of whether they are examples of testimony:
- someone telling you that your car has been stolen;
- seeing your car being stolen;
- reading a note from a friend telling you that your car has been stolen;
- remembering that your car has been stolen;
- seeing that your car is no longer in front of your house and inferring that it has been stolen.

2 Try to briefly state in your own words what reductionism about testimony holds, and why someone might endorse this view. Think of *four* beliefs that you hold which you are certain of but which would not meet the requirements laid down by reductionism.

3 Try to briefly state in your own words what credulism about testimony holds, and why someone might endorse this view. Is this view preferable to reductionism?

4 Why might one supplement one's credulism by appealing to some form of epistemic externalism? Describe what such a rendering of credulism would look like, and critically evaluate it. (Along the way, try to state clearly what the epistemic externalism/internalist amounts to.)

5 Explain, in your own words, why the problem facing memorial knowledge and justification is broadly analogous to the problem we have seen facing testimonial knowledge and justification. State what a reductionist and a credulist view would be as regards memory, and specify, where applicable, which view you find to be most plausible. (If you find neither view plausible, say why.)

• INTRODUCTORY FURTHER READING

Bernecker, Sven (2009) 'Memorial Knowledge', *The Routledge Companion to Epistemology*, (eds.) S. Bernecker & D. H. Pritchard, (New York: Routledge). A thorough and completely up-to-date overview of the main epistemological issues as regards memory.

Lackey, Jennifer (2006) 'Knowledge from Testimony', *Philosophy Compass* (Oxford: Blackwell). Not quite as up-to-date as Lackey (2009), but still a very helpful survey of the recent literature on the epistemology of testimony.

Lackey, Jennifer (2009) 'Testimonial Knowledge', *The Routledge Companion to Epistemology*, (eds.) S. Bernecker & D. H. Pritchard, (New York: Routledge). A thorough and completely up-to-date overview of the main epistemological issues as regards testimony.

• ADVANCED FURTHER READING

Coady, C. A. J. (1992) *Testimony: A Philosophical Study* (Oxford: Clarendon Press). This is the classic text on the epistemology of testimony which defends a credulist approach. Very readable (though perhaps not really introductory), with sections that apply the account of testimony offered to specific domains, such as legal testimony.

Lackey, Jennifer and Sosa, Ernest (eds.) (2005) *The Epistemology of Testimony* (Oxford: Oxford University Press). This is the latest collection of papers on the subject, containing articles from most of the leading figures in the field. Not for the novice, but essential reading if you want to develop your grasp of the epistemology of testimony and are already familiar with much of the background of the area.

Martin, C. B. and Deutscher, Max (1966) 'Remembering', *The Philosophical Review*, 75, 61–196. This is the classic article on the epistemology of memory, and can be found in many anthologies of epistemology articles. Note, however, that it is really quite difficult, and hence is not the sort of thing that you are likely to be able to follow on the first reading.

• FREE INTERNET RESOURCES

Adler, Jonathan (2005) 'Testimony, Epistemological Problems of', *Stanford Encyclopedia of Philosophy*, <http://www.seop.leeds.ac.uk/contents.html#t>. This is an outstanding and state-of-the-art entry on the epistemology of testimony, written by one of the experts in the field. It includes lots of detail about the debates in this area and a comprehensive list of references to other articles that might be of use.

Eng, David and Webb, Mark, *Social Epistemology Resources Webpage*, <http://ucsu.colorado.edu/%7Ebrindell/soc-epistemology/Bibliographies/Testimony/testimony.htm>. This is a solid overview of both the epistemology of testimony and some of the literature that you might find useful if you want to explore this debate further. The further reading is helpfully grouped into separate sections like 'expert testimony', 'reductionism and non-reductionism', and so on.

Green, Christopher (2008) 'Epistemology of Testimony', *Internet Encyclopedia of Philosophy*, <http://www.iep.utm.edu/e/ep-testi.htm>. A comprehensive and very recent survey of the issues regarding the epistemology of testimony. Not for beginners.

IMDb Internet Movie Database, <http://www.imdb.com/title/tt0120382/>. Learn more about the movie *The Truman Show*.

Morris, William Edward (2001) 'Hume', *Stanford Encyclopedia of Philosophy*, <http://www.seop.leeds.ac.uk/entries/hume/>. An excellent overview of the work of Hume.

Senor, Tom (2005) 'Epistemological Problems of Memory', *Stanford Encyclopedia of Philosophy*, <http://plato.stanford.edu/entries/memory-episprob/>. An excellent overview of the epistemological issues as regards memory by one of the leading figures working on this area.

Sutton, John, *Philosophy of Memory*, <http://www.phil.mq.edu.au/staff/jsutton/Memory philosophy.html>. An excellent resource of information relevant to the philosophy of memory.

Yaffe, Gideon (2003) 'Reid', *Stanford Encyclopedia of Philosophy*, <http://www.seop.leeds.ac.uk/entries/reid/>. An excellent overview of the work of Reid.

9

a priority
and inference

- A priori and empirical knowledge
- The interdependence of a priori and empirical knowledge
- Introspective knowledge
- Deduction
- Induction
- Abduction

A PRIORI AND EMPIRICAL KNOWLEDGE

A distinction that is common in philosophy is that between **a priori** and **empirical** knowledge (the latter is sometimes known as **a posteriori knowledge**). Very roughly, this distinction relates to whether the knowledge in question was gained independently of an investigation of the world through experience (what is known as an *empirical* inquiry). If it was, then it is a priori knowledge; if it wasn't, then it is empirical (or a posteriori) knowledge.

Suppose, for example, that I come to know that all bachelors are unmarried simply by reflecting on the meanings of the words involved (e.g., that 'bachelor' just means unmarried man, and thus it follows that all bachelors must be unmarried men). Given that I gained this knowledge simply by reflecting on the meanings of the words involved rather than by undertaking an investigation of the world, it is a priori knowledge.

Contrast my knowledge in this respect with my knowledge that the Tropic of Cancer is in the northern hemisphere, which I gained by looking in a reliable atlas. Since I gained this knowledge by making an investigation of the world (i.e., by looking up the Tropic of Cancer in an atlas), this knowledge is thus empirical knowledge.

Notice that the same distinction also applies to justification. A belief is a priori justified if that justification was gained independently of a worldly investigation (e.g., by reflecting on the meanings of the words involved). In contrast, a belief is empirically justified if that justification was gained via a worldly investigation (e.g., looking something up in an atlas).

One way in which this distinction is often made is to say that a priori knowledge (/justification) is knowledge(/justification) that one gains simply by sitting in one's armchair, whilst empirical knowledge(/justification) demands that one get out of one's armchair and make further (empirical) inquiries. In this way we can see that it is not only truths of meaning (e.g., all bachelors are unmarried) that one can have a priori knowledge of, but also other claims, such as logical and mathematical truths. For example, we do not need to make empirical inquiries in order to discern that two plus two equals four, since we can discover this simply by reflecting on our mathematical concepts.

Notice that any proposition which one can have a priori knowledge of one can also have empirical knowledge of. For example, I could come to know that all bachelors are unmarried men not by reflecting (in my armchair) on the meanings of the words involved but also by looking up the meaning of the word 'bachelor' in a dictionary (i.e., by getting out of my armchair and making an empirical inquiry). The converse of this is not true, however, in that it doesn't follow that any proposition which one can have empirical knowledge of one can also have a priori knowledge of. The only way to find out which hemisphere the Tropic of Cancer is in is by getting out of one's armchair and making an empirical investigation – this just isn't the sort of proposition that one can have a priori knowledge of.

• THE INTERDEPENDENCE OF A PRIORI AND EMPIRICAL KNOWLEDGE

Most of our knowledge, even that knowledge which is explicitly empirical, makes use of further knowledge which is both empirical and a priori. Imagine, for example, a detective who is trying to work out who committed a murder, and who discovers, via the reliable testimony of a witness, that one of the suspects – let's call him Professor Plum – was in the pantry at the time of the murder. Now the detective also knows that if someone is in one place at a certain time then they can't be in another place at the same time, and thus he infers that Professor Plum was not in the hallway at the time of the murder, something that may well be very salient to the investigation as a whole. (It might be known, for example, that the murder was committed in the hallway, and thus that Professor Plum is off the hook.)

In this case, the detective is making the following sort of inference, where 1 and 2 are premises from which a conclusion, C, is drawn:

1 Professor Plum was in the pantry at the time of the murder.

2 If Professor Plum was in the pantry at the time of the murder, then he wasn't in the hallway.

Therefore:

> C Professor Plum was not in the hallway at the time of the murder (and so is innocent).

Let's take it as given that both premises are known. The first premise of this inference, 1, is clearly empirical knowledge since it was gained by listening to the testimony of a witness. Premise 2, however, is not obviously empirical knowledge at all, since it seems to be something that you could discover without making any investigation of the world. That is, merely by reflecting on what it means to be located somewhere, you could realise that someone could not be in two places at once and thus that if Professor Plum is in one place (in this case the pantry), then he couldn't also simultaneously be in another place (in this case the hallway). Indeed, presumably, this is just how the detective came by this knowledge in this case, and so it is a priori knowledge. The conclusion is obviously empirical knowledge, however, since it was gained, in part, by making an empirical inquiry (i.e., listening to the testimony of a witness). So although the inference in this case leads to empirical knowledge, it also makes use of a priori knowledge as well.

• INTROSPECTIVE KNOWLEDGE

An important variety of a priori knowledge is gained by **introspection**. This is where we try to discover something by examining our own psychological states.

Suppose, for example, that I sought to decide whether I really wanted to get involved in a certain relationship, and I recognised that I had conflicting thoughts in this regard. One way in which I might try to resolve this issue could be to examine how I really feel about this person. The kinds of questions I might ask myself could be as follows: Do I enjoy her company? Does being around her make me happy, or make me anxious? Am I getting further involved in this relationship simply because I feel pressured to do so? In asking questions of this sort I will, with any luck, discover how best to proceed. Notice, however, that the kind of enquiry that I am conducting here is not an empirical enquiry, since I am not investigating the world at all. Rather I am 'looking into' myself and investigating what I find there. This is, after all, the kind of enquiry that one could undertake in one's armchair. This is introspection and when it yields knowledge – what is known as *introspective knowledge* – it is often the case that the knowledge it yields is a priori knowledge.

Introspection need not only be involved in settling affairs of the heart in the manner just described, since we use introspection all the time to settle more mundane issues. Suppose my partner, whilst fiddling with the gas fire, asks me whether I smell a gas leak. If I was unaware of smelling gas I might reflect further on the nature of my experiences to see if there is anything unusual about them. In doing so, I am introspecting my experiences and thereby examining them in order to extract new information.

Notice that when introspection is used in this kind of way, the knowledge that it yields is empirical knowledge. After all, the original experience (i.e., being in the room which may or may not contain a gas leak) was gained via interaction with the world. Nevertheless, there is a non-empirical component to the introspective knowledge gained in this case, since one is examining one's experience independently of gaining any further empirical information. In this way, for example, one might come to believe that there is a smell of gas in the room, even though one did not recognise this at the time (perhaps one was not looking out for a gas leak, and so merely noted that something smelt strange without further wondering what the smell was of).

• DEDUCTION

Consider again the argument we gave above:

1 Professor Plum was in the pantry at the time of the murder.

2 If Professor Plum was in the pantry at the time of the murder, then he wasn't in the hallway.

Therefore:

C Professor Plum was not in the hallway at the time of the murder (and so is innocent).

This is clearly a good argument for the conclusion, but what do we mean by 'good' here? Well, at the very least we mean that premises 1 and 2 support the conclusion, C, in the following sense: if the premises are true, then the conclusion must be true as well. In other words, it just isn't possible for the premises in this argument to be true and yet the conclusion be false, which is to say that the truth of the premises *entails* the truth of the conclusion. This is what is known as **validity**; this argument is valid.

This argument is more than just valid, however, since the premises are (we supposed above) also true. Suppose, as it happened, that Professor Plum had not been in the pantry at the time of the murder. One of the premises, 1, would then have been false. Nevertheless, it would still have been the case that *if* these premises had been true *then* the conclusion would have been true as well. You can thus have a valid argument even if it has false premises. If the premises are false, the argument is still a good argument in the sense of being valid, even though it gives us no reason for thinking that the conclusion is true because of the falsity of the premises. Since the argument considered above is both valid and has true premises, then it has an additional virtue: it is an argument that is not only good in the sense of being valid but also gives us reason for thinking that the conclusion is true. This virtuous property of arguments is known as **soundness**. Our argument is thus not only valid but also sound.

Arguments that are valid are known as **deductive** arguments. Deductive arguments are very important to the acquisition of knowledge since they enable one to expand one's knowledge. By having knowledge of the premises in the above argument one can thereby infer the conclusion and in doing so gain knowledge of a new proposition.

Moreover, valid arguments which lack true premises, and so are not sound, can still be epistemically useful. If I am justified in believing the premises of a valid argument, then, in most cases at least, I am justified in believing the conclusion of that argument. This is so even if, as it happens, one of the premises is, unbeknownst to me, false, which would mean that the conclusion might be false also (and so not a candidate for knowledge). In order to see this, notice that even if 1 in the argument above is in fact false, it would still follow that if I am justified in believing 1 (e.g., if I was told that 1 was the case by a reliable witness) and I am also justified in believing 2, then I would be justified in believing C. Accordingly, even if deductive arguments do not always extend knowledge, they do always extend justified belief.

• INDUCTION

Not all acceptable types of argument are deductive, however. Consider the following inference:

1 Every observed emu has been flightless.

Therefore:

C All emus are flightless.

This argument is clearly not deductive, since it is entirely possible, even granted the truth of 1, that there is an unobserved emu around somewhere that is not flightless. That is, since the premise can be true and yet the conclusion simultaneously be false, this argument is not a valid argument. Nevertheless, given that we have observed lots of emus across a suitable length of time and in lots of different habitats, then it does seem that this is an entirely legitimate inference to make.

That is, the argument seems perfectly acceptable provided that we interpret 1 along the following lines:

1* Lots of emus have been observed over many years and in a wide range of environments, and they have always been flightless.

Therefore:

C All emus are flightless.

The point about adding this detail to 1 is that inferences of this sort are only legitimate provided that the sample is sufficiently large and representative. If one had only seen a couple of emus, or only observed lots of emus in one very specific environment (e.g., at a particular lake), then the fact that they were flightless in this case need not be any indication at all that emus are, in general, flightless birds. So long as the sample is large and representative enough, however, then this style of reasoning seems perfectly acceptable. This sort of non-deductive reasoning is known as **induction**.

In the case of **deduction**, it is obvious why the reasoning is legitimate, since deductive inferences, being valid, preserve truth; if your premises are true then you can be assured that your conclusion is true also. Accordingly, it ought to be uncontentious to suppose that one can go directly from knowledge of the premises to knowledge of the conclusion. In the case of induction, however, this defence does not work since one might know the premises and yet lack knowledge of the conclusion because the conclusion is false. For example, if there were an unobserved emu somewhere which was not flightless, then one might know the premise in the above argument, legitimately infer the conclusion, and yet lack knowledge of the conclusion because it wasn't true.

Nevertheless, it is the case that good inductive arguments (i.e., ones which make an inference from a large and representative sample), like deductive arguments, always extend justified belief. If I am justified in believing the premise, 1*, of the above inductive argument, then I am justified in believing the conclusion, even if, as it happens, the conclusion is false. The reason for this is that good inductive arguments, while they do not have premises which entail the conclusion, do have premises which make that conclusion likely. They are thus very useful, albeit fallible, ways of forming true beliefs and thereby extending one's justified belief (and, hopefully, knowledge too).

• ABDUCTION

Not all non-deductive arguments have the same form as that just considered. Rather than proceeding from a large and representative sample to an unrestricted conclusion, some non-deductive arguments instead proceed from a single observed phenomenon to an explanation of that phenomenon, usually via the implicit use of connecting premises of some sort. For example, consider the following inference:

  1 There are feet exposed under the curtain in the hall.

Therefore:

  C There is someone hiding behind the curtain.

This seems like a perfectly legitimate form of reasoning. Moreover, like the inductive inferences considered above, the premise clearly does not entail the conclusion, as happens in a deductive argument. Crucially, however, this type of reasoning is very unlike the inductive inference above in that it does not make appeal to a large and representative set of observations. Instead, this style of argument, often known as **abduction**, usually proceeds, as in the case just outlined, from a single observed phenomenon to the best explanation of that phenomenon. This is why this style of reasoning is sometimes called **inference to the best explanation**.

Before we can evaluate this type of reasoning, we need to fill in the gaps here. Whilst it might seem that abductive inferences are as stark as the one just described, if one reflects on the example, one will quickly realise that there is much that is implicit. That is, we only infer that there is someone behind the curtain because of what else we know about the likelihood of there being feet behind the curtain without there being someone there to whom the feet belong. If, for example, we were in the unfortunate (and rather gruesome) situation of being in a room in which there were dismembered feet to be found, then it is unlikely that we would have so quickly inferred C from the observation contained in 1.

Once one makes this element of abductive inference explicit, however, it starts to look like a shorthand way of expressing a normal inductive argument. That is, why do we infer from the fact that we can see feet under the curtain that there is a person there? Well, because we know, from previous experience, that there is an observed regularity between feet being under the curtain and a person behind the curtain to whom the feet belong. When abductive inferences are just abbreviated versions of normal inductive inferences in this way, they pose no special problems.

Sherlock Holmes

Sherlock Holmes, the famous fictional detective of London's Baker Street, often reached his conclusions by making abductive inferences, much to his colleague Dr Watson's amazement. Simply by observing someone's clothing and demeanour, for example, Holmes would draw quite startling (and usually true) conclusions about that person.

In the story, *A Scandal in Bohemia*, for instance, Holmes deduces, simply from taking a good look at Watson, that he has got very wet recently and that his maid is careless. Holmes explains how he knows this by pointing out that the leather on the inside of Watson's left shoe is scored by six almost parallel cuts, as if caused by someone who has carelessly scraped round the edges of the sole in order to remove crusted mud from it. This suggests to Holmes that Watson has recently been out in very wet weather and that his maid has been careless in cleaning his shoes.

Holmes isn't obviously drawing on a series of observations of shoes in order to reach this conclusion, but rather regards the conclusion that he offers as being the best explanation of what he sees. It thus appears to be an abductive inference.

Not all abductive inferences can easily be construed as normal inductive inferences in disguise, however. Imagine, for example, that one came across a wholly unusual phenomenon for the first time, such as a corn circle in a field. There are numerous possible explanations for this phenomenon – from the relatively mundane, such as that it was caused by freak atmospheric conditions, to the quite bizarre, such as that Martians created the circles as a sign to humankind. Which explanation should one choose? Clearly, one cannot make appeal to any observed regularity in this case because, by hypothesis, this is the first time that this sort of phenomenon has been observed. On normal inductive grounds alone, then, one should hold one's fire and wait for further information before one forms a judgement.

That said, I think most people would regard the simplest and most conservative explanation of this phenomenon to be preferable to any explanation which would involve one making radical adjustments to one's beliefs. That is, it seems common sense to explain this phenomenon in terms of freak atmospheric conditions if one can, rather than by resorting to explaining it in terms of Martian activity. This reflects the fact that in ordinary life we tend to treat the best explanation of a phenomenon as being that explanation which, all other things being equal, is the simplest one that is most in keeping with what we already believe. The problem with this kind of regulative principle on abductive inference is that there seems no good reason for thinking that explanations which are simple and conservative in this way are more likely to be true than complex or unconservative explanations.

In any case, the only grounds we could have for thinking that it is legitimate to use such regulative principles in abductive inference could be inductive grounds for thinking that simplicity and conservatism have helped us to get to the truth in the past. It seems then that if abductive inference is to be legitimate at all, then it must reduce to an inductive inference at some point, however complicated the 'reduction' might be. That is, despite the apparent differences between abductive and normal inductive inferences, abductive inferences always seem to make implicit use of further information or regulative principles which, if properly employed at any rate, are inductively grounded.

If that's right, then abductive inferences will be acceptable just so long as the corresponding inductive inferences are acceptable; more generally, abduction is an acceptable form of inference if induction is. As we will see in Chapter 10, however, there is in fact cause to doubt whether induction is a legitimate way of drawing inferences, and so both induction and abduction are problematic.

• CHAPTER SUMMARY

- We began by noting a distinction between a priori and empirical knowledge. The former is knowledge that you have gained without having to investigate the world (i.e., armchair knowledge), while the latter is gained, at least in part, via a worldly investigation.

- An important kind of a priori knowledge is gained by introspection, which is where we 'look inwardly' and examine our own psychological states rather than 'look outwardly' and investigate the world. As we saw, however, not all introspective knowledge is a priori knowledge.
- We then looked at different kinds of inference. In particular, we made a distinction between inferences that are deductive and inferences that are inductive. The former kind of inference is where one moves from premise(s) to conclusion, where the premise(s) *entail* the conclusion (i.e., given that the premise(s) are true, the conclusion must also be true).
- Inductive arguments, in contrast, are inferences from premise(s) which provide support for the conclusion without actually entailing it (i.e., the premise(s) could be true without the conclusion being true). We noted that good inductive arguments are ones that provide strong support for the conclusion, and this will usually mean that their premises appeal to a representative sample in providing support for the conclusion.
- Finally, we noted that many non-deductive inferences do not seem to have the same form as normal inductive inferences, even though they involve premise(s) which do not entail the conclusion. Instead, these inferences involve making an inference regarding what is the best explanation of a certain phenomenon – what is known as an abductive inference. Nevertheless, despite their superficial differences, it seems that any legitimate form of abductive inference will be an abbreviated version of an inductive inference.

● STUDY QUESTIONS

1. Explain, in your own words, the distinction between a priori and empirical knowledge. Give two examples of each type of knowledge, and explain why they are of that type.
2. What is introspection? Give an example of your own of introspective knowledge, and say whether the knowledge in question is a priori or empirical.
3. What is a deductive argument? Give an example of your own of a deductive argument.
4. What is the difference between an argument which is merely valid and one that is, in addition, sound? Give an example of your own to illustrate this distinction.
5. What is an inductive argument, and how is it different from a deductive argument? Give an example of your own of an inductive argument which you think is a good argument. Say why you think this argument is a good argument.
6. What is an abductive argument, and how is it different from a normal inductive argument? Why might one think that abductive arguments, at least when cogent, are in fact normal inductive arguments in disguise?

• INTRODUCTORY FURTHER READING

Bonjour, Laurence (2005) 'A Priori Knowledge and Justification, Recent Work on', *Routledge Encyclopedia of Philosophy*, (ed.) E. Craig, (London: Routledge), <http://www.rep.routledge.com/article/P060?ssid=244041654 andn=2#>. A recent survey of the issues regarding a priori knowledge and justification in the recent literature, written by one of the leading figures in the debate. Well worth a look.

Bonjour, Laurence (2009) 'A Priori Knowledge', *The Routledge Companion to Epistemology*, (eds.) S. Bernecker & D. H. Pritchard, (New York: Routledge). This covers similar ground to Bonjour (2005), but is more up-to-date.

Jenkins, Carrie (2008) 'A Priori Knowledge: Debates and Developments', *Philosophy Compass* (Oxford: Blackwell). A very useful up-to-date survey of the contemporary literature. It can be a little demanding in places, but overall is accessible enough to just about count as 'introductory' further reading.

Vogel, Jonathan (2005) 'Inference to the Best Explanation', *Routledge Encyclopaedia of Philosophy*, (ed.) E. Craig, (London: Routledge), <http://www.rep.routledge.com/article/P025>. This is a nice clear entry on abduction.

• ADVANCED FURTHER READING

Casullo, Albert (2003) *A Priori Justification* (Oxford: Oxford University Press). This is the classic book on a priori knowledge and justification from the recent literature. Not for beginners.

Lipton, Peter (1991) *Inference to the Best Explanation* (London: Routledge). A very readable overview of the issues. Well worth reading if you want to find out more about abductive arguments.

• FREE INTERNET RESOURCES

'Deductive and Inductive Arguments', *Internet Encyclopedia of Philosophy*, <http://www.iep.utm.edu/d/ded-ind.htm>. A neat overview of the distinction between inductive and deductive arguments.

Kind, Amy (2005) 'Introspection', *Internet Encyclopedia of Philosophy*, <http://www.iep.utm.edu/i/introspe.htm>. A clear introduction to the issues surrounding introspection.

Russell, Bruce (2007) 'A Priori Justification and Knowledge', *Stanford Encyclopedia of Philosophy*, <http://plato.stanford.edu/entries/apriori/>. A comprehensive and completely up-to-date survey of the literature on this topic.

'Sherlock Holmes', *Wikipedia*, <http://en.wikipedia.org/wiki/Sherlock_Holmes>. Some further information on the fictional detective Sherlock Holmes, including a quite sophisticated discussion of his distinctive style of reasoning.

'Validity and Soundness', *Internet Encyclopedia of Philosophy*, <http://www.iep.utm.edu/v/val-snd.htm>. A neat overview of the notions of validity and soundness.

10
the problem of induction

- The problem of induction
- Responding to the problem of induction
- Living with the problem of induction I: falsification
- Living with the problem of induction II: pragmatism

THE PROBLEM OF INDUCTION

As we saw in Chapter 9, it is very important to be able to account for the legitimacy of inductive inferences since we use them all the time to acquire knowledge. Think of the activity of the scientist when she is conducting her experiments. Here the inferences involved are almost exclusively inductive, since they often move from a premise which concerns an observed, though representative, sample, to an entirely general claim which goes beyond the restricted claim found in the premises.

For example, that a certain liquid is observed to have a particular boiling point in lots of relevant conditions (e.g., in normal atmospheric conditions) and across a large number of trials is good reason for thinking that, in general, it has that boiling point, even though it is consistent with the experiments conducted that it sometimes boils at a different temperature. If induction is not a legitimate way of gaining knowledge, then this would seem to preclude us from gaining scientific knowledge of this sort, and much else besides. Our dependence on inductive inferences in this way has been shown to be problematic, however, by a famous argument – due to David Hume (1711–76) – that appears to show that inductive reasoning is unjustified.

We noted in Chapter 9 that inductive inferences seem entirely legitimate provided that the sample used is sufficiently large and representative. Recall the 'emu' example that we gave there, and what we said about it. Here's the basic inference again:

1 Every observed emu has been flightless.

Therefore:

C All emus are flightless.

As we noted, this inference seems perfectly acceptable just so long as the observations of emus were made in a representative range of cases (in lots of different environments and circumstances, say), and that there was a sufficiently large number of observations (e.g., just a couple of observed emus would not do). That is, we need to read 1 as something like 1*:

1* Lots of emus have been observed over many years and in a wide range of environments, and they have always been flightless.

The inductive inference from 1* to C does seem to be a good inference because, given the sorts of observations in play in 1*, C seems very likely to be true.

The issue that Hume raised, however, was how we could be sure that regularities that are observed within a representative sample (e.g., between being an emu and being a flightless bird) should increase the likelihood that the unrestricted generalisation (i.e., that all emus are flightless birds) is true. Seemingly, our only defence for this claim is an inductive one (i.e., that representative samples have supported such unrestricted generalisations in the past). But if that's the case, then this means that inductive inferences are only justified provided they make use of the conclusions of further inductive inferences. Accordingly, there can be no non-circular way of justifying induction (i.e., no way of justifying it which does not itself make appeal to a further inductive inference).

Let's break this argument down into stages. Hume's first point is that the inference from 1* to C in the inductive argument above is problematic unless it is supplemented with a further premise, namely:

2 That a certain regularity has been observed across a sufficiently large and representative sample means that it is likely that the regularity applies in general.

With this premise in play, there is no mystery about why we can legitimately infer C from 1*, since the representativeness of the sample at issue in 1* will ensure, in line with 2, that the conclusion is likely to be true. But how, if at all, do we know 2? Intuitively, the only way one could know such a claim is via another inductive inference:, by observing a correlation between observed regularities across sufficiently large and representative samples and the unrestricted regularity itself. But that means that an inductive inference is only legitimate provided it makes use of a further claim which is itself gained via induction. Accordingly, concludes Hume, the epistemic support we have for inductive inferences is circular, since they only generate justified belief in the conclusion provided one already makes use of a further inductive inference. As a result, there could be no non-circular justification of induction.

• RESPONDING TO THE PROBLEM OF INDUCTION

It is not altogether obvious how one should respond to an argument of this sort. One line of response might be to claim that such a fundamental epistemic practice as induction does not stand in need of justification, and thus that we can legitimately employ it without worrying about whether a non-circular justification is available. This does seem rather ad hoc, however, and is hardly an intellectually satisfying approach to the problem.

Another possibility is to claim that just so long as induction works, it does not matter whether we are in possession of non-circular reasons for thinking that it is a legitimate way of arguing. That is, the thought would be that just so long as a premise like 2 is true then it can be legitimately employed in an inductive argument – it doesn't matter whether we have any good independent reasons for thinking that it is true. Such a move might be made by one who endorses epistemic externalism (i.e., one who holds that one can be justified in holding a belief, and thus have knowledge, even whilst lacking supporting grounds, just so long as certain 'external' conditions obtain, such as that one forms one's belief in a reliable fashion). In this case, the epistemic externalist would hold that we can be justified in holding a belief in the conclusion of an inductive argument even though, granted the **problem of induction**, we lack any good reason for thinking that this belief is true, just so long as induction is in fact a reliable way of forming one's beliefs.

This type of move will not appeal to everyone. In particular, it will not appeal to epistemic internalists who think that in order to be justified in holding a belief, one must always be in possession of appropriate supporting grounds. The problem for the epistemic internalist, however, is to explain how our widespread induction-based beliefs are justified given that, as Hume seems to have shown, there are no non-circular grounds available in support of these beliefs. The choice between the two views is thus very stark indeed.

• LIVING WITH THE PROBLEM OF INDUCTION I: FALSIFICATION

Interestingly, not everyone thinks that it is vital that we respond to the problem of induction by finding a way of resolving it. Instead, some argue that this is a problem that we can live with.

Perhaps the most famous proponent of a view of this sort is **Karl Popper** (1902–94), who argued that the problem of induction was not nearly as pressing as it might at first seem because we don't in fact make use of inductive inferences all that often. In particular, he claimed that science, properly understood, does not make use of inductive inferences at all, but instead proceeds deductively.

In order to see what Popper means by this, consider again the inference that we looked at above concerning emus:

1* Lots of emus have been observed over many years and in a wide range of environments, and they have always been flightless.

Therefore:

C All emus are flightless.

This is clearly an inductive inference since the truth of the premise is compatible with the falsity of the conclusion (i.e., the premise makes the conclusion *probable*, but does not entail it). Moreover, it also seems to accurately represent the way in which a scientist might go about discovering that all emus are flightless – that is, observe lots of emus in lots of different conditions and then draw a general conclusion about whether or not they can fly.

Karl Popper (1902–94)

Good tests kill flawed theories; we remain alive to guess again.

Popper (attributed)

Karl Popper was born in Austria but spent most of his academic life working in Britain. His most famous philosophical contribution was the advocacy of the process of **falsification** as an alternative to induction when it came to understanding science. He claimed that the methodology of science was not to slowly and inductively build up a case for a generalisation, but rather to formulate bold generalisations and then seek to refute them by finding counter-examples to the generalisation.

Popper claimed that the mark of a scientific theory was that it was *falsifiable* – that is, that there was some observation or set of observations which would show that it was false. With this benchmark for what constitutes a scientific theory in mind, Popper argued against certain theories which purported to be scientific but which weren't, Popper claimed, falsifiable. The two theories that Popper focused upon in this regard were Marxism and psychoanalysis. In both cases, argued Popper, any apparent counter-evidence to the view is always explained away so that nothing is ever allowed to count decisively against the theory. But that just goes to show, claimed Popper, that such views are not falsifiable and hence not scientific theories at all.

Popper claims, however, that in fact science proceeds not in this inductive fashion at all but rather by making bold generalisations and then trying to *falsify* them (i.e., by trying to show that the bold generalisation is false). When successful, this process is what Popper calls *falsification*. For example, to take the emu case just described, the scientist who suspects that all emus are flightless will boldly put forward this hypothesis for testing. 'Testing' the hypothesis, however, does not mean looking for evidence in its favour, but rather looking for decisive evidence *against* it. In this case, for instance, it will mean looking for an emu which can fly.

Notice the form of the inference that would take place if one were to falsify an hypothesis in this way – that is, if one were to discover a flying emu. First we have our bold hypothesis:

H All emus are flightless.

We also have our definitive counterevidence to H, the observation of a flying emu:

1 There exists a flying emu.

From this observation we can conclude that the bold hypothesis, H, is false, since this states that all emus are flightless:

C Not all emus are flightless.

What is important about this inference from 1 to C, however, is that it is entirely deductive, not inductive. If there does indeed exist a flying emu then it follows that not all emus are flightless; this conclusion is not merely likely, given the premise, but *must* be the case.

Popper's idea is thus that by offering bold hypotheses which they try to falsify, scientists are in effect proceeding deductively rather than inductively. That is, they do not try to find lots of evidence which supports, albeit inconclusively, the conclusion of an inductive inference; rather they make a bold generalisation which they then try to falsify conclusively, where if this falsification takes place they can deductively conclude that the bold generalisation is false.

If Popper is right on this score, then it follows that we needn't be quite as troubled by the problem of induction as we might have thought we should be, since it is not as if as much of our knowledge of the world – gained through science – is dependent upon induction as we originally supposed. But does Popper's rather radical solution to the problem work?

There are a number of problems with Popper's proposal; we shall here consider the two main ones. The first problem arises because if we understand our scientific knowledge in the way that Popper suggests, it's not clear that we have all that much scientific knowledge. As it happens, no one has ever observed a flying emu (as far as we know at any rate). Do we not know, then, that all emus are flightless? Not according to Popper. If we found a flying emu then we could deductively come to know that *not all* emus are flightless, but knowing that *all* emus are flightless would require induction, and recall that by Popper's lights we haven't legitimated our use of *that*. It seems, then, that we can never know the unfalsified generalisations that scientists make; we can only know the falsity of those generalisations that have been shown to be false. It seems, then, that we lose a lot of our knowledge on the Popperian view after all.

The second problem with Popper's proposal arises because it is not obvious that scientists are able to deduce the falsity of one of their bold generalisations simply by observing what seems to be a decisive counter-example to the generalisation. Consider again the case of the emus. Suppose that for many centuries people had observed that emus were flightless, and so came to believe that all emus are flightless. Now suppose that one day a scientist comes into the room and claims that she's just seen a flying emu. How would you respond?

Well, for one thing, you certainly wouldn't abandon your belief that all emus are flightless just on the basis of this one instance of testimony. After all, given the long history of observations of flightless emus, other explanations of what this scientist seems to have observed seem far more preferable. At the uncharitable end of the spectrum, one might suspect that the scientist was simply wrong in her observation, or perhaps even deceitful. Even if one trusts the scientist, however, there are still ways in which one could challenge the observation. One could note that there are birds in the area which can look a lot like emus in certain conditions. More radically, one might simply assert that whatever this creature was that was flying, it couldn't have been an emu, since it is characteristic of emus that they don't fly, and so it must have been a different creature entirely, perhaps a new type of bird not seen before, one that is just like an emu in every respect except that it flies.

The point about all of this is that one isn't obliged to take any observation at face value. Moreover, there seems nothing essentially irrational about objecting to the observation in the sorts of ways just outlined provided that the generalisation called into question by the observation is sufficiently well confirmed by other observations. The problem, however, is that if there is rational room for manoeuvre regarding whether one accepts an observation at face value, then it appears as if there is even less scientific knowledge on the Popperian view than we thought, since, unless one accepts the observation at face value, one can't make the relevant deductive inference to the denial of the bold generalisation and so come to know that the generalisation is false. That is, the upshot of this objection is that not only does this view prevent us from knowing that any generalisation about the world is true, it also doesn't follow on this view that we necessarily have much in the way of knowledge that many generalisations about the world are false either.

• LIVING WITH THE PROBLEM OF INDUCTION II: PRAGMATISM

A very different way of living with the problem of induction is offered by Hans Reichenbach (1891–1953). Reichenbach agrees with Hume that there is no justification for induction. However, Reichenbach argues that it is nevertheless rational, at least in one sense of that term, to make inductive inferences. In essence, Reichenbach's idea is that induction is rational because if we don't employ induction then we are guaranteed to end up with very few true beliefs about the world, while if we do use induction then we at least have the chance to form lots of true beliefs about the world through our inductive inferences. That is, if anything is going to work, then it is going to be induction, so it is in this sense rational to use induction, even though we have no justification for thinking that it does work. Reichenbach therefore offers a practical – or *pragmatic* – response to the problem of induction, rather than an epistemic response.

Touching the Void

Touching the Void is a famous documentary made in 2003. It is a dramatic retelling of a real-life incident involving two mountain climbers who face disaster after one of them has an accident on the mountain Siula Grande in the Peruvian Andes. One of the most spectacular scenes in the film concerns the moment when the main protagonist has to make a choice between certain death and the unknown. He has fallen deep into the heart of a glacier and is now hanging there in the darkness unable, due to his injuries, to climb out. The choice he is faced with is either to hang there in the darkness until he eventually passes out and dies, or else cuts the rope and let himself fall deeper into the darkness of the glacier below him. For all he knows, the fall would kill him, but, equally, there is always the possibility that he might survive the fall. The gamble pays off in that the hero survives the fall and then miraculously finds a way out of the glacier.

According to Reichenbach, the choice made by this climber is essentially the same as that facing us as regards induction. Just as the climber has no reason to think that cutting the rope will benefit him, we have no reason to trust induction. Nevertheless, given the alternatives involved, cutting the rope is the most rational thing to do since it leaves open the *possibility* of survival. In the same way, trusting induction is the most rational thing to do given the choices facing us in light of the problem of induction, according to Reichenbach, since it is only by employing induction that we have any hope of systematically forming true beliefs about the world.

In order to understand Reichenbach's point, consider one of the examples that he uses: the rationality of someone who is terminally ill, and with very little time left, choosing to try a new experimental operation even though there is not, at present, any reason to think it will save his life. The point is that in this case the choice is between certain death and the faint possibility of life. Given that the agent is faced with this choice, it is rational that he should opt for the operation even though he has no good grounds for thinking that it will be successful. If anything will save the agent's life, it will be this operation.

Likewise, according to Reichenbach, we face the choice between not using induction and losing all chance of gaining lots of true beliefs about the world through these inferences, or using it and potentially gaining lots of true beliefs about the world. With the choice so framed, using induction even though one lacks a justification for this style of inference seems perfectly rational.

With our discussion of epistemic rationality in mind from Chapter 5, notice that the kind of rationality in play here is not obviously an epistemic rationality.

Reichenbach is, after all, quite clear that we have no good grounds for thinking that our trust in our inductive inferences will be rewarded with true beliefs. In this sense, then, Reichenbach's advice to us to trust induction should remind us of Pascal's wager. Recall that the point of this wager was, in essence, that since what one gains (i.e., infinite life) by believing in God if the belief is true is enormous relative to the losses (i.e., the inconvenience of having the belief) involved if the belief is false, hence it is rational to believe in God's existence. Like Reichenbach's defence of induction, then, Pascal's wager doesn't offer us a reason to think that a certain claim is true (e.g., that God exists), only that we have most to gain by groundlessly supposing that it is true.

There is a key difference, however, between Reichenbach's defence of induction and Pascal's wager, which is that while Pascal's wager is not aimed at all at the goal of gaining true beliefs about God's existence – it is just concerned to show us which belief in this regard is most in our interest to believe – Reichenbach's defence of induction *is* aimed at the goal of gaining true beliefs, albeit in a roundabout way. That is, Reichenbach is saying that if gaining lots of true beliefs is what you are interested in, then the best thing to do is trust induction, even though we lack a justification for induction. So while such a belief in induction is not directly epistemically rational (i.e., it is not supported by grounds in favour of the truth of that belief), it is *indirectly* epistemically rational in that belief in induction is, according to Reichenbach, the sort of thing that an epistemically rational person should believe.

With this point in mind, it may be that Reichenbach's way of dealing with the problem of induction is not quite so merely pragmatic as many (including Reichenbach himself) have supposed.

• CHAPTER SUMMARY

- We began by looking at Hume's problem of induction. This problem arises because it seems impossible to gain a non-circular justification for induction. This is because inductive inferences are only legitimate provided we are already entitled to suppose that observed regularities provide good grounds for the generalisations we inductively infer from those regularities. The trouble is that our grounds for this supposition themselves depend upon further inductive inferences (i.e., that we have found the connection between observed regularities and the relevant generalisations to hold in the past). But if this is right, then our justification for making any particular inductive inference will itself be at least partly inductive, and this means that there can be no non-circular justification for induction.

- One way in which commentators have responded to the problem of induction is by arguing that such a fundamental epistemic practice does not stand in need of justification, but we noted that this was not a very intellectually satisfying way of responding to the problem. A better approach, one that is in the same spirit, is to defend induction on epistemic externalist grounds. In this view, our lack of adequate grounds in support of induction need be no bar to gaining justified beliefs using induction just so long as induction is, as a matter of fact, reliable. We noted that those epistemologists who adhere to epistemic internalism will not find such an approach very plausible.

- We then considered one way of responding to the problem of induction which is due to Popper. This held that the problem of induction did not undermine as much of our knowledge as we thought because most apparently inductive knowledge – in particular, most scientific knowledge – is in fact gained via deduction. Popper argues that rather than make tentative inferences from observed regularities, scientists in fact formulate bold hypotheses which they then try to decisively refute, or *falsify* – a process which is deductive rather than inductive. We noted two problems facing this view: it seemed to undermine a great deal of our scientific knowledge after all; and it wasn't clear that we could make sense of scientific methodology in terms of falsification anyway.

- Finally, we looked at Reichenbach's *pragmatic* way of living with the problem of induction. On this proposal, one concedes that one lacks a justification for induction, but argues that, nonetheless, employing induction is the most rational thing to do. This is because if any method of inference is going to get us true beliefs about the world, it will be induction. We can thus be assured that induction is the best method available, even if we have no justification for it, and thus, since we have to form beliefs about the world, it is rational to use induction.

● STUDY QUESTIONS

1 Try to describe, in your own words, the problem of induction. Use a particular inductive inference which would otherwise seem legitimate as an illustration of the problem.
2 How might an epistemic externalist respond to the problem of induction? Do you find such an approach plausible? Explain and defend your answer.
3 What does Popper mean when he says that the methodology of science is one of falsification, rather than induction, and why is falsification a deductive process? Give an example to illustrate your points. Is Popper right, do you think? If he is right, does this help us live with the problem of induction? Explain and defend your answer.
4 What does Reichenbach mean when he says that employing induction is rational, even though we lack a justification for induction? How is Reichenbach's approach to the rationality of employing induction similar to Pascal's wager, and how is it different?

● INTRODUCTORY FURTHER READING

Bird, Alexander (2009) 'Inductive Knowledge', *The Routledge Companion to Epistemology*, (eds.) S. Bernecker & D. H. Pritchard, (New York: Routledge). A clear and completely up-to-date summary of the epistemological issues regarding induction. Ideally, to be read in conjunction with Gemes (2009).

Bonjour, Laurence (1993) 'Problems of Induction', *A Companion to Epistemology*, (eds.) J. Dancy and E. Sosa, (Oxford: Blackwell). An excellent overview of the issues regarding the problem of induction.

Gemes, Ken (2009) 'Skepticism about Inductive Knowledge', *The Routledge Companion to Epistemology*, (eds.) S. Bernecker & D. H. Pritchard, (New York: Routledge). A clear and completely up-to-date summary of the literature regarding the problem of induction. Ideally, to be read in conjunction with Bird (2009).

Kaplan, Mark (1998) 'Induction, Epistemic Issues in', *Routledge Encyclopaedia of Philosophy*, (ed.) E. Craig, (London: Routledge), <http://www.rep.routledge.com/article/P024?ssid=185698882andn=2#>. A comprehensive overview of the issues as regards induction, by one of the leading figures in the field.

● ADVANCED FURTHER READING

Swinburne, Richard (ed.) (1974) *The Justification of Induction* (Oxford: Oxford University Press). This is a classic collection of important papers on the problem of induction. Note that some of these papers are not for beginners.

• FREE INTERNET RESOURCES

Huber, Franz (2008) 'Confirmation and Induction', *Internet Encyclopedia of Philosophy*, <http://www.iep.utm.edu/c/conf-ind.htm>. This entry is only really suitable for more advanced readers, but does repay careful study.

The Karl Popper Web, <http://www.eeng.dcu.ie/~tkpw/>. A webpage devoted exclusively to Popper.

Thornton, Stephen (2005) 'Karl Popper', *Stanford Encyclopedia of Philosophy*, <http://plato.stanford.edu/entries/popper/>. Excellent overview of the philosophy of Popper, including plenty of information about Popper's views on falsification and induction.

'Touching the Void', *IMDb Internet Movie Database*, <http://www.imdb.com/title/tt0379557/>. Find out more about the movie *Touching the Void*.

Vickers, John (2009) 'The Problem of Induction', *Stanford Encyclopedia of Philosophy*, <http://plato.stanford.edu/entries/induction-problem/>. An excellent overview of the literature on the problem of induction. Note that it is quite difficult in places.

11

a case study: moral knowledge

- The problem of moral knowledge
- Scepticism about moral facts
- Scepticism about moral knowledge
- The nature of moral knowledge I: classical foundationalism
- The nature of moral knowledge II: alternative conceptions

THE PROBLEM OF MORAL KNOWLEDGE

In the four previous chapters we have looked at several of the main ways in which one gains knowledge. The purpose of this chapter is to consider how what we have learned about the sources of knowledge might apply to a particular – and, as we will see, *putative* – kind of knowledge: *moral knowledge*. Moral knowledge, if it exists, is knowledge of propositions which concern moral truths (if there are any). It is certainly common to suppose that we have an awful lot of moral knowledge. To take a hackneyed example in philosophical circles, don't we all know that kicking a small child for fun is wrong? But it is clearly a moral judgement that we are making here; hence if this is knowledge, then it is a paradigm case of moral knowledge. The problem though, as we will see, is that it is hard even to make sense of the idea of moral facts, let alone knowledge of these facts. In particular, even if there are moral facts, it is difficult to explain how one would come by such knowledge.

SCEPTICISM ABOUT MORAL FACTS

What is certainly true is that if there are moral facts, they are not like other kinds of facts. In particular, moral facts, if they exist, seem to lack the sort of objectivity that most other facts are thought to have. Take, for example, a normal empirical fact such as that water boils at roughly 100°C. Admittedly, there is *something* subjective about this fact (so expressed anyway) in that it involves a system of measurement, yet the system of measurement we employ is in a certain sense up to us. But subjectivity of this sort is both inevitable and also benign. After all, which other system of measurement are we to use, if not our own? Moreover, notice that if an alien were to come down and make this measurement with a different system of measurement, they would – wouldn't they? – gain the same result, albeit one expressed in a different way. The point is that in the relevant sense empirical facts of this sort are *objective* in that they don't, in any essential way, depend on our cognitive input, but are simply determined by the way things are. Put another way, what makes empirical facts true is the nature of the world and not us.

Compare a scientific discourse with a discourse where taste or opinion is what is important, such as one regarding what is funny. Here it doesn't seem so obvious to say that there is a genuine fact of the matter. Suppose, for example, that I think that the Woody Allen film *Bananas* is hilarious, while you think that it isn't remotely funny. Is it clear that one of us is right and one of us is wrong (i.e., that for one of us what is believed is a fact, whereas for the other what is believed is not a fact)? Of course, it is a fact that *I think* that *Bananas* is a funny film (just as it's a fact that you don't think this), but that's not what we're arguing about, which is whether it is a funny film *simpliciter*. In practice, we would probably just agree to disagree. But that in itself seems to suggest that this is not a dispute about 'objective' facts of the sort found in a scientific dispute. After all, we don't think it reasonable for two scientists with opposing views to simply agree to disagree!

This seems to suggest that there isn't a real disagreement here at all – that is, a disagreement over an 'objective' fact. For notice that if in saying that *Bananas* is funny, I am simply saying that *I think* it is funny, and in saying that Bananas is not funny, you are simply saying that *you think* it isn't funny, then we aren't really disagreeing at all, but just expressing our subjective opinions. If this is the right way to understand disputes over what is funny, however, then it is odd that we should argue about this kind of topic at all, since by definition there would be no way of ever resolving such a dispute as there is no objective fact at issue. But that is just to emphasise that disputes about what is funny are nothing like scientific disputes since there clearly is something objectively at issue in the latter case.

The foregoing seems to suggest that we should be careful about treating all statements as being on par in terms of whether they are attempting to state that something is a fact. Plausibly, when a scientist states that a certain liquid boils at a certain temperature, she is expressing her conviction that it is an objective truth that this liquid boils at this temperature. In contrast, when it comes to other kinds of statements, such as regarding what we find funny or which films we like, we are not saying that what we believe is a fact, but rather just expressing personal views.

So what are we to make of moral statements? Are they like statements about what is (/what we find) funny, which arguably simply express subjective opinions rather than aiming to express objective facts? or are they like scientific statements, which arguably do aim to express objective facts? Well, if there are such things as moral facts, it is hard to see why they would be objective in the same way as scientific facts. Let's take the clichéd example noted above that kicking a small child for fun is wrong. This truth – if it is a truth – is subjective in at least the sense that if creatures like us who cared about the things that we care about never existed, then this wouldn't obviously be true at all.

Suppose, for example, that we humans had evolved in such a way that we don't feel pain. Would it still be true that kicking a small child for fun is wrong? Perhaps not. It depends very much on whether the putative wrongness of kicking a small child for fun relates to the potential pain felt by the small child who is kicked. But if human beings don't feel pain, then this can't be a reason for thinking that kicking a small child for fun is wrong. Let's suppose for the sake of argument that the reason why we think kicking a small child for fun is wrong is indeed because this act would cause pain. It follows that there is a sense in which this statement expresses something subjective, in that its truth is at best relative to the kind of creatures we are (i.e., creatures who feel pain). In contrast, the fact that water boils at roughly 100°C is not subjective in this way, since it is something that intuitively would have been true regardless of whether any creatures like ourselves existed.

But that moral statements are 'subjective' in this sense does not put them on a par with statements about what is funny, even if it does mean that they are not quite objective in the sense of a scientific statement. The simple fact is that we humans do indeed feel pain, and given this fact, and the moral relevance of pain, it follows that it is a truth that kicking a small child for fun is wrong – remember that we are taking it as given that this is the reason why this is wrong. Put another way, although moral statements are subjective in the sense that they are contingent on the kind of creatures we have turned out to be, given that we are this kind of creature, they are objective; any creature that was like us in the relevant ways should have the same moral code.

If this is right, then there is a kind of objectivity that attaches to moral statements, in that they are not purely subjective like statements about what we find funny. After all, statements about what is funny are arguably *completely* subjective in that they are wholly dependent upon the tastes of the individual person concerned. In contrast, in this view moral statements don't purely express the opinions of the people who are involved, but rather express common human truths.

This line of defence against scepticism about moral truth might initially look attractive, but it is important to realise that its scope is severely limited. After all, while it might be a common truth about human beings that we feel pain, and feeling pain is at best unpleasant, arguably one can't account for the truth of the wide range of moral statements that we make by appeal to this fact alone. Take moral statements that appeal to notions like that of a human right, for example, such as the right to free speech. Suppose I claim that it is wrong to suppress free speech, even when the speech in question is offensive to most people. Lots of people think that something like this claim is true (i.e., that free speech is a universal human right), but it is hard to account for the truth of this by appealing only to our common aversion to pain. After all, the exercise of this free speech is, on the face of it, causing a great deal of pain, and hence should on this account be treated as immoral.

More generally, the crux of the matter is that while there may well be a basis in our common humanity to account for the 'objectivity' of some moral statements, the simple fact remains that there is an awful lot of disagreement about morality. Moreover – and this is the most worrying facet of this problem for the defender of moral truths – this disagreement often breaks down along familiar demographic lines (e.g., culture, race, gender, and so on). So, for example, some cultures think that obedience to recognised authority should take precedence over one's personal liberties, while for other cultures the reverse is the case and one's personal liberties are regarded as sacrosanct. The concern, then, is that moral statements simply express our subjective tastes, where these are culturally determined. So, while it may seem as if moral statements express universal truths when we speak to people like us, once we start to speak to other people (who are different only in their cultural background) and discover that they have radically different moral views, we realise that the 'objectivity' of moral statements is in fact just a locally shared subjectivity in disguise.

We are thus back where we started with the idea that moral statements don't express objective facts but rather subjective sentiments. Note, however, that if there are no moral facts then there is nothing to be known in the first place, and hence moral knowledge is impossible. Those who argue for this quite radical philosophical position are usually called **moral expressivists**. The reason for this is that if you hold that there are no such things as moral facts, you need to offer an explanation of what it is that we are doing when we confidently assert moral claims. The explanation offered by the expressivist is that what we are doing is not asserting (something which we take to be) a fact – as one would do when one asserts that water boils at roughly $100°C$ – but rather expressing a sentiment. For example, to assert that kicking a small child for fun is wrong is to express one's own feeling that one shouldn't do such a thing. In effect, then, such an assertion is equivalent to saying that one feels that one shouldn't kick babies for fun. Crucially, though, expressions of feelings are not normally thought of as assertions.

A good analogy in this regard is with injunctions, such as 'Shut that door'. Although a statement of an injunction might superficially look like an assertion, no one would on reflection regard this statement as an assertion. One is, after all, clearly not trying to say something true, but rather simply trying to make something happen (i.e., to get the door to close). Some expressivists have argued that moral claims should be interpreted as injunctions rather than assertions. In this view, saying that kicking small children for fun is wrong, one is in effect saying something like 'Don't kick small children for fun'. Rather than trying to say that something is the case (i.e., that kicking small children for fun is morally wrong), one is simply registering one's displeasure at this sort of thing and trying to ensure – by, in effect, issuing an order – that others do not act in a fashion that would generate this displeasure.

An advantage of thinking about moral claims in this way is that the expressivist can explain why we might initially suppose that we are committed to the existence of moral facts even though (according to the expressivist anyway) they don't exist. As a result, one doesn't need to engage with the above issue of explaining why moral facts, were they to exist, are so different to normal empirical facts. The challenge to those who believe in the existence of moral facts is thus to explain why we shouldn't think of moral statements along expressivist lines.

● SCEPTICISM ABOUT MORAL KNOWLEDGE

Suppose that we can resist the expressivist view and convincingly argue that there are moral facts. As noted above, this wouldn't suffice to show that moral knowledge is possible, since it could still be the case that these are facts that we are unable to know. One issue here is the diversity of moral opinion that we noted above. Some people think that abortion can sometimes be morally permissible, while others think that it is clearly immoral. Some think that animal experimentation can sometimes be morally permissible, while others think that it is always immoral. Some think that taxation is a form of theft and hence immoral, but many others disagree. And so on. Now of course one can find disagreements occurring in lots of different domains. Even amongst the best scientists, for example, there can be disagreements, and yet scientific inquiry (as conducted by the top scientists at any rate) is meant to be a para-digmatically good way of acquiring knowledge. But if the existence of such dis-agreements in science does not undermine our confidence that there is scientific

---

A. J. Ayer (1910–89)

The propositions of philosophy are not factual, but linguistic in character – that is, they do not describe the behaviour of physical, or even mental, objects; they express definitions, or the formal consequences of definitions.

A. J. Ayer, *Language, Truth and Logic*

In his seminal book, *Language, Truth and Logic* (published in 1936, when he was only 26 years old), the British philosopher **A. J. Ayer** put forward a philosophical position which entails a robust form of scepticism about moral facts. Ayer was a logical positivist, and as such he argued that for a proposition to be meaningful it had to be capable of being empirically verified. This meant that you needed to have some way of demonstrating, through experience, that the proposition was either true or false, at least in principle. Moral 'facts', however, do not meet this requirement, or so argued logical positivists like Ayer. For how would one go about empirically demonstrating that a moral statement was true or false? Accordingly, in this view moral statements are strictly speaking nonsense. Note, however, that it is not just moral facts that are under threat by the lights of this view. Think, for example, of the kinds of statements made in aesthetics (e.g., that Woody Allen has made some good films). Aren't these statements equally immune to empirical verification? In fact, much of philosophy gets called into question as well – logical positivists were particularly suspicious of metaphysical claims. Indeed, embarrassingly for logical positivism, the very statement of the view fails to satisfy its own criteria, for how would one go about empirically verifying the statement that all meaningful statements are empirically verifiable? Hence the very statement of logical positivism is by its own lights nonsense too.

knowledge, then why should the existence of disagreements about morality make us sceptical about moral knowledge?

Notice, however, that the disagreements one finds in science are very different from those found with regard to morality. To begin with, the extent of the disagreement is not the same; there are far more moral disagreements than there are scientific disagreements. That this is so reflects two further differences between science and morality. First, morality is, as we noted above, very much culture-relative in that one's moral views tend to be shaped by the culture that one was raised in; yet different cultures can have strikingly different moral codes. In contrast, there is no analogue to this in science, which is arguably not at all culture-relative. To return to our example of the boiling point for water, for instance, while two distinct cultures might have a different system of measurement that they apply in this case, so long as they are carrying out their experiments properly they will reach equivalent conclusions.

Second, in the scientific case it is usually clear to both parties what would resolve the dispute (e.g., what evidence would be required to settle the issue one way or the other). If a scientist were for some reason sceptical that water boils at 100°C then we could convince her by doing the appropriate experiment to illustrate this fact. When it comes to morality, however, this is rarely the case. Indeed, both parties to a moral dispute might agree on all the relevant empirical facts yet still have opposing moral opinions. In the debate about the morality of abortion, for example, both parties might agree on such issues as the nature of conception, what the foetus is able to experience at different stages of development, and so on, yet still disagree about whether abortion can be morally permissible. If that's right, it is very unclear how one could ever settle an entrenched moral dispute.

A natural way to respond to at least the first point is to argue that some cultures have better moral codes than others. We might regard some cultures as being morally inferior, for example, on account of how a greater number of their moral beliefs are false. Indeed, if there are moral facts then on the face of it there seems no reason why there couldn't be moral progress (just as there is scientific progress). As we progress as a society, we shake off prejudices of old and become more enlightened, thereby enhancing our body of moral knowledge. Some cultures might thus simply have moral codes that are more developed down the road of moral progress than other societies.

The worry about this response, however, is how to defend it without slipping into a narrow moral parochialism. The problem is that every culture tends to suppose that its moral code is superior to all others, so how are we to be sure that our moral code really is the ascendant one that we take it to be? In short, how can we be sure that it isn't us who employ the 'primitive' moral code while the culture that we look down upon from a moral point of view is the one employing a progressive moral code?

This point highlights that the really important consideration that counts against moral knowledge is the second worry just raised regarding the difficulty of resolving moral disagreements. After all, if there were an objective way of resolving moral disagreements, we wouldn't need to worry about the problem of moral parochialism.

Like the scientist, we could just put our moral code to the objective test and find out whether it really is superior to the alternative moral codes offered by other cultures. That there is no objective test of this sort that we could subject our moral beliefs to means that we are cast adrift on this score, with no sure way to guide us through the moral challenges posed to us by alternative moral codes.

• THE NATURE OF MORAL KNOWLEDGE I: CLASSICAL FOUNDATIONALISM

So far we have seen some pretty formidable obstacles to the idea that there is moral knowledge. Let us suppose, however – these concerns notwithstanding – that we do have moral knowledge. What would be the best epistemological account of this knowledge?

Perhaps the most natural model of moral knowledge treats such knowledge as involving a fairly complex inference which makes appeal to fundamental and universal moral truths – otherwise known as moral principles – and the concrete features of the case in hand. For example, that one should, all other things being equal, try to alleviate the suffering of others might be one such universal moral truth. That one should, all other things being equal, respect the sanctity of human life may be another possible universal moral truth. These universal moral truths wouldn't all by themselves tell us what we should do in any particular situation, however. For one thing, we would also need to bring our knowledge of the specifics of the case to bear. For another, these universal moral truths may well conflict with one another, prima facie anyway, and so one would need to consider how much weight to accord each truth (actually, they don't really conflict, as we explain below).

Let's look at how this might work in practice. Suppose that you see an attempted suicide take place, as a woman throws herself from a bridge into the cold driving water of a river. What should you do? Well, from a purely practical point of view (i.e., a point of view where one puts moral issues to one side), the answer would seem to be straightforward: you should walk on by, or at least do as little as possible to ensure that you are not subject to the practically troublesome censure of your fellow citizens – that is, you should phone the emergency services, say, and act suitably concerned about the fate of the woman, but nothing more. But the question we're interested in is what you should do from a specifically moral point of view. Here, the answer isn't so clear. For consider the moral 'truths' that you might appeal to in order to make a decision.

For example, as noted above, you might agree that there is a moral principle to the effect that you should try to alleviate suffering, all other things being equal (call this *principle one*). So, the given that this person will clearly suffer in the cold water of the river would seem to suggest that you should jump in to save her. Similarly, that one should, all other things being equal, respect the sanctity of human life (call this *principle two*) may be another possible reason to take the plunge. But wait, before you strip off your expensive trousers and dive in, consider some other moral principles that you most likely hold. One moral principle will surely be that – as ever, all other things being equal – one should respect the considered views of others (call this *principle three*). Another will probably be that one has a duty to look after one's own well-being, all other things being equal (call this *principle four*). The trouble is that, on the face of it at least, four principles are in conflict with each other. After all, principles one and two seem to suggest that you should jump in, while principles three and four suggest that you should, respectively, (i) defer to (what seems to be) the considered view of the agent concerned and (ii) value your own good self which would be put in danger by this act of heroism.

Of course, these principles are not actually in conflict because they all have this 'get-out' clause of 'all other things being equal'. Presumably, the kind of cases in which all things are not equal will include those cases where there is a prima facie tension between the applicable moral principles. In such cases, one needs to decide how to weigh the conflicting demands made by these principles. How would you do it? Well, for one thing you would first need to get a good sense of what the relevant facts are. Here are some (but by no means all) of the morally salient questions that one might ask:

- Did the person in question really choose to throw herself off the bridge?
- Was her decision to do this her considered view, made in a clear state of mind with due consideration for the consequences of her action?
- To what extent will this course of action cause her suffering? (For example, will the fall kill her instantly?)
- What are one's chances of saving her, were one to attempt to do so?
- What are one's chances of being harmed oneself, and to what extent, were one to try to save her?

In each case the issue in question is straightforwardly factual in nature, but what answer one gives to these questions will affect on how one weighs up the conflicting demands of these moral principles. After all, if the person concerned is lost anyway (e.g., if she was killed on impact) then clearly principles one, two, and three are in effect inoperative here, since, respectively, (i) you're simply not in a position to alleviate this person's suffering, (ii) you're not in a position anymore to respect her human life since it is no more, and (iii) you're not in a position to respect (or disrespect, for that matter) her considered judgements about what is best for her. So with all that in mind you are free, it seems, to follow principle four and make sure you are looking after your own well-being.

In practice, of course, one probably wouldn't be in a position to offer a confident answer to any of these questions. And yet, from a moral point of view, one would be required to act, and would be morally judged on the basis of the choice that one made. Given that it is often the case that moral judgements involve such complex evaluations of the relative weight of moral principles in light of a range of facts about the nature of the situation, it is no wonder that making the right moral judgements is so darned hard.

With the foregoing in mind, we start to get a picture of how moral knowledge might come about. But what does this tell us about what the structure of moral knowledge is? Well, on the face of it at least, it would seem to suggest that a kind of foundationalism would be appropriate. After all, moral principles do seem to occupy a foundational role in this picture of moral knowledge. That is, knowledge of these principles appears to be epistemically basic in that one does not need to base one's belief in these principles on other beliefs that one holds. In particular, it seems that one can know these propositions a priori simply by reflecting on them, and a priori knowledge is often regarded as paradigmatically epistemically basic.

In contrast, our knowledge of particular moral truths (e.g., as what the morally right action is on a specific occasion) seems to be essentially non-foundational. For to gain such knowledge it appears that we need to undertake a complex inference which takes into account both one's non-moral knowledge, such as one's empirical knowledge of the relevant facts of the situation, and also one's (putatively) foundational moral knowledge of the relevant moral principles. So it seems that the right epistemology of moral knowledge is straightforwardly foundationalist. In particular, it seems that moral knowledge is either acquired through a priori reasoning (as when one gains moral knowledge of a foundational moral truth) or through a mix of a priori reasoning and empirical investigation (as when one gains moral knowledge of a non-foundational particular moral truth by considering the specific details of the case in light of the relevant moral principles). The form of foundationalism in play is thus classical foundationalism – of the sort that we considered in Chapter 4 – in that the foundations are *self-justifying*. That is, the thought is that a priori knowledge is a kind of knowledge which, in virtue of the manner in which it was acquired, does not require additional independent epistemic support.

• THE NATURE OF MORAL KNOWLEDGE II: ALTERNATIVE CONCEPTIONS

Although many are attracted to this classical foundationalist conception of moral knowledge, there is reason to think that it may not be the right way of thinking about moral knowledge. One challenge to this conception of moral knowledge comes from the coherentist who argues that while this view is right to treat our moral knowledge of particular moral truths as being essentially inferential, they are wrong in thinking that there is any foundational moral knowledge. In particular, they dispute that our knowledge of moral principles is a priori in the fashion that the foundationalist picture suggests.

But if a priori knowledge of moral principles is not possible, then on what basis does one acquire this knowledge? The coherentist answer is to say that knowledge of these principles is in effect gained by considering particular cases. That is, one has a body of relevant beliefs about moral matters, and one adjusts them in light of a range of relevant factors that one encounters. In this view, moral principles are just rather general moral beliefs that one holds with great conviction, but this doesn't mean that they are thereby epistemically basic, or that they are not gained through an inferential process that involved empirical beliefs.

For the coherentist about moral knowledge, then, the (defeasible) starting point for moral knowledge might well be one's judgements about a range of cases that such-and-such action was either morally right or wrong. In light of such judgements, one might then formulate some general moral principle which one thinks captures what is common to the moral judgements that one is making, where this moral principle is itself regarded as provisional relative to what further moral judgements one makes about particular cases. In this way, or so the coherentist argues at any rate, one can capture how moral knowledge is in fact acquired. Rather than any particular moral claim being foundational, there is instead a constant interplay in terms of the moral beliefs that we hold, either regarding moral principles or more specific moral beliefs, such that no particular moral belief ever plays a foundational epistemic role in our system of moral belief. But provided that one in this way forms one's moral beliefs in a suitable fashion (and those beliefs are also true of course), then, argues the coherentist, one can gain moral knowledge.

Coherentism is not the only alternative to classical foundationalism when it comes to moral knowledge. In particular, there is also a non-classical foundationalism account available. The idea behind this proposal is that it is possible to know moral truths directly. Indeed, the claim made by proponents of this view is that moral knowledge, rather than being (at least for the most part anyway) inferential knowledge which is gained via reason (whether on the model that the classical foundationalist or the coherentist supposes), is rather better thought of as being (in paradigm cases anyway) more akin to a kind of perceptual knowledge, at least as such knowledge is conceived of by direct realism (*see* Chapter 7).

Before we start to ask how plausible this conception of moral knowledge is, it's important to first note that one key thing in its favour is that it seems to accord very well with how we *think* we gain moral knowledge. In particular, when one examines paradigm cases in which moral knowledge is acquired, it does not seem at all right to say that an inference was either actually involved or required. Rather, it seems that one is often able to simply 'see' that a certain act is morally right or wrong.

For example, when you see someone clearly doing something despicable, such as kicking a small child for fun, it seems odd to think that any kind of inference, even a very quick one, is required to form one's judgement that this act is wrong. Moreover, such spontaneous moral judgements often seem to count as knowledge even if one is unable to offer independent reasons (e.g., an appeal to a general moral principle which is applicable in this case) in favour of this judgement. Indeed, if one's moral judgement were challenged, one would usually just re-assert that the act in question is clearly morally wrong (probably with a degree of puzzlement, for, one might ask, what kind of person doesn't realise that hurting small children for fun is wrong?).

Interestingly, not only does it seem that we don't usually undertake inferences when acquiring moral knowledge but that in a wide range of cases if one actually undertook such an inference then this would be a sign of some sort of moral corruption on the part of oneself. That is, we expect decent people to respond instinctively to paradigm cases of morally good and morally bad acts, such that, for example, they are immediately in support of the former and immediately repulsed by the latter, and act accordingly. Indeed, the use of the emotive word 'repulsed' is entirely appropriate here, since our moral judgements – particularly about concrete cases – do often go hand-in-hand with an emotional response.

So, for example, if one sees someone hurting a small child for fun, one does not merely form the view that this act is wrong, but one actually feels angry that it is happening and (where feasible) one does what one can to stop it. More generally, I think we would be very worried about the moral character of someone who saw a wicked act take place and formed her moral judgement in a cool, unemotional fashion (or, for that matter, who only formed an emotional response after considering the rational basis for her judgement). To see this, imagine the concrete case of witnessing a small child being hurt purely for someone's amusement. Now imagine that one is with someone who has no immediate moral or emotional response to this scene and only decides that what she is seeing is morally wrong, and hence acts (and feels?) accordingly, once she has reflected, say, on the fact that this cruel act contravenes what she takes to be a moral principle. Wouldn't one be at least puzzled by, if not more than a little concerned about, this person?

If this is the right way to think about moral knowledge, however, then it does seem that we should take the idea that we can (sometimes, at least) directly see that an act is morally right or wrong at face value. In one respect, then, moral knowledge, at least in paradigm cases, would be akin to perceptual knowledge in that it is acquired directly, without the need for further independent rational support, simply by observing the phenomenon in question. This would clearly be a very different way of thinking about moral knowledge than that offered by classical foundationalist and coherentist accounts. But what kind of epistemology of moral knowledge would it be?

A natural way of thinking about moral knowledge in this model would be along the kind of lines suggested by virtue epistemology. Recall that we noted in Chapter 6 that virtue epistemologists hold that knowledge is true belief that is acquired via the reliable epistemic virtues, and possibly also cognitive faculties, of the agent. Virtue epistemology offers an attractive account of perceptual knowledge because it can make sense of how our reliable cognitive faculties could be understood as able to directly enable us to gain knowledge even though one had no independent rational basis for the target belief (just as a chicken-sexer could conceivably gain knowledge while lacking a rational independent basis for her belief). Accordingly, one might opt to try to account for moral knowledge along the very same lines, and argue that moral knowledge can be directly gained via the employment of one's reliable epistemic virtues and cognitive faculties even though the agent concerned may lack any independent rational basis for this knowledge. That is, just as our perceptual virtues enable us to skilfully, but directly, gain perceptual knowledge, so our moral virtues enable us to skilfully, but directly, gain moral knowledge.

The result would be a kind of epistemic externalism about moral knowledge. It would be a kind of foundationalism, in the minimal sense, that some beliefs are appropriately epistemically supported even though they are not supported by further beliefs, but it would be very different from a classical foundationalism which treated the foundational beliefs as self-justifying. For what is in fact justifying these foundational beliefs by the lights of this alternative foundationalist account are 'external' facts (in particular, facts about how the belief was formed, about the reliability of the belief-forming process in play, and so on).

Notice that the strength of this account of moral knowledge is also what makes it problematic. For while this proposal has the advantage of allowing us to directly gain moral knowledge in certain cases even though we lack any independent rational support for our belief, one might by the same token argue that there is something troubling about the very idea of such directly gained moral knowledge. When it comes to knowledge gained by perceptual faculties, it is far more natural to think of this knowledge as potentially completely direct in this way, but this is because we are born with these capacities, and hence they predate our rational powers. If we do possess moral faculties, however, then it is hard to see how they could be innate. For one thing, if that were the case then it would be very puzzling why one's moral code tends to vary with the culture in which one was raised. The problem, however, is that if one conceives of our moral faculties in such a way that one acquires, and then refines, these faculties over time as one matures as a person then it is hard to see how one's moral knowledge, insofar as it really is moral knowledge, could possibly lack independent rational support. For wouldn't one over time acquire reasons to believe, for example, that one has a reliable ability to detect moral truths of the relevant kind?

So even if one can overcome the kind of problems that have made many think that moral knowledge is impossible, there is still a challenge remaining to explain what moral knowledge would be were it to be possible. In particular, one needs to tread a fine line between, on the one hand, avoiding the danger of over-intellectualising moral knowledge and, on the other hand, offering a sufficiently sophisticated story about moral knowledge such that we are willing to regard it as bona fide.

• CHAPTER SUMMARY

- We began by noting that it is far from obvious that there is any such thing as a moral fact, and that if there are no moral facts then it immediately follows that there can be no moral knowledge. Part of the worry about moral facts is that they don't seem to be objective in a way that 'real' facts, like scientific facts, are. For example, one's moral judgements seem to largely reflect one's cultural upbringing.

- If one holds that there are no moral facts, then one is a moral expressivist. Moral expressivists hold that moral statements do not express facts but rather perform a very different role instead (e.g., expressing one's support for a certain action or one's desire to stop certain actions from taking place).
- Even if one rejects moral expressivism and argues that there are moral facts, it still doesn't follow that there is moral knowledge since it could be that it is impossible to know these facts. The differences between a moral discourse and a scientific discourse might give one grounds for thinking that this is the case. For example, whereas scientific disagreements seem to be in their nature resolvable, moral disagreements are often completely intractable.
- Assuming that there is such a thing as moral knowledge, we then explored what the right epistemology of such knowledge might be. The first proposal we considered was a classical foundationalist theory which held that we had a priori knowledge of basic moral principles which, when coupled with our empirical knowledge of the particular circumstances of the case in hand, enabled us to appropriately form moral judgements about what to do in specific cases. One problem with this view was that it seemed to over-intellectualise what is required for moral knowledge.
- The second proposal that we considered was coherentism. This view held that there are no foundational moral beliefs, and even one's beliefs in moral principles would be open to revision if suitable counter-evidence were to come to light.
- The final proposal we looked at was a type of virtue epistemology which allowed that we could, in certain cases, directly gain moral knowledge – even though one had no independent rational basis for one's belief – just so long as one appropriately employed one's epistemic virtues. We saw that such a view may be problematic in that moral knowledge – unlike, say, perceptual knowledge – does seem to essentially involve the possession of appropriate supporting reasons.

• STUDY QUESTIONS

1 Try to give a possible example of each of the following:
   - a scientific fact;
   - a moral fact;
   - an aesthetic fact (e.g., regarding whether something is funny).
   Try to list some potential differences between the three kinds of facts, and explain why these differences might be thought to call the existence of moral facts into question.
2 What is moral expressivism? Do you find it compelling?
3 Explain, in your own words, why the existence of moral facts is compatible with scepticism about moral knowledge.
4 Describe, and critically evaluate, at least two grounds for scepticism about moral knowledge.
5 Describe the classical foundationalist account of moral knowledge. Is it plausible, do you think?

6 Describe the coherentist account of moral knowledge. How does it differ from the classical foundationalist account of moral knowledge? Is it preferable, do you think?

7 Describe the virtue epistemic account of moral knowledge. Critically evaluate whether this approach offers an account of moral knowledge which is most in keeping with our ordinary ways of thinking about moral knowledge.

8 Should we aim to offer an epistemology of moral belief which accords with our ordinary thinking about moral knowledge? If so, why? If not, why not?

• INTRODUCTORY FURTHER READING

Audi, Robert (2009) 'Moral Knowledge', *The Routledge Companion to Epistemology*, (eds.) S. Bernecker & D. H. Pritchard, (New York: Routledge). An excellent and completely up-to-date summary of the main issues regarding moral knowledge.

Sayre-McCord, Geoffrey (1998) 'Moral Knowledge', *Routledge Encyclopaedia of Philosophy*, (ed.) E. Craig, (London: Routledge), <http://www.rep.routledge.com/article/L056?ssid=1039426977&n=1#>. An extremely accessible overview of the main issues as regards moral knowledge.

• ADVANCED FURTHER READING

Audi, Robert (1999) 'Moral Knowledge and Ethical Pluralism', *The Blackwell Guide to Epistemology*, (eds.) J. Greco & E. Sosa, 271–302, (Oxford: Blackwell). A sophisticated and quite comprehensive overview of ethical epistemology. Not for the beginner.

Lemos, Noah (2002) 'Epistemology and Ethics', *The Oxford Handbook of Epistemology*, (ed.) P. K. Moser, 479–512, (Oxford: Oxford University Press). An excellent treatment of epistemological issues in ethics. Not for the beginner.

• FREE INTERNET RESOURCES

Campbell, Richmond (2007) 'Moral Epistemology', *Stanford Encyclopaedia of Philosophy*, <http://plato.stanford.edu/entries/moral-epistemology/>. An excellent overview of the main issues regarding moral epistemology.

Sinnott-Armstrong, Walter (2002) 'Moral Skepticism', *Stanford Encyclopaedia of Philosophy*, <http://plato.stanford.edu/entries/skepticism-moral/>. A very good, albeit quite sophisticated, discussion of the various types of moral scepticism.

Tramel, Peter (2005) 'Moral Epistemology', *Internet Encyclopaedia of Philosophy*, <http://www.iep.utm.edu/m/mor-epis.htm>. A good overview of the main issues regarding moral epistemology.

Part III

do we know

anything at all?

12

scepticism about other minds

- The problem of other minds
- The argument from analogy
- A problem for the argument from analogy
- Two versions of the problem of other minds
- Perceiving someone else's mind

THE PROBLEM OF OTHER MINDS

We take it for granted in our everyday lives that we are not alone in the universe; that there are other people who inhabit this place with us. As we will see, however, once one starts to reflect on the matter, it isn't entirely obvious what entitles us to this belief. Why are we so sure that there are other people out there, people who have minds like our own?

The problem confronting our knowledge of other minds is that, on the face of it at least, we don't actually observe other minds in the way that we observe objects like trees and cars. After all, one's mind seems to be something that *underlies* one's body and one's bodily behaviour such that, although one's behaviour manifests one's mind, simply observing an agent's behaviour is not the same as observing their mind. Accordingly, the thought runs, in order to know that someone is minded we have to do more than merely observe their behaviour; we also have to infer that there is something underlying that behaviour and giving rise to it – namely, a mind.

If this picture of how we come to know that there are other minds is correct, then scepticism about the existence of such minds is just around the corner (i.e., the view that knowledge that other minds exist is impossible). After all, if we have to *infer* the existence of other minds from observed behaviour, then the question naturally arises as to whether that observed behaviour could be manifested even though there is no mind underlying the behaviour. Perhaps the 'people' that one interacts with on a daily basis are nothing more than unminded automata or zombies who have no thoughts and feelings at all. How would we tell the difference? (This is particularly troubling in the case of zombies, where there is no obvious underlying physical difference.) This difficulty concerning how we know that there are other people who have minds like we do is called the **problem of other minds**.

THE ARGUMENT FROM ANALOGY

So how might one respond to the problem of other minds? Perhaps the most famous line of response – a version of which is usually credited to **John Stuart Mill** (1806–73) – makes use of a form of inductive reasoning known as an **argument from analogy**. Essentially, the idea behind this approach to the problem of other minds is to maintain that we can come to know that there are other minds by observing how the behaviour of others mirrors that of our own (where we know that we are minded). The thought is that since we know that we have minds, it follows that the behaviour of others which is similar to our own shows that these others have minds too.

John Stuart Mill (1806–73)

If all mankind minus one were of one opinion, and only one person were of the contrary opinion, mankind would be no more justified in silencing that one person, than he, if he had the power, would be justified in silencing mankind.

Mill, *On Liberty*

The English philosopher and economist, John Stuart Mill, was one of the most influential men of his day. Like his father, James Mill (1773–1836), Mill was a prominent liberal reformer committed to *utilitarianism* – the view that actions are morally right to the extent to which they promote the greatest happiness in the greatest number of people. He was a member of the British parliament and forcefully argued for the rights of women.

The starting-point for this argument is our knowledge both of the existence and nature of our own minds. After all, we cannot seriously doubt that we have a mind, since who then would be doing the doubting? (This is the point of Descartes '*cogito*': 'I think, therefore I am'.) Moreover, it is also held that there cannot be any troubling sceptical argument concerning our access to what is going on in our own minds because this access is *privileged*. That is, we have immediate non-inferential access to what is going on in our own minds – what we are thinking and feeling – and this means that our knowledge in this regard is entirely secure (at least if any knowledge is). It follows that we can put our knowledge of our own minds together with our knowledge of how we, as minded creatures, behave, to determine what sort of behaviour a minded creature should have.

For example, we might notice that when we are in pain, as when we accidentally burn ourselves on a match, we respond in certain ways (e.g., by calling out). Suppose we notice a number of these correlations between external stimuli (e.g., the burning of a match, the tickle of a feather), external response (e.g., calling out, giggling), and the associated mental state (e.g., pain, pleasure). Suppose further that we observe other apparently minded people behaving in the same ways in response to the same stimuli (i.e.,they call out when burnt by matches and giggle when tickled with feathers). Wouldn't we then be entitled to inductively infer that there are other minds just like our own?

Here is the form of the inductive argument that is being used here:

A1 There are patterns in my behaviour in response to external stimuli which reveal that I am having mental states of a certain sort (e.g., my crying out in response to being burnt by a match indicates that I am in pain).

A2 This same behaviour in response to external stimuli is exhibited by others.

AC These others experience the same mental states that I do, and so are minded, just like me.

On the face of it, this looks like a good way of responding to the problem of other minds.

• A PROBLEM FOR THE ARGUMENT FROM ANALOGY

Although initially persuasive, the argument from analogy runs into problems on closer inspection. For one thing, the style of argument being employed here is not a good one, even if we set aside the more general worries one might have about inductive arguments that we looked at in Chapter 10. Compare the argument given above to the following inductive argument:

1 Box A is brown and it contains a book.

2 Boxes B, C and D are brown.

C Boxes B, C and D contain a book.

Clearly, this is a very bad style of argument in that the mere fact that one brown box contains a certain item does not give us any reason to believe that any other brown box contains that sort of item. The problem with this argument is that it only considers a particular instance of a brown box, an instance which we have no reason to think is representative of brown boxes in general. As we noted in Chapter 10, however, good inductive arguments are always ones that reason from *representative* premises to conclusions. Accordingly, we cannot reason from this instance to a more general conclusion that applies to any brown box we care to pick.

Notice that the following argument would be OK:

1* Lots of brown boxes have been observed over many years and in a wide range of environments and they have all contained books.

2 Boxes B, C, and D are brown.

C Boxes B, C, and D contain a book.

If it is indeed true that we have observed a representative range of brown boxes and found them all to have a book in them, then there is no problem in justifiably concluding that any other brown box we find will also have a book in it. The trouble is, however, that the argument from analogy is more akin to the first of these 'brown box' arguments than the second. The reason for this is that it begins with the observation of a correlation in a single case (between my behaviour and my mindedness) and draws conclusions about the relationship between behaviour and mindedness in general. But that is a very bad way of reasoning, as the first 'brown box' argument shows.

If we were entitled to suppose that our case is somehow representative of minds in general, so that what holds for my mind would hold for others, then we could properly use an argument from analogy to draw conclusions about the existence of other minds. But how would we come by such a supposition without in the process simply assuming that which is to be shown (i.e., that there are other minds out there which are like my own)?

This is not the only problem facing the argument from analogy, but it is the most decisive one. One cannot legitimately infer simply that there are other minds on the basis of one's own case.

• TWO VERSIONS OF THE PROBLEM OF OTHER MINDS

As if the problem of other minds as it is presented above weren't bad enough, there is a second difficulty lurking here. This is that, even if we could come to know that there exist other minds, it isn't at all clear how we could come to know that these other minds are like our own. That is, there are two problems here which can easily be run together if one isn't careful. The first is whether any other minds exist, regardless of what those minds are like. The second is whether, given that other minds exist, those minds are like our own.

Clearly, one could answer the first problem without having any answer to the second. In order to see this point, take it for granted for a moment that there are indeed other minds. Now ask yourself how you can be sure that other people's minds are like your own? A standard motif of science fiction movies, for example, is that of the alien taking over someone's mind. In such a case, we have someone who may well nearly always behave as she used to, but who no longer thinks and feels like a human but like an alien. How would we tell the difference if there was nothing in the alien's appearance or behaviour to give the game away?

Invasion of the Body Snatchers

The main premise of the 1956 film *Invasion of the Body Snatchers* is that people are being quietly replaced by alien duplicates. In many ways, though not in all ways, these aliens act just like the people they have replaced, which is what makes it so difficult to tell the alien duplicates apart from the 'real' people. Presumably, while these aliens look and act like real people, they do not experience the world as we do. This raises the question, central to this section of the chapter, of how we can be sure that others are minded in the specific way that we suppose them to be; how do we know that they feel pain like we do, for example? After all, the alien duplicates act just like we act, so it seems that we cannot tell what their minds are like just by observing their behaviour. But if we can't do it in this way, then how can we do it?

Indeed, we don't need to consider science fiction movies in order to get an example of this sort of 'deviant' mindedness. After all, some people are colour-blind, for example, and so see colours very differently to 'normal' people. Others have unusual senses of taste and hearing, perhaps being unable to taste/hear things that others can taste/hear, or tasting/hearing them differently. Often we can tell that this is happening because it has an impact on someone's behaviour. For example, if a certain fruit that tastes sweet to others tastes very sour to them, then they will respond with disgust upon tasting it. We can easily imagine cases, however, in which another person experiences the world very differently and yet this difference does not manifest itself in experience. For instance, suppose that someone sees red as blue and vice versa. Accordingly, they would grow up calling what they experience as blue 'red', and vice versa. Would this ever come to light? It might in that it might affect how they respond to other colours on the spectrum, for example. Equally, however, it might not in that this person might just go through life systematically mistaking red for blue and blue for red. If this is possible, however, then it raises the question of how certain we can be that we are all experiencing the world in the same way. Perhaps we have just learned to categorise the world in a standard way, even though the subjective natures of our experiences are in fact very different from case to case?

• PERCEIVING SOMEONE ELSE'S MIND

One way in which one might respond to the problem of other minds – in both its forms – is to question its guiding premise that our knowledge of other minds is by its nature inferential. After all, common sense would seem to suggest otherwise on this score. Suppose I see someone writhing in agony on the ground before me. Do I really need to make an *inference* in order to know that he is in pain? Can't I just see, directly, that he is in pain?

The thought is thus that perhaps, at least when it comes to some very clear-cut cases, I could know that someone is having a certain experience – of being in pain, say – simply by looking at them. And if I can know what kind of experience someone is having in this direct way, then presumably I can also come to know that this person is a creature with a mind that is capable of experiences in the first place. That is, I can come to know, without inference, both that there is someone else with a mind and that the experiences that this person has are at least in certain respects like mine. If this is right, then the worry that the inference involved in the argument from analogy is unsound does not get a grip, at least not on these select cases of direct knowledge of other people's minds.

At first pass, this proposal might look like mere dogmatism, but notice that this sort of view is structurally very similar to the direct realism as regards perceptual knowledge that we looked at in Chapter 7. One of the key motivations for direct realism was the thought that we should resist the inference from the fact that our perceptual experience could be undetectably misleading to the claim that what we are directly aware of in perceptual experience is only the way the world seems to us rather than the way the world is. Although it is true that in deceived cases, such as the scenario in which I am visually presented with a mirage of an oasis, I am not directly aware of the world but only with the way the world appears, this should not be thought, says the direct realist, to entail that in non-deceived cases, such as that in which I am actually looking at an oasis in the distance, I am not directly acquainted with objects in the world.

One might apply the same line of reasoning here. There clearly are cases in which one might make a judgement about what someone is experiencing and be wrong. Moreover, we can certainly conceive of cases in which one makes a judgement that something has a mind – a robot, say – when in fact it doesn't. Conceding this much, however, doesn't by itself ensure that you can never know what someone else is experiencing – or, indeed, that they have a mind – just by observing them. Why should the cases in which one's judgements go wrong dictate whether one has knowledge in cases where one's judgements go right? Of course, such knowledge, if it is possessed, is bound to be fallible – we could be wrong. But then we are usually happy to grant knowledge in the absence of **infallibility**, so why not here?

• CHAPTER SUMMARY

- The problem of other minds concerns the fact that it seems that we are unable to observe another person's mind in the same way that we can observe physical objects like tables and chairs. So how, then, do we know that there are other minds in the first place?
- One way to try to resolve this problem is to make use of the argument from analogy which notes correlations between our behaviour and our mental states and thereby inductively draws conclusions about the mental states of others who behave in ways that are similar to how we behave.
- The style of reasoning employed in the argument from analogy is defective, however, since one cannot legitimately reason from a correlation that holds in a single (and apparently unrepresentative) case to a general conclusion that applies to many cases.
- We then distinguished two closely related problems that are involved in the problem of other minds. The first (noted above) is whether other minds exist. The second is whether, given that other minds exist, these minds are like our own. As we noted, it could be that we are able to know that there are other minds, but are nevertheless unable to know that these minds are like our own. This is because it seems possible that other people might experience the world very differently from how I experience it, but in such a way that these differences in subjective experience are undetectable to others.
- Finally, we looked at one way in which one might respond to the problem of other minds (in both its forms), which is to hold that we can, at least sometimes, have direct knowledge of another person's mind. For example, if I see someone writhing around on the ground before me, I could come to know, without needing to make any inference, that this person is in pain. We noted that such a view is very controversial.

• STUDY QUESTIONS

1 Why might it be thought problematic to suppose that one can know that there are other minds? What is it about our beliefs in the existence of other minds that makes them suspect?

2 What is the argument from analogy, and how is it supposed to resolve the problem of other minds? What difficulties does this argument face? Does this argument succeed in showing that we can have knowledge of other minds?

3 Explain, in your own words, why there is a difference between doubt about the existence of other minds, and doubt that others have minds like one's own. What special reasons might there be to doubt the latter?

4 Is it plausible to suppose that one can directly observe someone else's pain, and thereby come to know, without inference, that they are in pain? If one could, then how would this help us resolve the problem of other minds?

● INTRODUCTORY FURTHER READING

Avramides, Anita (2009) 'Skepticism about Knowledge of Other Minds', *The Routledge Companion to Epistemology*, (eds.) S. Bernecker & D. H. Pritchard, (New York: Routledge). An authoritative and completely up-to-date introduction to the problem of other minds, written by an expert in the field. Essential reading.

Hyslop, Alec (1998) 'Other Minds', *Routledge Encyclopedia of Philosophy*, (ed.) E. Craig, (London: Routledge), <http://www.rep.routledge.com/article/V022?ssid=44 4735708&n=1#>. An excellent introduction to the problem of other minds. Very accessible.

Skorupski, John (1989) *John Stuart Mill* (London: Routledge). A classic introduction to the philosophy of Mill.

● ADVANCED FURTHER READING

Avramides, Anita (2001) *Other Minds* (London: Routledge). An excellent book-length treatment of the problem of other minds.

Skorupski, John (ed.) (1998) *The Cambridge Companion to John Stuart Mill* (Cambridge: Cambridge University Press). A good source of more advanced material for those who wish to learn more about the philosophy of Mill.

● FREE INTERNET RESOURCES

Hyslop, Alec (2005) 'Other Minds', *Stanford Encyclopedia of Philosophy*, <http://plato.stanford.edu/entries/other-minds/>. A good overview of the problem of other minds.

'Invasion of the Body Snatchers', *IMDb Internet Movie Database*, <http://www.imdb.com/title/tt0049366/>; <http://www.imdb.com/title/tt0077745/>. Read more about the 1956 version of the film *Invasion of the Body Snatchers*, and the 1978 remake.

'John Stuart Mill', *Internet Encyclopedia of Philosophy*, <http://www.utm.edu/research/iep/ m/milljs.htm>. A good overview of the life and work of Mill.

Thornton, Stephen (2004) 'Solipsism and the Problem of Other Minds', *Internet Encyclopedia of Philosophy*, <http://www.iep.utm.edu/s/solipsis.htm>. A good overview of the problem of other minds.

Wilson, Fred (2005) 'John Stuart Mill', *Stanford Encyclopedia of Philosophy*, <http://plato.stanford.edu/entries/mill/>. An excellent overview of the life and work of Mill.

13

radical scepticism

- The radical sceptical paradox
- Scepticism and closure
- Mooreanism
- Contextualism

THE RADICAL SCEPTICAL PARADOX

In Chapter 12 we looked at scepticism about other minds, which is the view that we know very little about other minds (both about whether there are other minds and also about what their minds are like given that they do exist). This chapter is also devoted to scepticism, but of an even more dramatic form. Whereas the scepticism of the previous chapter was restricted to a certain domain, the kind of scepticism that we will be looking at here holds that it is impossible to know anything much at all about the world around you, or at least anything of any consequence. Because it is so dramatic and general in scope, this type of scepticism is known as **radical scepticism**.

As it is usually understood, radical scepticism is not supposed to be thought of as a philosophical position (i.e., as a stance that someone adopts) as such, but rather it is meant as a challenge which any theorist of knowledge must overcome. That is, radical scepticism is meant to serve a *methodological* function. The goal is to show that one's theory of knowledge is scepticism-proof, since if it isn't – if it allows that most knowledge is impossible – then there must be something seriously wrong with the view. Accordingly we are not to think of the 'sceptic' as a person – as someone who is trying to convince us of anything – but rather as our intellectual conscience which is posing a specific kind of problem for our epistemological position in order to tease out what our view really involves and whether it is a plausible stance to take.

There are two main components to sceptical arguments as they are usually understood in the contemporary discussion of this topic. The first component concerns what is known as a sceptical hypothesis. A sceptical hypothesis is a scenario in which you are radically deceived about the world and yet your experience of the world is exactly as it would be if you were not radically deceived. Consider, for example, the fate of the protagonist in the film *The Matrix*, who comes to realise that his previous experiences of the world were in fact being 'fed' into his brain whilst his body was confined to a large vat. Accordingly, whilst he seemed to be experiencing a world rich with interaction between himself and other people, in fact he was not interacting with anybody or any *thing* at all (at least over and above the tubes in the vat that were 'feeding' him his experiences), but was instead simply floating motionlessly.

The Matrix

The Matrix, a 1999 film starring Keanu Reeves, is the first part of a trilogy. The film follows the story of a computer hacker called Neo, played by Reeves, who discovers that his experiences of the world are in fact entirely artificial, and that he is instead floating in a vat of nutrients and being 'fed' his experiences. In this nightmarish scenario, supercomputers have enslaved the human race and now use the 'essences' of humans as a power source. Neo escapes from the vat in which he has been floating and leads a rebellion against the supercomputers.

The problem posed by sceptical hypotheses is that we seem unable to know that they are false. After all, if our experience of the world could be exactly as it is and yet we are the victims of a sceptical hypothesis, then on what basis could we ever hope to distinguish a genuine experience of the world from an illusory one? The first key claim of the sceptical argument is thus that we are unable to know that we are not the victims of sceptical hypotheses.

The second component of the sceptical argument involves the claim that if we are unable to know the denials of sceptical hypotheses, it follows that we are unable to know very much at all. Right now, for example, I think that I know that I am sitting here at my desk writing this chapter. Given that I do not know that I am not the victim of a sceptical hypothesis, however, and given that if I were the victim of a sceptical hypothesis the world would appear exactly the same as it is just now even though I am *not* presently sitting at my desk, then how can I possibly know that I am sitting at my desk? The problem is that, so long as I cannot rule out sceptical hypotheses, I don't seem able to know very much at all.

We can roughly express this sceptical argument in the following way:

1 We are unable to know the denials of sceptical hypotheses.

2 If we are unable to know the denials of sceptical hypotheses, then we are unable to know anything of substance about the world.

C We are unable to know anything of substance about the world.

Two very plausible claims about our knowledge can thus be used to generate a valid argument which produces this rather devastating radically sceptical conclusion. In this sense, the sceptical argument is a **paradox** (i.e., a series of apparently intuitive premises which validly entail an absurd), and thus *counter-intuitive*, conclusion.

One might think that the weakest link in this argument is the second premise, on the grounds that it is far too much to ask of a knower that she be able to rule out radical sceptical hypotheses. Why should it be, for example, that in order to be properly said to know that I am sitting at my desk right now I must first be able to rule out the possibility that I am not being 'fed' my experiences by futuristic supercomputers that are out to deceive me? Surely all that I need to do in order to have knowledge in this case is to form my belief in the right kind of way and for that belief to be supported by the appropriate evidence (e.g., that I can see my desk before me). To demand more than this seems perverse, and if scepticism merely reflects unduly restrictive epistemic standards then it isn't nearly as problematic as it might at first seem. We can reject *perverse* epistemic standards with impunity – it is only the *intuitively correct* ones that we need to pay serious attention to.

Nevertheless, there is an additional way of motivating premise 2, one that makes its truth seem entirely uncontentious. This is done by employing a principle known as the **closure principle**. Here it is, in outline:

The closure principle

If I know one proposition, and I know that this proposition entails a second proposition, then I know the second proposition as well.

For example, if I know that I am sitting here in my office right now, and I also know that if I am sitting in my office right now then I can't be standing up next door, then it seems that I must also know that I am not standing up next door. So expressed, the principle seems entirely unremarkable.

Notice, however, that it follows from the fact that one is seated at one's desk in one's office that one is not encased in a large vat being 'fed' the experiences as if one were sitting at one's desk (aside from anything else, if one were in the vat then one wouldn't be *seated* at all, but *floating* in the nutrients contained therein). Accordingly, given the closure principle, it follows that if I know that I am currently seated in my office then I also know that I am not encased in a large vat being 'fed' experiences that are designed to deceive me. However, as the sceptic points out in premise 1 of her argument, that seems precisely the kind of thing that I could never know. As a result, concludes the sceptic, it must be that I don't know that I am presently seated in my office either.

In effect, what the sceptic's use of the closure principle does is make knowledge of normal 'everyday' propositions (i.e., the sort of propositions which we would usually regard ourselves as unproblematically knowing) contingent upon knowledge of the denials of sceptical hypotheses. Moreover, since the principle is so plausible, it makes this connection seem entirely intuitive. That is, the demand that I should know the denials of sceptical hypotheses seems now to be the product of entirely reasonable epistemic standards, not perverse ones. The trouble is, of course, that with this demand in place, the sceptical conclusion appears irresistible.

• SCEPTICISM AND CLOSURE

What is one to do about this sceptical argument? One possibility might be to respond by rejecting the closure principle, although this is easier said than done. After all, how could such a plausible principle be false? How could it be that I could know one proposition, know that it entails a second proposition, and yet fail to know that entailed proposition? Indeed, the only instances where this kind of principle seems at all problematic is when it is employed in sceptical arguments, and this suggests that perhaps the reason why we find the closure principle problematic here is simply that it is helpful to the sceptic. If this is right, then the move to deny this principle smacks of desperation.

Nevertheless, there are motivations that can be offered in defence of rejecting this principle, at least as the sceptic employs it. One way in which some have gone about rejecting the closure principle is by appeal to the fallibilist intuition that in knowing something I only need to be able to rule out all *relevant* possibilities of error, and don't have to rule out *all* possibilities of error. Taking 'rule out' here to mean 'know to be false', this means that in order to know something I only need to know that a restricted range of error possibilities are false, not that all of them are (that would be **infallibilism**). The complaint raised by fallibilists against the closure principle, however, is that it demands that we know the falsity of even far-fetched – and thus, intuitively, *irrelevant* – error possibilities, such as sceptical hypotheses, and hence that there is something deeply suspect about it.

Although superficially appealing, this line of argument is not that persuasive on closer inspection. Notice that the closure principle is entirely compatible with **fallibilism**. This principle does not demand that you know that all error possibilities are false, but only those error possibilities which are known to be incompatible with what you know, which is a much weaker claim. One cannot therefore reject the closure principle solely on fallibilist grounds.

Everything thus rests on the further claim being made here about relevance: that sceptical hypotheses are far-fetched and therefore of their nature irrelevant. The problem with this suggestion is that it is hard to see just what, besides a blank statement of intuition, could justify the thought that sceptical hypotheses are irrelevant. Indeed, why doesn't the fact that we know that they are inconsistent with our everyday beliefs, such that those beliefs cannot be true if the sceptical hypotheses obtain, make them relevant?

A different tack taken by fallibilists in order to attack the closure principle has been to suggest that the mark of knowledge is that one has a true belief which is *sensitive* to the truth in the following sense:

The sensitivity principle

If an agent knows a proposition, then that agent's true belief in that proposition must be sensitive in the sense that, had that proposition been false, she would not have believed it.

For example, consider a case in which no one thinks that the agent has knowledge, such as a Gettier case like the 'stopped clock' example. In this case, we have an agent who forms a true belief about what the time is by looking at a stopped clock, one that just happens to be showing the right time. The agent in this case clearly doesn't know what the time is, even if her belief is justified, since it's just a matter of luck that her belief is true. One way of fleshing out this idea that the belief in this case is just too luckily true to count as knowledge is to notice that it is a belief which is insensitive. After all, had what the agent believed been false – if the time had been a minute earlier or later, for example, but everything else had stayed the same – then she would have carried on believing what she does regardless, even though it is no longer true. In contrast, someone who finds out what the time is by looking at a working clock will form a sensitive belief about what the time is, since were the time to have been different (but everything else had stayed the same), then the clock would have displayed a different time and the agent would therefore have formed a different (and likewise true) belief about what the time is. In short, a sensitive belief is one that changes as the facts change so that one does not end up with a false belief, while an insensitive belief is one that doesn't so change.

What is interesting about the **sensitivity principle** is that while most of our everyday beliefs are sensitive to the truth, our anti-sceptical beliefs, such as our belief that we are not brains in vats, are not sensitive. My belief that I am presently sitting at my computer writing this, for example, is sensitive since, were this to be false, but everything else the same – such as if I were standing up next to my computer, for example – then I wouldn't any longer believe that I was sitting; I'd believe that I was standing instead. In contrast, think of my belief that I am not a brain in a vat. Were this belief to be false – so that I was indeed a brain in a vat – then I would carry on believing it regardless. Indeed, it is explicitly part of how we characterise sceptical hypotheses that our beliefs in their falsehood are insensitive in this way.

If the sensitivity principle captures something essential about knowledge, therefore, then we can account for why we feel that we can know an awful lot of propositions which we think we know even while failing to know the denials of sceptical hypotheses. Of course, this would necessitate denying the closure principle, and that's a high price for any theory of knowledge to pay – perhaps *too* high – but notice that we would at least have *motivated* the denial of this principle in terms of how it conflicts with another epistemological principle (i.e., the sensitivity principle) which we have also seen is quite intuitive.

• MOOREANISM

A very different sort of response to this argument might be to try to use the closure principle to your own anti-sceptical advantage. The general idea is that one can employ the closure principle in order to show that we do know the denials of sceptical hypotheses after all, because we know lots of mundane claims which entail the falsity of these hypotheses.

For example, I seem to be sitting at my desk right now and everything appears to be entirely normal. In these circumstances we would typically grant, provided that what I believe is true of course, that I do know that I am seated at my desk. As noted above, however, if we grant knowledge in this case then it follows, given that I know that I cannot be both sitting at my desk and floating in a vat of nutrients, that I must know that I am not floating in a vat somewhere being 'fed' misleading impressions of the world. The anti-sceptical thought that might arise at this point is thus to contend that, despite first impressions, we *do* know that we are not the victims of sceptical hypotheses after all and, moreover, we know this precisely *because* of our knowledge of rather mundane things (such as that we are seated) and the truth of the closure principle. Something like an anti-sceptical argument of this form is often associated with the remarks made about scepticism by **G. E. Moore**, and thus this approach to scepticism is often referred to as **Mooreanism**.

This way of trying to turn the closure principle back against the sceptic is really quite dubious, however. For one thing, what is at issue is whether we do know anything of substance, and thus it seems somewhat question-begging to make use of an instance of knowledge in order to show that we can know the denials of sceptical hypotheses after all, especially since we have already seen that the sceptical claim that we cannot have such knowledge is very plausible.

G. E. Moore (1873–1958)

I can prove . . . that two human hands exist. How? By holding up my two hands, and saying, as I make a certain gesture with the right hand, 'Here is one hand', and adding, as I make a certain gesture with the left, 'and here is another'.

Moore, *Proof of an External World*

G. E. Moore was a distinguished British philosopher – he spent his entire academic career at Cambridge University – who was very influential on twentieth-century philosophy. His work influenced both Ludwig Wittgenstein and Bertrand Russell, but unlike Wittgenstein and Russell, Moore's philosophical approach was very much to defend common sense rather than advance any grand philosophical theses. In epistemology this manifested itself with Moore's astonishingly direct response to the problem of scepticism. In ethics, another area of philosophy where his work has had long-lasting impact, his common-sense approach led him to claim that goodness could not be defined, contrary to the many definitions of goodness offered by ethicists.

Moreover, given the plausibility of the sceptical premise regarding our inability to know the denials of sceptical hypotheses, the current state of play seems to be less a victory to Mooreanism as merely a further problem for one's theory of knowledge that needs to be resolved. How could it be that we can know the denials of sceptical hypotheses given that there appears to be nothing in our experiences which could possibly indicate to us that we are not in such a scenario? The Moorean cannot simply assert that we have such knowledge without also explaining how such knowledge could come to be possessed – but that is far more difficult than it might at first seem.

Nevertheless, there are ways of giving Mooreanism some further motivation in this regard. One way of doing this is by allying the view to some form of direct realism, of the kind we saw in Chapter 7. Recall that the direct realist claimed that we directly experience the world, and thus argued that we should not conclude from the fact we are unable to tell the difference between cases where we are not deceived and counterpart deceived cases (i.e., cases where everything seems the same, such as the brain in a vat case) that we do not directly experience the world in non-deceived cases. In this picture, then, the thought is that our experiences in the non-deceived cases are not the same as in deceived cases, even though we cannot tell the difference between them. If this picture is right, it could go some way to supporting Mooreanism since it undermines the sceptical claim that we can't possibly know the denials of sceptical hypotheses given that our experiences would be exactly the same even if such hypotheses obtained.

That said, the support offered Mooreanism by this move is limited. After all, the chief worry that the sceptic raises is not that our experiences are the same in counterpart deceived and non-deceived cases, but rather that we cannot tell the difference between such cases, and there is nothing in direct realism (at least as we have just described the view) which undermines *that* claim.

With this in mind, Mooreans often take a different tack and try to show how we can know the denials of sceptical hypotheses even though we are unable to tell such cases apart from counterpart non-deceived cases. To do this, they often propose a condition on knowledge that goes something like as follows:

The safety principle

If an agent knows a proposition, then that agent's true belief in that proposition must be *safe* in the sense that it couldn't have easily been false (alternatively: were the agent to continue believing that proposition in similar circumstances, then the belief would almost always still be true).

Informally, the idea behind the **safety principle** is to capture the intuition that knowledge cannot be lucky. Think of the skilled archer that we looked at in Chapter 1. What constitutes such a skill is that the archer can usually hit the target in a wide range of relevant conditions, and that's what sets a skilled archer apart from someone who only just happens to hit the target by luck. We noted in Chapter 1 that we can think of knowledge in terms of this metaphor, where the arrow is belief and the target is truth. The idea is that knowledge arises when our beliefs hit the target of truth through skill and not through luck.

The safety principle offers a way of cashing-out this archery analogy. After all, one way of expressing the difference between the skilled archer who hits the target and the clumsy archer who hits the target is that the clumsy archer (but not the skilled archer) could very easily have missed. (Alternatively, there are lots of similar circumstances in which the clumsy archer misses the target, while only very few in which the skilled archer misses the target.) Similarly, someone who genuinely knows, rather than someone who merely happens to truly believe, has a belief that could not have easily been false (were that belief to be formed in similar circumstances, then it would usually still be true).

In order to see this, contrast someone who finds out what the time is by looking at a reliable working clock with someone who finds out what the time is by looking at a broken clock, albeit one which, as it happens, is showing the right time. In the first case, the true belief is safe in that a belief about the time formed in similar circumstances (e.g., where the time was slightly different) would continue to be true. In contrast, the true belief in the second case is unsafe, since there are lots of similar conditions in which the agent forms a belief about the time and yet her belief is false (e.g., situations in which the time is slightly different).

What is interesting about the safety principle from our point of view is that it lends some support to the Moorean claim that we are able to know the denials of sceptical hypotheses. Even though I may lack any good reason for thinking that I'm not a brain in a vat – I wouldn't be able to tell the difference between being a brain in a vat and not being a brain in a vat after all – just so long as circumstances are pretty much as I take them to be, then my true belief that I'm not a brain in a vat won't be unsafe. This is because there won't be any similar circumstances in which I form this belief and my belief is false for the simple reason that if the world is pretty much as I take it to be then there are no similar circumstances in which I am a brain in a vat – this sort of thing only happens in circumstances that are very different from the ones I'm in. If this line of thought is granted, then it might be possible to allow that we can know the denials of sceptical hypotheses, even though we lack good grounds for these beliefs, and if we can grant *that* then the motivation to deny the closure principle as a way of dealing with the sceptical problem subsides. (Notice that, so construed, Mooreanism is clearly committed to some form of epistemic externalism, since it is allowing that we can have knowledge of the denials of sceptical hypotheses even while lacking good grounds in favour of our beliefs in the denials of sceptical hypotheses.)

One might want to object to this line of thought by saying that we can't simply presuppose that the world is pretty much as we take it to be, since once we presuppose that then we've already sidestepped the sceptical problem. This presupposition is not nearly as contentious as it might at first seem, however. To begin with, notice that no one disputes that if we are victims of sceptical hypotheses then we don't know very much. The interesting question is whether, *even if we're not so deceived*, we are able to know very much, and to this question the sceptic replies negatively. The sceptic is therefore claiming that *whatever* circumstances we find ourselves in, we are unable to know very much (including that we are not the victim of a sceptical hypothesis); if this is right, it follows that we can assume anything we like about what circumstances we are in without dodging the sceptical challenge.

Even if this objection is not fatal, however, one might still worry about the idea that we can possess anti-sceptical knowledge in this way. After all, the analogy with the skilled archer suggests that we gain knowledge in virtue of forming beliefs in a way which involves being responsive to how the world is, and yet on this view anti-sceptical knowledge seems to be gained even though there is no responsiveness to the world at all. (Remember that the Moorean grants that we can't tell the difference between everyday life and a sceptical hypothesis.) In short, the worry one might have regarding such knowledge is that it involves no skill at all, and thus is in this sense only luckily true, even though it may well involve a safe true belief.

• CONTEXTUALISM

One final anti-sceptical theory that we will look at is **contextualism**. This view holds that the key to resolving the sceptical problem lies in recognising that knowledge is a highly context-sensitive notion. Think for a moment about other terms that we use that might plausibly be thought to be context-sensitive, such as 'flat' or 'empty'. For example, if, in normal circumstances, I tell you that the fridge is empty, then you will understand me as saying that it's empty of food, and not that it's empty of *anything* – it contains *air*, after all. Similarly, if, in normal circumstances, I tell you that the table is flat, I mean that it's not especially bumpy, and not that there are no imperfections *whatsoever* on the surface of the table. In different contexts, however, what is meant by calling something 'flat' or 'empty' could change. When a scientist requests a 'flat' table to put her highly sensitive instrument on, for example, she probably has in mind something an awful lot flatter than the sort of table that we would normally classify as 'flat'.

Suppose for a moment that 'knows' is also context-sensitive in this way. One way in which this might have import for the sceptical problem could be if the sceptic was using the term in a more demanding way than we usually use it, just as the scientist is using a more demanding conception of what counts as a 'flat' surface in the example just offered. In this way, just as we can consistently grant that a table is 'flat' by our everyday standards even though it might not meet the scientist's more exacting standards, so we can, it seems, grant that we 'know' an awful lot relative to our everyday standards even though we may not count as knowing very much relative to the sceptic's more exacting standards.

More specifically, the contextualist thought is that whereas in normal contexts we count an agent as having knowledge just so long as she is able to rule out mundane non-sceptical possibilities of error, what the sceptic does is raise the standards for knowledge such that in order to count as having knowledge, that agent must in addition be able to rule out far-fetched sceptical possibilities of error. Accordingly, the contextualist claims that while we have lots of knowledge relative to everyday standards, this claim is entirely compatible with the sceptical claim that we lack knowledge relative to more demanding sceptical standards.

On the face of it, this is a neat resolution of the problem. For one thing, we don't have to deny the closure principle on this view, since provided we stick within a single context – whether everyday or sceptical – we'll either have knowledge both of everyday propositions and the denials of sceptical hypotheses or lack knowledge both of everyday propositions and the denials of sceptical hypotheses (i.e., there will be no context in which one knows the former without also knowing the latter). Moreover, we can respond to the sceptical problem while conceding that there is *something* right about scepticism – the sceptic is, after all, perfectly correct if her argument is understood relative to more exacting sceptical standards.

On closer inspection, however, the contextualist response to scepticism is not nearly so compelling. For one thing, consider again the analogy with terms like 'flat' and 'empty'. Hasn't science shown us that, strictly speaking, *nothing* is every really flat or empty (because every surface has *some* imperfections, no matter how small, and there are no vacuums in nature)? Of course, we talk as if there are flat surfaces and empty containers, but in fact when we think about it we realise that nothing really corresponds to these ascriptions of flatness and emptiness – we are just talking loosely. Accordingly, if we follow through the analogy with 'knows', then the natural conclusion to draw is that we don't really know anything – because no one could rule out *all* possibilities of error, including sceptical error possibilities – even though we often talk, loosely, as if we do know a great deal.

At the very least, then, it seems that contextualists must be careful what analogy they draw when they say that knowledge is highly context-sensitive. But even if there are context-sensitive terms which better fit the contextualist picture, there will still be other problems outstanding. In particular, perhaps the most pressing difficulty is that it just isn't clear that the sceptical problem does trade on high standards. After all, the sceptical claim is that we have no good grounds at all for thinking that we're not the victims of sceptical hypotheses, not that we have good grounds but the grounds we have aren't good enough. If this is right, then it is hard to see how appealing to different epistemic standards will help since it seems to follow, *relative to any epistemic standards that you care to choose*, that we lack knowledge of the denials of sceptical hypotheses, and this will mean, given the closure principle, that we lack everyday knowledge as well, again relative to any epistemic standards that you care to choose.

Relatedly, if we really can make sense of the idea that we can know the denials of sceptical hypotheses, relative to *any* normal epistemic standard, then it is not clear what the motivation for contextualism would be. Why not simply opt for a form of Mooreanism which maintains that we know the denials of sceptical hypotheses and leave the matter at that? That is, why not stop with Mooreanism rather than going further and opting for contextualism which holds *both* that we can know the denials of sceptical hypotheses *and* that knowledge is a highly context-sensitive notion?

So while superficially appealing, the contextualist response to scepticism, like the other responses that we have looked at, is far from being unproblematic.

• CHAPTER SUMMARY

- Radical scepticism is the view that it is impossible to know very much. We are not interested in the view because anyone positively defends it as a serious position, but rather because examining the sorts of considerations that can be put forward in favour of radical scepticism helps us to think about what knowledge is.
- One dominant type of sceptical argument appeals to what is known as a sceptical hypothesis. This is a scenario which is indistinguishable from normal life but in which one is radically deceived (e.g., the possibility that one is a disembodied brain floating in a vat of nutrients being 'fed' one's experiences by supercomputers).
- Using sceptical hypotheses, the sceptic can reason in the following way. I'm unable to know that I'm not the victim of a sceptical hypothesis (since such a scenario is indistinguishable from normal life), and thus it follows that I can't know any of the propositions which I think I know which are inconsistent with sceptical hypotheses (e.g., that I'm presently writing this chapter).
- We noted that this argument seems to rest on the closure principle, which roughly holds that if you know one proposition (e.g., that you are sitting at a computer typing), and know that it entails a second proposition (e.g., that you are not a brain in a vat), then you also know that second proposition. One way of responding to the sceptical argument is thus to deny this principle, and therefore hold that one can know 'everyday' propositions (e.g., that you are sitting at a computer) even while being unable to know anti-sceptical propositions (e.g., that you are not a brain in a vat).
- Given the plausibility of the closure principle, we saw that denying it is easier said than done. One way in which epistemologists have tried to motivate this claim is by arguing that knowledge is essentially concerned with having *sensitive* true beliefs (i.e., true beliefs which, had what is believed been false, the agent would not have held. This is known as the sensitivity principle. Most of our 'everyday' beliefs are sensitive, but our anti-sceptical beliefs are not.

- If one wishes to retain the principle of closure, then one possibility is to opt for Mooreanism and hold that we can know the denials of sceptical hypotheses. One way of doing this is by appealing to a form of direct realism, though we saw that this sort of motivation for Mooreanism is not all that helpful on closer inspection. A more promising way of supporting the idea that we can know the denials of sceptical hypotheses is by saying that knowledge is essentially concerned with having *safe* true beliefs (i.e., true beliefs which could not have easily been false). This is known as the safety principle. It is possible for our anti-sceptical beliefs to be safe; thus, if knowledge is essentially concerned with safety, we might be able to know such propositions.
- Finally, we looked at the contextualist response to the sceptical problem which held that knowledge is a radically context-sensitive notion. In this view, while the sceptic is right to contend, relative to her very demanding epistemic standards, that we are unable to know very much, this claim is consistent with our possessing lots of knowledge relative to the more relaxed standards in operation in normal contexts. One problem that we noted for this proposal is that it is not obvious that the sceptical argument does trade on high epistemic standards in this way. Indeed, it seems that the sceptical argument goes through relative to *all* epistemic standards, not just very austere ones.

● STUDY QUESTIONS

1 What is a sceptical hypothesis, and what role does it play in sceptical arguments? Try to formulate a sceptical hypothesis of your own and use it as part of a radical sceptical argument.
2 What is the closure principle, and what role does it play in sceptical arguments? Give an example of your own of an inference that is an instance of this principle.
3 What is the sensitivity principle? Why do proponents of this principle hold that we need to reject the closure principle?
4 What is the safety principle, and what role does it play as part of a Moorean anti-sceptical argument? In the light of this principle, critically assess the Moorean claim that we are able to know the denials of sceptical hypotheses.
5 What is the contextualist response to scepticism? Do you find it persuasive? If so, try to think of some reasons why others might not be persuaded. If not, then try to state clearly why you think the view is problematic.

● INTRODUCTORY FURTHER READING

Greco, John (2007) 'External World Skepticism', *Philosophy Compass* (Oxford: Blackwell). A sophisticated, yet still accessible, survey of the main issues as regards scepticism of the variety that concerns us in this chapter. Very up-to-date.

Luper, Steven (2009) 'Cartesian Skepticism', *The Routledge Companion to Epistemology*, (eds.) S. Bernecker & D. H. Pritchard, (New York: Routledge). An authoritative and completely up-to-date survey of the kind of scpeticism that is of interest to us in this chapter.

Steup, Matthias and Sosa, Ernest (eds.) (2005) *Contemporary Debates in Epistemology* (Oxford: Blackwell). This volume contains a number of sections that would be relevant to the topics covered in this chapter. See especially the exchange between Fred Dretske and John Hawthorne on the closure principle; the exchange between Earl Conee and Stewart Cohen on contextualism; and the exchange between Jonathan Vogel and Richard Fumerton on scepticism.

• ADVANCED FURTHER READING

Baldwin, Tom (1990) *G. E. Moore* (London: Routledge). A classic overview of the philosophy of Moore.

DeRose, Keith and Warfield, Ted (eds.) (1999) *Skepticism* (New York: Oxford University Press). A first-rate collection of recent papers on scepticism.

Greco, John (ed.) (2008) *The Oxford Handbook of Skepticism* (Oxford: Oxford University Press). A comprehensive collection of articles on scepticism. First-rate, and very up-to-date.

Pritchard, Duncan (2005) *Epistemic Luck* (Oxford: Oxford University Press). This book gives an extended overview of the state of play as regards scepticism in the recent philosophical literature, and also sets out a fully-fledged anti-luck epistemology (i.e., an epistemology that explicitly understands knowledge in terms of non-lucky true belief).

• FREE INTERNET RESOURCES

Baldwin, Tom (2004) 'G. E. Moore', *Stanford Encyclopedia of Philosophy*, <http://plato.stanford.edu/entries/moore/>. An excellent introduction to Moore's philosophy, this page also contains some useful links to further internet resources devoted to Moore.

Black, Tim (2006) 'Contextualism in Epistemology', *Internet Encyclopedia of Philosophy*, <http://www.iep.utm.edu/c/contextu.htm>. An excellent overview of the issues relating to contextualism, by one of the main figures in the contemporary debate.

Brueckner, Tony (2004) 'Brains in a Vat', *Stanford Encyclopedia of Philosophy*, <http://plato.stanford.edu/entries/brain-vat/>. A useful account of the 'brains-in-a-vat' sceptical hypothesis and its implications for epistemology.

IMDb Internet Movie Database, <http://www.imdb.com/title/tt0133093/>. More information about the movie *The Matrix*.

Klein, Peter (2005) 'Skepticism', *Stanford Encyclopedia of Philosophy*, <http://plato.stanford.edu/entries/skepticism/>. A superb overview of the literature on scepticism, written by one of the world's foremost epistemologists.

Pritchard, Duncan (2002) 'Skepticism, Contemporary', *Internet Encyclopedia of Philosophy*, <http://www.iep.utm.edu/s/skepcont.htm>. An accessible introduction to the literature on scepticism.

14

˙truth and objectivity

- Objectivity, anti-realism, and scepticism
- Truth as the goal of inquiry
- Authenticity and the value of truth
- Relativism

• OBJECTIVITY, ANTI-REALISM, AND SCEPTICISM

Right back at the beginning of this book, in Chapter 1, I noted that I was going to take it as given that truth is *objective* in the following sense: for at least most of the propositions about the world that you believe, your thinking that they are true does not make them true. As I said there, whether or not the world is round has nothing to do with whether or not we think that it is, but simply depends upon the shape of the earth.

Objectivism of this ilk goes hand-in-hand with a kind of fallibilism, such that no matter how good your reasons are for believing that the world is a certain way, it could still be that it isn't that way; you could be wrong. Objectivism about truth thus goes together with what we might term 'epistemic modesty'. Notice, though, that epistemic modesty is not the same as scepticism, even though the two can often be confused. After all, that there is always the possibility of error does not by itself mean that you are unable to know very much – the latter only follows from the former if one advances a form of infallibilism about knowledge, the view that knowledge requires that one can eliminate *all* possibilities of error. But why would anyone hold such an austere thesis? Provided that we are fallibilists about knowledge, then there is no direct entailment from epistemic modesty to scepticism. (In any case, as we saw in Chapter 13, you don't need infallibilism to generate the sceptical problem, since fallibilists face that problem too.)

Even though such objectivism about truth does not directly license scepticism, one might think that the root cause of scepticism lies in a strong version of this thesis. Take a *strong* version of objectivism to hold that it is *always* possible that what you believe about the world could be false. In contrast, take a *weak* version of objectivism to hold simply that what we believe about the world right now could be false. Weak objectivism, but not strong objectivism, is consistent with the thought that the truth of the matter as regards what the world is like cannot *ultimately* outstrip our best formed judgement in this respect. That is, it may be that right now it is possible that most of our beliefs are false, but once we have got the best grounds available for believing what we do, it cannot any longer be possible that what we believe is false. People who hold such a thesis are known as **anti-realists**, and they are often characterised as holding that the truth is just our best opinion, and therefore cannot be different from it. For example, one way in which some anti-realists often express this point is by saying that the truth is what we discover at the *end of inquiry* – whatever we think is the case when we reach this point *is* the case, and that's the end of the matter.

Although superficially it may appear as if **anti-realism** will help us with the sceptical problem, it isn't at all clear on closer inspection just how it is supposed to help. We are right now, I take it, not at the end of inquiry, and so it is certainly possible that our beliefs can be radically in error and thus that we do not know very much. Scepticism is still a live possibility for us, then, and so we need to deal with it. But even when we do reach the end of inquiry, such that there is then no difference between best opinion and the truth, how would we know this point has been reached such that we can be confident that the possibility of massive error has now passed? After all, new evidence can always come along which could call our previous best opinion into doubt, so how could we be sure that such evidence is not around the corner? Without any decisive indication that the end of inquiry has been reached, however, it is of no comfort at all to be told that there is no gap between the truth and best opinion for the sceptic to exploit once we reach this stage.

● TRUTH AS THE GOAL OF INQUIRY

The motivation for anti-realism about truth thus does not obviously come from any inherent ability it might have to help us resolve the sceptical problem. Where proponents of anti-realism are on stronger ground is when they claim that the **realist** notion of truth inherent in a commitment to strong objectivism – one that can always outstrip best opinion, such that it is always possible that best opinion is wrong – is in some sense an 'idle cog' when it comes to our inquiries. Suppose that all the evidence really is in as regards a certain subject matter, such as quantum physics, and that this evidence points towards a certain class of propositions as being true. According to the realist, our beliefs in these propositions could still be wrong, and so our best opinion could come apart from the truth of the matter. But, claims the anti-realist, why should we care about this possibility? That is, if all the evidence points towards one proposition, and will never point towards any other proposition, then why not just treat the target proposition as true and leave the matter at that?

In short, the thought is that a notion of truth which extends beyond our best opinion is *necessarily* irrelevant to our inquiries. It certainly cannot be something, the anti-realist claims, that we aspire to in inquiry, since inquiry will always fall short of truth in this sense. What we aspire to in inquiry must thus be best opinion, but since the difference between truth and best opinion cannot possibly make any difference to us, why not just treat best opinion as the truth and forget about this idle cog, the realist conception of truth? As the anti-realist sometimes puts it, if there is no difference to tell, then why think that there is a difference at all?

It's not altogether clear how best to understand this argument. One way of understanding it might be as follows: if the truth is indistinguishable from best opinion, then the truth can't be something that we should value over best opinion. Although this inference has a superficial appeal, it is not all that compelling once you start to think about it. Imagine that we're all being systematically deceived by a demon who is continually frustrating our efforts at finding out how the world is – preventing us from gaining the evidence we need in order to form our beliefs properly, for example. In such a case, wouldn't we want to say that best opinion was just wrong, even though it was indeed best opinion such that it could never be improved upon? And doesn't it *matter* that our beliefs would be wrong in this case, even though we can never tell that they're wrong?

In general, the fact that two things are indistinguishable does not mean that they are of the same value. Imagine two books: one the first ever produced on the first ever printing press; and the other an exact replica constructed in recent times by lasers. It could be that these two books got mixed up a long time ago and no one can now tell – nor will ever be able to tell – which is which. Still, wouldn't we want to say that the book produced on the first ever printing press is of more value, even though we'll never know which it is? If you share this intuition then I think you should resist the inference from the fact that we can't tell truth and best opinion apart to the conclusion that best opinion and truth are just as valuable (such that we might as well just treat best opinion as the truth and leave the matter at that).

Another way of understanding the anti-realist's argument could be as follows: the fact that we can't tell truth and best opinion apart means that the goal of inquiry must in fact be the latter rather than the former. But why should best opinion have any precedence over truth in this regard? I take it that the underlying thought here is that where two goals are indistinguishable, we should regard ourselves as aspiring for the easier of the two to achieve, which in this case is best opinion rather than truth. Since we can't tell the difference between truth (as the realist conceives of it) and best opinion, and since we know that we can in principle attain best opinion, we should regard ourselves as aiming for best opinion rather than truth.

Now this sort of inference might be acceptable in lots of cases, but it's not clear that it applies here. After all, we only care about best opinion because best opinion is a reliable guide as to what the truth is. Accordingly, if we shift our aim to best opinion, then what could be our reason for desiring it now? And note that it is no good saying here that in the anti-realist view best opinion *is* the truth, since if that's the case then that we value the truth can't offer any *independent* reason for why we care about best opinion. Moreover, if best opinion *is* the truth then how do we go about determining that it is best opinion, for don't we determine best opinion in terms of whether it is likely to be true? For example, don't we judge the expert opinion of an astronomer about the position of Pluto in the night sky as better than my untutored opinion on the grounds that her opinion has a greater likelihood of being true? But if that's right – if we assess and value best opinion in terms of its propensity to lead us to the truth – then how can best opinion just be the truth?

None of this suffices to show that anti-realism is wrong, of course, since we are only considering some of the most basic considerations that can be advanced in its favour. But it does indicate that we should be wary of drawing any quick conclusions about truth on the basis of the kinds of considerations that most immediately seem to favour anti-realism. In fact, I think that anti-realism is an important philosophical thesis since it poses a standing challenge to realism which the latter must deal with if it is to be accepted, and that is to explain why we value, or at least should value, a realist conception of truth. It is this issue that I want to explore in its own right in the next section.

• AUTHENTICITY AND THE VALUE OF TRUTH

Think again about the two indistinguishable books mentioned above: the one that was the first book produced on the first ever printing press and an exact replica. We clearly value the former book over the latter, and value it because of how it was produced – but why? I think the answer lies in how in many areas of life – indeed, I would suggest, in the most important areas of life – we value what is *authentic*.

In order to see this, think again of the kind of life lived by the brain in a vat that we looked at in the previous chapter. This scenario is explicitly set up so that we can't tell the difference between being a brain in a vat and not being a brain in a vat who has similar experiences. Presumably, the anti-realist will say that since you can't tell the difference between the two cases, then it really shouldn't matter to you whether you are a brain in a vat. Crucially, however, it *does* matter! You might initially be suspicious of this claim, but if so, imagine for a moment that you're given a choice between living your life inside a vat and living a 'real' life outside of the vat. Indeed, imagine in addition if you like that the envatted life will be more enjoyable – you will never come to harm and all your dreams will seem to come true, for instance. Even so, would you really *choose* the envatted life? After all, remember that such a life is entirely fake – the relationships that you form in this envatted world are not real, after all, but fake, and none of your apparent achievements are real. Wouldn't such a life be pretty pointless, even if undetectably so?

What I'm suggesting is that the kind of life that we want to lead is an authentic life – one that is in touch with the world – where the relationships that we form are genuine and the achievements we strive for real. This means, of course, that we have to face the hardship of having relationships that go awry and sometimes see our goals go unrealised; but an authentic life, even one full of hardship, is still of more value than a fake life of empty pleasure. Indeed, I would go so far as to suggest that the underlying reason why we care about resolving the sceptical problem is because we recognise that a good life is a life in which one is not radically deceived and in fact knows a great deal. It is thus imperative that one has some assurance that one is not the victim of a sceptical hypothesis.

In short, I'm claiming that it is because we value authenticity that we value truth, and value it over mere best opinion, even when we cannot tell the difference.

• RELATIVISM

With this point in mind, we will close by considering a view about truth which is radically non-objective. The **relativist** holds that what you think is true is true. This view is much more radical than anti-realism – which holds that truth is best opinion – since on this picture truth just *is* opinion, best or otherwise. Notice that in this view two opposing propositions can be true at the same time. You may think that the earth is flat while I think that it is round. According to the relativist, we are *both* right. (This won't happen on the anti-realist view because although the end of inquiry may not produce a verdict on every proposition, it certainly wouldn't generate two conflicting verdicts.)

Relativism is clearly false because it is self-undermining. For example, if relativism is true then it follows that the opinions of the realist about truth are just as true as the opinions of the relativist. But it is part of the very essence of realism to deny relativism since in this view merely thinking that something is the case does not make it the case (which is what the relativist holds). It therefore follows that they can't both be right, and thus the fact that the relativist is forced to concede the truth of the realist's opinions about truth means that he is driven down a logical cul-de-sac. If relativism is true, then so is realism. But if realism is true, then relativism is false. So relativism must be false.

People can sometimes be led into relativism because they confuse it with either scepticism or anti-realism. They confuse it with the latter because both anti-realism and relativism reject the strong form of objectivism advanced by the realist. Notice, however, that while anti-realism is a problematic thesis, it is not obviously false in the way that relativism is. It is thus important to keep the two views well apart.

In contrast, people often confuse relativism with scepticism because the worry about whether we are able to know anything of substance gets illicitly converted into the thought that in terms of truth, anything goes. But that there is a problem about how we gain knowledge of the truth does not mean that there is no gap at all between what you think is true and what is true. In any case, the sceptical problem cannot possibly be thought to be a motivation for relativism, since there could be no sceptical problem for the relativist as in this view there is no gap between truth and belief for the sceptic to trade on.

Moreover, it is not as if we can make sense of the idea of relativism being a *response* to the sceptical problem since so construed it is more like a complete capitulation rather than a counter-attack. Even if we can make sense of the idea that your belief that the earth is flat is just as true as my belief that the earth is round (and I don't think we can), we surely can't make sense of the idea that we can both have *knowledge* of these inconsistent propositions. As we've noted at various junctures in this book, knowledge is non-lucky true belief, analogous to the success at hitting the target exhibited by the skilled archer. If one gets to the truth just by believing it, then there is no sense any more to belief aiming at the truth, and thus no sense to the idea that knowledge results when one gets to the truth in a non-lucky fashion – where one's aim is skilful. It would be like living in a world in which every arrow that gets fired hits its target, no matter where it is fired. In such a world, there could be no skill of archery. Similarly, if the relativist is right, there is no knowledge.

We care about getting things right, and that's why we care about the truth, and thus about knowing the truth. According to relativism, however, there just is no sense to the idea of 'getting things right', since what you think is so *is* so, and thus there is nothing to care about. I'm not sure that anyone actually is a relativist (although some claim to be), because anyone who puts a modicum of thought into what the view is about will surely realise that it is self-defeating. But if there is such a person, then it ought to be clear that endorsing such a view cuts that person off from some of the most important values that make life worthwhile. In particular, if one does not care about the truth, then one does not care about authenticity either since the two go hand-in-hand, and yet the good life is clearly an authentic life.

We began this book by considering the value of knowledge, and we end it on a similar note. We care about knowledge because knowledge is crucial to a worthwhile, valuable life. The questions of epistemology may be abstract, but their importance to our lives is vital.

• CHAPTER SUMMARY

- To say that truth is objective is to say that merely thinking that the world is a certain way does not entail that it is that way. We noted that such objectivism goes hand-in-hand with fallibilism, since the key idea behind objectivism is that our beliefs can be wrong.
- We distinguished between a strong form of objectivism, which holds that it is always possible for our beliefs to be wrong, and a weak form of objectivism, which merely holds that what we believe right now could be wrong. The former view we called realism about truth, and it holds that the truth can in principle outstrip our best inquiries – no matter what reasons we have for thinking that the world is a certain way, it is always possible that it is not that way. In contrast, weak objectivism is consistant with anti-realism, the view that truth cannot ultimately outstrip best opinion.
- One motivation for anti-realism comes from the thought that a realist conception of truth is in some sense an idle cog in inquiry. As we saw, it is not clear how we are

to make sense of this sort of argument for anti-realism. For one thing, even when two things are indistinguishable, it can still be the case that we care about the difference, and so that we can't distinguish between truth and best opinion need not mean that we shouldn't value the former over the latter. Moreover, unless we distinguish between truth and best opinion, it isn't at all clear why we should value best opinion in the first place, since the value of best opinion seems to derive from the fact that it is a reliable guide to the truth.

- Still, the anti-realist does pose an important challenge to the realist, which is to explain why we value truth given that it can on this view undetectably outstrip best opinion. I argued that the answer to this question lies in the fact that we value *authenticity*, even when such authenticity is undetectable. (A fake life as a brain in a vat is of less value than a real life outside of the vat, even if it would be impossible to tell the two lives apart.)
- Finally, we looked at relativism, the view that truth is just what you think it is. Such a view is self-defeating since it follows on this proposal that what the realist thinks about truth is also true, which is just to say that relativism is false. We also noted that the relativist can neither make any sense of our ever possessing knowledge, nor of why we should care about truth if it is understood in this way.

• STUDY QUESTIONS

1 What does it mean to say that truth is objective? Give two examples of propositions which everyone once thought were true but later found out to be false. Why does objectivism about truth go hand-in-hand with fallibilism?
2 Describe, in your own words, the realism/anti-realism distinction concerning truth. Offer two arguments for each position.
3 Think about the brain in a vat. Is a life lived in this way any less valuable than a life (with essentially the same experiences) lived outside the vat? Defend your answer.
4 What is relativism about truth? Why is this view self-defeating?

• INTRODUCTORY FURTHER READING

Blackburn, Simon (2005) *Truth: A Guide for the Perplexed* (Harmondsworth: Allen Lane). A very readable introduction to the issues as regards the philosophy of truth. Perhaps the best place to start for the interested reader.

Boghossian, Paul (2009) 'Objectivity and Relativity', *The Routledge Companion to Epistemology*, (eds.) S. Bernecker & D. H. Pritchard, (New York: Routledge). A sophisticated introduction to the epistemological issues raised by relativism.

Lynch, Michael (2009) 'Truth', *The Routledge Companion to Epistemology*, (eds.) S. Bernecker & D. H. Pritchard, (New York: Routledge). An accessible and completely up-to-date survey of the main issues as regards the philosophy of truth.

• ADVANCED FURTHER READING

Lynch, Michael (2005) *True to Life: Why Truth Matters* (Cambridge, Mass.: MIT Press). A very readable introduction to the issues as regards the philosophy of truth.

O'Grady, Paul (2002) *Relativism* (Chesham: Acumen). A very nice overview of the issues surrounding relativism.

• FREE INTERNET RESOURCES

Dowden, Bradley and Swartz, Norman (2006) 'Truth', *Internet Encyclopedia of Philosophy*, <http://www.iep.utm.edu/t/truth.htm>. A thorough introduction to the issues regarding truth.

Glanzberg, Michael (2006) 'Truth', *Stanford Encyclopedia of Philosophy*, <http://plato. stanford.edu/entries/truth/>. A comprehensive overview of the issues as regards truth, though quite technical in places. Not for the beginner.

Miller, Alexander (2005) 'Realism', *Stanford Encyclopedia of Philosophy*, <http://plato. stanford.edu/entries/realism/>. An excellent overview of the philosophical literature on realism, taking in not just realism about truth but realist views in philosophy more generally.

Swoyer, Chris (2003) 'Relativism', *Stanford Encyclopedia of Philosophy*, <http://plato. stanford.edu/entries/relativism/>. A very sophisticated survey of the issues as regards relativism which also offers a neat taxonomy of the kinds of relativist position that are available.

general further reading

● REFERENCE WORKS

Bernecker, Sven and Pritchard, Duncan (eds.) (2009) *The Routledge Companion to Epistemology* (London: Routledge). A mammoth, completely up-to-date collection of articles on all the key areas of epistemology.

Blaauw, Martijn and Pritchard, Duncan (2005) *Epistemology A–Z* (Edinburgh: Edinburgh University Press). A short and inexpensive dictionary of epistemology.

Craig, Edward (ed.) (2000) *Routledge Encyclopedia of Philosophy* (London: Routledge). A general reference work in philosophy, not specific to epistemology. It does contain lots of epistemology-specific entries though, and is also available on the internet to subscribers.

Dancy, Jonathan and Sosa, Ernest (eds.) (1993) *A Companion to Epistemology* (Oxford: Blackwell). A very full list of entries. Very useful to have to hand.

Greco, John and Sosa, Ernest (eds.) (1999) *The Blackwell Guide to Epistemology* (Oxford: Blackwell). A series of introductory articles on the main topics in epistemology. A very good collection of papers.

Moser, Paul K. (ed.) (2002) *The Oxford Handbook of Epistemology* (Oxford: Oxford University Press). Contains lots of essays on the main topics in the area, written by the key figures involved.

Steup, Matthias and Sosa, Ernest (eds.) (2005) *Contemporary Debates in Epistemology* (Oxford: Blackwell). An excellent idea: the main figures in the literature offer alternative perspectives on a key issue, and then respond to each other's articles. Very up-to-date.

● TEXTBOOKS

Audi, Robert (1998) *Epistemology: A Contemporary Introduction to the Theory of Knowledge* (London: Routledge). An excellent textbook, though perhaps a little advanced in places.

Bonjour, Laurence (2000) *Epistemology: Classic Problems and Contemporary Responses* (Totowa, N.J.: Rowman & Littlefield).

Bonjour, Laurence and Sosa, Ernest (2003) *Epistemic Justification: Internalism vs. Externalism, Foundations vs. Virtues* (Oxford: Blackwell). It is not quite true to say that this is a textbook, since it in fact features two opposing essays from the main contributors, along with a critique and response from each contributor to the other. Nevertheless, an excellent way of getting an overview of some of the key issues in the contemporary literature.

Chisholm, Roderick (1989) *Theory of Knowledge* (Englewood Cliffs, N.J.: Prentice-Hall). This is an old classic (the original edition of which dates back to 1966), and is perhaps the most influential book in epistemology of the last 50 years. While inevitably a little dated now in terms of its scope, it is a model of clarity and still well worth working through today.

Craig, Edward (1990) *Knowledge and the State of Nature: An Essay in Conceptual Synthesis* (Oxford: Clarendon Press). A rather idiosyncratic approach to epistemology, though *very* interesting, even if missing many of the key issues central to contemporary epistemology.

Dancy, Jonathan (1985) *Introduction to Contemporary Epistemology* (Oxford: Blackwell). For a long time one of the best epistemology textbooks around, though now a little dated, and quite difficult in places.

Feldman, Richard (2003) *Epistemology* (Englewood Cliffs, N.J.: Prentice Hall).

Fumerton, Richard (2006) *Epistemology* (Oxford: Blackwell). A very readable and up-to-date overview of the area, though misses out on some of the main trends in contemporary epistemology.

Hetherington, Stephen (1996) *Knowledge Puzzles: An Introduction to Epistemology* (Boulder, Colo.: Westview Press).

Landesman, Charles (1997) *An Introduction to Epistemology* (Oxford: Blackwell).

Lehrer, Keith (1990) *Theory of Knowledge* (Boulder, Colo.: Westview Press).

Lemos, Noah (2007) *An Introduction to the Theory of Knowledge* (Cambridge: Cambridge University Press).

Morton, Adam (1997) *A Guide Through the Theory of Knowledge* (Oxford: Blackwell). Very readable, and pitched at a very accessible level. Misses out some key features of the contemporary literature though.

Pojman, Louis P. (2001) *What Can We Know?: An Introduction to the Theory of Knowledge* (Belmont, Calif.: Wadsworth).

Pollock, John and Cruz, Joseph (1999) *Contemporary Theories of Knowledge* (Totowa, N.J.: Rowman & Littlefield). Very influential. Surprisingly, though, it is now starting to look a little dated.

Pritchard, Duncan (2009) *Knowledge* (London: Palgrave Macmillan). This book is written for advanced undergraduates and aims to offer an opinionated overview of some of the main themes in contemporary epistemology.

Steup, Matthias (1996) *An Introduction to Contemporary Epistemology* (Englewood Cliffs, N.J.: Prentice-Hall).

Welbourne, Michael (2002) *Knowledge* (Chesham: Acumen). Short and readable, though sticks quite closely to the author's own epistemological theory.

Williams, Michael (2001) *Problems of Knowledge: A Critical Introduction to Epistemology* (Oxford: Oxford University Press). Very readable and *very* thought-inspiring, if a little idiosyncratic in places.

• ANTHOLOGIES

Alcoff, Linda (ed.) (1998) *Epistemology: The Big Questions* (Oxford: Blackwell). A good selection of articles, with more breadth than most collections, but as a consequence not quite so much depth.

Bernecker, Sven (ed.) (2006) *Reading Epistemology* (Oxford: Blackwell). A nice collection of articles, each of which is accompanied by a very useful commentary from the editor.

Bernecker, Sven and Dretske, Fred (eds.) (2000) *Knowledge: Readings in Contemporary Epistemology* (Oxford: Oxford University Press). An excellent and well-priced anthology of articles.

Gendler, Tamar Szabo, and Hawthorne, John (eds.) *Oxford Studies in Epistemology* (Oxford: Oxford University Press). This is a new series of anthologies in epistemology containing cutting-edge work in the area. Not for the beginner.

Huemer, Michael (ed.) (2002) *Epistemology: Contemporary Readings* (London: Routlege).

Moser, Paul K. and Vander Nat, A. (eds.) (2003) *Human Knowledge: Classical and Contemporary Approaches* (Oxford: Oxford University Press). Very comprehensive, with good coverage of some of the relevant historical texts.

Neta, Ram and Pritchard, Duncan (eds.) (2009) *Arguing About Knowledge* (London: Routledge). This collection aims to cover the main themes in epistemology by offering a selection of articles which present a 'for and against' treatment of the relevant positions.

Pojman, Louis P. (ed.) (2003) *The Theory of Knowledge: Classical and Contemporary Readings* (Belmont, Calif.: Wadsworth). Very comprehensive, with good coverage of some of the relevant historical texts. Expensive though.

Sosa, Ernest (ed.) (1994) *The International Research Library of Philosophy, Vol. 9: Knowledge and Justification* (2 vols) (Aldershot: Dartmouth Publishing Company). Very comprehensive, though not the sort of book to purchase – look out for it in your nearest library.

Sosa, Ernest and Villanueva, Enrique (eds.) (2004) *Philosophical Issues 14: Epistemology* (Oxford: Blackwell). Good selection of papers, though a little tricky to get hold of – look out for it in your nearest library.

Sosa, Ernest *et al* (eds.) (2008) *Epistemology – An Anthology* (Oxford: Blackwell). An excellent and well-priced anthology of articles which has recently been updated to include a number of new articles on recent developments in the epistemological literature.

Tomberlin, James (ed.) (1988) *Philosophical Perspectives 2: Epistemology* (Oxford: Blackwell). Good selection of papers, though difficult to get hold of – look out for it in your nearest library.

Tomberlin, James (ed.) (1999) *Philosophical Perspectives 13: Epistemology* (Oxford: Blackwell). Good selection of papers, though again a little tricky to get hold of – look out for it in your nearest library.

• INTERNET RESOURCES

Certain Doubts Weblog, <http://www.missouri.edu/~kvanvigj/certain_doubts/>. A weblog entirely devoted to discussion of epistemological issues. Well worth a visit.

Craig, Edward (ed.) (2000) *Routledge Encyclopaedia of Philosophy*, <http://www.rep. routledge. com/views/home.html>. This is the internet version of the main encyclopedia of philosophy currently available. You'll need a subscription to access it, though most universities subscribe to this service so if you belong to a university library then you should be able to get access to it this way. An excellent resource, fully searchable, and with lots of good entries on epistemology. (A paper version of this encyclopedia is also available – see p.159.)

Epistemic Value Weblog, <http://epistemicvaluestirling.blogspot.com/>. A weblog specifically devoted to epistemology, though with a special focus on issues to do with the value of knowledge.

'Epistemology', *Wikipedia*, <http://en.wikipedia.org/wiki/Epistemology>. A very good introduction to the main topics in epistemology which also covers issues to do with the definition of knowledge. It also has an excellent list of further internet resources.

Epistemology Page, <http://pantheon.yale.edu/%7Ekd47/e-page.htm>. An excellent webpage which is maintained by Keith DeRose, one of the world's foremost epistemologists. Contains lots of useful information, including an extremely thorough list of the main epistemologists and their relevant publications.

Epistemology Research Guide, <http://www.ucs.louisiana.edu/~kak7409/Epistemological Research.htm>. This excellent webpage is maintained by Keith Korcz and contains lots of useful information, such as a fairly comprehensive list of the free online papers in epistemology that are available.

Internet Encyclopedia of Philosophy, <http://www.iep.utm.edu/>. The second-best completely free internet encyclopedia of philosophy available – not quite as comprehensive or authoritative as the *Stanford Encyclopedia of Philosophy* (see below), but still contains some good entries on epistemology.

Stanford Encyclopedia of Philosophy, <http://www.seop.leeds.ac.uk/contents.html>. The best completely free internet encyclopaedia of philosophy available. It's continually being updated, and has many great articles on epistemology.

glossary of terms

Abduction
Consider the following inference, an instance of abductive reasoning:

1 There are feet exposed under the curtain in the hall.

Therefore:

C There is someone hiding behind the curtain.

This seems like a perfectly legitimate form of inductive reasoning which proceeds from a premise which supports, but which does not entail, the conclusion. Unlike most other inductive reasoning, however, this abductive inference does not make appeal to a large and representative set of observations. Instead, it simply proceeds from a single observed phenomenon to the best explanation of that phenomenon. This is why abduction is sometimes called 'inference to the best explanation'. *See also* **induction**.

Ability knowledge
This is often referred to as 'know-how', since it involves knowing how to do something, such as ride a bike or swim. It is usually contrasted with propositional knowledge, which is knowledge of a proposition. The two types of knowledge are treated differently because, intuitively at least, one might know how to do something (e.g., swim) without having any relevant propositional knowledge (e.g., without knowing that you can swim, perhaps because you forgot that you could until you fell in the water). *See also* **propositional knowledge**.

Agrippa (*c.* 100)
See p. 34.

Agrippa's trilemma
According to Agrippa's trilemma, there are only three options available to us when it comes to responding to the challenge to show how our beliefs are supported:

1 say that our beliefs are unsupported; or

2 say that our beliefs are supported by an infinite chain of justification (i.e., one in which no supporting ground appears more than once); or

3 say that our beliefs are supported by a circular chain of justification (i.e., one in which a supporting ground appears more than once).

None of these options is particularly appealing, however, and this is why this challenge is posed as a *trilemma* (i.e., as presenting us with a choice between three unpalatable options, one of which we must choose). *See also* **coherentism**; **foundationalism**; **infinitism**.

Anti-realism/realism

The anti-realism/realism distinction as it is used in this book concerns truth. (Philosophers sometimes use these terms to refer to debates about other philosophical topics.) The realist about truth holds that truth can, in principle, outstrip our capacity to know it, such that even one's best opinion of what the truth is (e.g., the kind of opinion formed at the end of inquiry) could nevertheless be false. **Anti-realists** deny this claim, holding that there can be no distinction between the truth and best opinion.

A posteriori knowledge
See **a priori/empirical knowledge**.

A priori/empirical knowledge

The distinction between a priori and empirical knowledge – note that the latter is sometimes known as *a posteriori* knowledge – relates to whether the knowledge in question was gained independently of an investigation of the world (what is known as an *empirical* inquiry). If it was, it is a priori knowledge; if it wasn't, it is empirical knowledge. For example, my knowledge that Minsk is the capital of Belarus is empirical knowledge because I gained it by making an investigation of the world (e.g., I looked it up in an atlas). In contrast, my knowledge that all bachelors are unmarried is a priori knowledge, because I gained it by reflecting on what the words mean and so no investigation of the world was required (though note that I could have gained this knowledge empirically, by asking someone, for example).

Argument from analogy

The argument from analogy is a famous response to the problem of other minds that is often attributed to John Stuart Mill (1806–73). The problem of other minds arises because it seems that we are unable to directly observe that others are minded in the way that we are. Essentially, the idea behind this approach to the problem of other minds is to maintain that we can come to know that there are other minds by observing how the behaviour of others mirrors that of our own (where we know that we are minded). The thought is that since we know that we have minds, it follows that the behaviour of others which is similar to our own shows that these others have minds too. The argument from analogy is thus an inductive argument which proceeds from observations regarding our own minds and our own behaviour to draw conclusions about what is giving rise to similar behaviour in others. *See also* **other minds, problem of**.

Argument from illusion

Consider the visual impression caused by a genuine sighting of an oasis on the horizon and contrast it with the corresponding visual impression of an illusory sighting of an oasis on the horizon formed by one who is hallucinating. Here is the crux: *these two visual impressions could be exactly the same*. The problem, however, is that it seems that if this is the case then what we experience in perception is not the world itself, but something that falls short of the world, something that is common to both the 'good' case in which one's senses are not being deceived (and one is actually looking at an oasis) and the 'bad' case in which one's senses are being deceived (and one is the victim of an hallucination). This line of reasoning, which makes use of undetectable error in perception in order to highlight the indirectness of perceptual experience, is known as the argument from illusion. It suggests an 'indirect' model of perceptual knowledge, such that what we are immediately aware of when we gain such knowledge is a sensory impression – a *seeming* – on the basis of which we then make an inference regarding how the world is. *See* **indirect realism**.

Aristotle (384–322 BC)
See p. 59.

Ayer, A.J. (1910–89)
See p. 116.

Berkeley, George (1685–1753)
See p. 74.

Chicken-sexer
A chicken-sexer is, so the story goes at any rate, someone who, by being raised around chickens, has acquired a highly reliable trait which enables them to distinguish between male and female chicks. Crucially, however, chicken-sexers tend to have false beliefs about how they are doing what they do because they tend to suppose that they are distinguishing the chicks on the basis of what they can see and touch. Tests have shown, however, that there is nothing distinctive for them to see and touch in this regard, and that they are actually discriminating between the chicks on the basis of their smell.

Note that there may not actually be any chicken-sexers. The point of the example is merely to test our intuitions about what we should say about these cases – in particular, whether we should allow that the beliefs that the chicken-sexer is forming amount to knowledge. If one holds that reliability is all important – as reliabilism, a version of epistemic externalism, claims – then one ought to regard the chicken-sexer as having knowledge. In contrast, if you think that mere reliability by itself isn't enough for knowledge – because, for example, one needs to have some reason for thinking that one is reliable, which is what epistemic internalists typically demand – then one should regard the chicken-sexers as lacking knowledge. *See also* **epistemic externalism/ internalism; reliabilism**.

Chisholm, Roderick (1916–99)
See p. 21.

Classical foundationalism
Classical foundationalism is a form of foundationalism which holds that some beliefs – the foundational beliefs – do not require further justification because they are *self-justifying*. For example, if a belief was found to be completely immune to rational

doubt, and therefore certain and self-evidently true, then it might plausibly be regarded as self-justifying and so a foundational belief by the lights of classical foundationalism. *See also* **foundationalism**.

Closure principle
This principle states that if one knows one proposition, and one knows that this proposition entails a second proposition, then one knows the second proposition as well. So, for example, if I know that Paris is the capital of France, and I know that if Paris is the capital of France then it is not the capital of Germany, then I also know that Paris is not the capital of Germany.

Cognitive faculties
One's perceptual faculties, such as one's eyesight, are cognitive faculties, in that, when working properly in an environment for which they are suited at least, they enable you to reliably gain true beliefs, in this case about your environment. In general, a cognitive faculty is a natural and innate faculty which enables you to gain true beliefs reliably. *See also* **epistemic virtues**.

Coherentism
Coherentists respond to Agrippa's trilemma by arguing that a circular chain of supporting grounds *can* justify a belief, at least provided that the chain is large enough. *See also* **Agrippa's trilemma**.

Contextualism
Contextualism is the view that 'knowledge' is a highly context-sensitive term, and that this can help us resolve certain fundamental problems in epistemology, such as the problem of radical scepticism. Think for a moment about other terms that we use that might plausibly be thought to be context-sensitive, such as 'empty'. For example, if, in normal circumstances, I tell you that the fridge is empty, then you will understand me as saying that it's empty of food, and not that it's empty of *anything* (it contains *air*, after all). Suppose for a moment that 'knows' is also context-sensitive in this way. It could then be that in one context 'knows' means one thing, while in another context it means another. More specifically, it could be that 'knows' picks out quite demanding epistemic standards in one context, but quite weak epistemic standards in another. It is this last suggestion that is particularly relevant to the problem of radical scepticism, since the thought is that the sceptic is using the term in a more demanding way than we usually use it. Accordingly, we can, it seems, grant that we know an awful lot relative to our everyday standards even while simultaneously granting that we may not count as knowing very much relative to the sceptic's more exacting standards. More precisely, the contextualist thought is that whereas in normal contexts we count an agent as having knowledge just so long as she is able to rule out mundane non-sceptical possibilities of error, what the sceptic does is raise the standards for 'knowledge' such that in order to count as having knowledge the agent must be able to in addition rule out far-fetched sceptical possibilities of error (i.e., rule out sceptical hypotheses). Accordingly, the contextualist claims that while we have lots of knowledge relative to everyday standards, this claim is entirely compatible with the

sceptical claim that we lack knowledge relative to more demanding sceptical standards. *See also* **scepticism**.

Credulism

Credulism is primarily a thesis as regards the epistemology of testimony that is usually attributed to Thomas Reid (1710–96). In this regard credulists hold, in contrast to reductionists, that one can be justified in holding a testimony-based belief even though one lacks any independent grounds in support of that belief. Credulism has also been applied to other types of belief, such as belief formed via memory. Here credulists argue that one can be justified in holding a memory-based belief even though one lacks any independent grounds in support of that belief. *See also* **reductionism**; **testimony**.

Criterion, problem of the

Suppose I want to offer a definition of knowledge. One way I might do this is by first gathering together lots of instances of knowledge (i.e., cases in which an agent has knowledge) and working out what all these cases have in common. The problem with this strategy, however, is that if I don't already know what the distinguishing marks – or *criteria* – of knowledge are, then how am I supposed to identify cases of knowledge in the first place? Accordingly, one might think that the right thing to do is *first* identify what the criteria for knowledge are and then use this knowledge to identify instances of knowledge. The problem now, however, is that unless I'm already able to identify instances of knowledge, then it's not clear how I would go about determining what the criteria for knowledge are. We are thus stuck, it seems, in a very small circle, and this is the problem of the criterion. In order to identify cases of knowledge, one needs to know what the criteria for knowledge are; but in order to identify the criteria for knowledge, one needs to be able to identify cases of knowledge. It seems, then, that in order to offer a definition of knowledge one must either groundlessly assume that one can identify cases of knowledge, or else groundlessly assume that one knows what the criteria for knowledge are. Neither option seems particularly appealing. *See also* **methodism**; **particularism**.

Deduction

A deductive argument is an argument where the premises *entail* the conclusion (i.e., where, if the premises are true, the conclusion must be true also). *See also* **induction**.

Deontic epistemic rationality

According to this conception of epistemic rationality, you are epistemically rational if you form your beliefs responsibly by your own lights. This means that if you blamelessly use the wrong epistemic norms – for example, if you blamelessly think that coin-tossing is a good way of deciding a defendant's guilt, and employ this method – then your belief is still epistemically rational. A non-deontic epistemic rationality, in contrast, would insist that the epistemically rational agent use the right epistemic norms. *See also* **epistemic norm**; **epistemic rationality**.

Descartes, René (1596–1650)

See p. 37.

Direct realism

Direct realism is a thesis about perceptual experience which has ramifications for perceptual knowledge. It holds that, at least in non-deceived cases, what we are aware of in perceptual experience is the external world itself. That is, if I am genuinely looking at an oasis on the horizon right now, then I am directly aware of the oasis itself, and thus I can have perceptual knowledge that there is an oasis before me without needing to make an inference from the way the world seems to how it is. *See* **argument from illusion; indirect realism**.

Empirical

See **a priori/empirical knowledge**.

Empirical knowledge

See **a priori/empirical knowledge**.

Empiricism

In its strongest guise, empiricism is the view that all knowledge – or, at least, all knowledge of any substance at any rate – should be traced back to sensory experience. Proponents of this view – empiricists – are thus suspicious of any knowledge which does not seem to depend on knowledge of the world, such as logical knowledge. Accordingly, they either deny that such knowledge exists, or else deny that it is knowledge of substance and so claim that it is in a certain sense trivial. Proponents of (some form of) empiricism include John Locke (1632–1704), George Berkeley (1685–1753), and David Hume (1711–76); collectively, these three philosophers are known as the *British empiricists*.

Epistemic externalism/internalism

In essence, the distinctive demand made by epistemic internalism is that when an agent has justified belief/knowledge, that agent must be able to offer good grounds in favour of what she believes. Epistemic externalism, in contrast, resists this demand and thus allows, at least in some cases, that an agent can have justified belief/knowledge and yet be unable to offer good grounds in favour of what she believes. *See also* **chicken-sexer**.

Epistemic internalism

See **epistemic externalism/internalism**.

Epistemic norm

An epistemic norm is a rule which one follows in order to gain true beliefs. That one should take care when weighing up evidence, and be as impartial as possible as one does so, is an example of an epistemic norm, since following this rule enables one to have a better chance of getting to the truth.

Epistemic rationality

This is a form of rationality that is aimed at gaining true belief. For example, a person who weighs up the evidence carefully in forming a belief about whether she can jump a ravine is being epistemically rational since she is trying to find out what the truth of the matter is, and is employing a good method in this regard. In contrast, someone who knows that she can't comfortably jump the ravine, but who, despite this, manages to convince herself that she can because she knows that only a committed jump will stand any chance of success – she has to jump this ravine, say, and she doesn't want to die trying – is not being epistemically rational (though she may be being rational in other regards).

Epistemic virtues

An epistemic virtue (sometimes called an *intellectual virtue*) is a character trait which makes you better suited to gaining the truth. An example of such a trait might be *conscientiousness*. An agent who is conscientious in the way in which she forms her beliefs (i.e., she is careful to avoid error and takes all available evidence into account) will be more likely to form true beliefs than someone who is unconscientious. *See also* **virtue epistemology**.

Epistemology

This is the name given for the theory of knowledge. Those who study epistemology – known as *epistemologists* – are also interested in those notions closely associated with knowledge, such as justification and rationality.

External world, problem of the

According to the argument from illusion, all that I am directly aware of in perceptual experience is how the world appears, not how it is independently of how it appears. If all that I am directly aware of in perceptual experience is the way the world appears, however, then this opens up the possibility that the way the world appears might be no guide at all to how the world is (there is nothing about my experiences that would indicate that this is not the case after all). This is the problem of the external world (i.e., a world 'external' to our experience of it). *See* **argument from illusion**; **indirect realism**.

Fallibilism

Fallibilism is the view that one can have knowledge even while having a belief in what one knows which is fallible. *See also* **fallibility**; **infallibilism**.

Fallibility

If one's belief is fallible, then it could be in error (though it might not be). *See also* **fallibilism**; **infallibility**.

Falsification

This is a rather radical response to the problem of induction, put forward by Karl Popper (1902–94). Popper claimed that good scientific reasoning did not make use of induction at all, as most assume, but rather employs a process he called falsification. This is where the scientist puts forward a bold hypothesis and then seeks to refute that hypothesis definitively by discovering a counter-example. For example, the scientist might propose that all emus are flightless (because no flying emu has yet been observed), and then set about trying to find a flying emu. If such an emu were found, then the hypothesis would be shown to be false. Notice, however, that the inference that would then be made would be deductive rather than inductive, since if a flying emu does exist then this *entails* that the hypothesis that all emus are flightless is false. *See also* **induction, problem of**.

Foundationalism

Foundationalists respond to Agrippa's trilemma by arguing that some beliefs can be justified without being supported by any further beliefs. In this way, the chain of justification can come to an end with beliefs that serve the special role of providing a foundation for other beliefs. One version of foundationalism, classical foundationalism, holds that these foundational beliefs are able to play this role because they are *self-justifying*. *See also* **Agrippa's trilemma; classical foundationalism**.

Gettier cases

Gettier cases are scenarios in which an agent has a justified true belief and yet lacks knowledge because it is substantially due to luck that the belief in question is true. A good instance of a Gettier case is the 'stopped clock' example. In this scenario we are asked to imagine an agent who forms her belief about what the time is by looking at a stopped clock that she has every reason for thinking is working. Crucially, however, she happens to look at the clock at the one time in the day when it is showing the right time, and so forms a true belief as a result. Her belief is thus both true and justified, yet it isn't a case of knowledge since it is just luck that her belief is true given that the clock is not working. Gettier cases show that the three-part, or *tripartite*, account of knowledge that analyses knowledge into justified true belief is unsustainable.

Hume, David (1711–76)

See p. 83.

Idealism

Idealism is the view that there is no external world (i.e., no world that is independent of our experience). In its simplest form, the view is not very appealing since it entails that the world ceases to exist when it is not being experienced. (For example, in order for a tree to fall in a forest, it is essential that there be someone present to perceive it fall.) In order to make the view more appealing, philosophers have supplemented the view in various ways. For example, George Berkeley (1685–1753) gets around some of the more counter-intuitive aspects of the view by arguing that God is always present and perceives everything, and thus the world does not cease to exist when it is not being experienced. Some other ways of modifying idealism transform it into a very different thesis. For example, the form of idealism – called transcendental idealism – that is proposed by Immanuel Kant (1724–1804) maintains that while it is impossible to ever experience the external world, nevertheless we can know, through reason, that such a world must exist. In this sense, then, the view is not strictly speaking an idealist view at all.

Indirect realism

According to the argument from illusion, one's experiences when one is perceiving normally could be exactly the same as the experiences one would have were one to be deceived in some way (e.g., if one were having an hallucination). Indirect realists embrace the conclusion of this argument by claiming, in opposition to direct realists, that one never directly experiences the world in perception. Instead, one experiences only how the world seems to one, and on this basis one must make inferences regarding how the world is independently of how it appears. *See* **argument from illusion**; **direct realism**.

Induction
An inductive argument is any argument where the premises, while offering support for the conclusion, do not *entail* the conclusion. Lots of scientific knowledge is gained inductively – the scientist makes a series of observations (say, regarding how every emu she comes across is a flightless bird) and on this basis draws a conclusion that goes beyond what she has observed (that all emus are flightless). The premise in this inference, however (that all observed emus are flightless), is entirely consistent with the falsity of the conclusion (i.e., it is consistent with the possibility of there being an unobserved flying emu). *See also* **deduction**.

Induction, problem of
This problem, the discovery of which is usually credited to David Hume (1711–76), concerns the fact that it seems impossible to gain a non-circular justification for induction. This is because inductive inferences are only legitimate provided we are already entitled to suppose that observed regularities provide good grounds for the generalisations we inductively infer from those regularities. The trouble is, our grounds for this supposition themselves depend upon further inductive inferences (i.e., that we have found the connection between observed regularities and the relevant generalisations to hold in the past). But if this is right, then our justification for making any particular inductive inference will be itself at least partly inductive, and this means that there can be no non-circular justification for induction. *See also* **induction**.

Infallibilism
Infallibilism is the view that in order to have knowledge one must have a belief which is infallible. *See also* **fallibilism**; **infallibility**.

Infallibility
If one's belief is infallible, then it could not be in error. *See also* **fallibility**; **infallibilism**.

Inference to the best explanation
See **abduction**.

Infinitism
Infinitists respond to Agrippa's trilemma by holding that an infinite chain of justification can justify a belief. *See also* **Agrippa's trilemma**.

Instrumental value
This is a kind of value that accrues to something in virtue of the fact that it serves some valuable goal. A thermometer is instrumentally valuable, for example, because it helps us to find out something of importance to us (i.e., what the temperature is). *See also* **intrinsic value**.

Intrinsic value
This is the kind of value that accrues to something solely in virtue of the kind of thing that it is, rather than because of some further goal that this thing might serve. Friendship is intrinsically valuable, for example. We don't value our friends because they are useful to us (though having friends is undoubtedly useful), but simply because they are our friends. If you valued someone just in terms of what they can do for you (e.g., help you to make more money), then you wouldn't count as their true friend. *See also* **instrumental value**.

Introspection
Introspection is a kind of 'inner' observation where we try to find out something by examining our own psychological states. For example, one might introspect one's own psychological states in order to try to determine whether one prefers the taste of one wine over another.

Kant, Immanuel (1724–1804)
See p. 75.

Locke, John (1632–1704)
See p. 72.

Methodism
A term coined by Roderick Chisholm (1916–99) to describe one historically popular way of responding to the problem of the criterion. According to this problem, if we try to understand what knowledge is we immediately face a dilemma. Either we must assume that we can independently come to know what the criteria for knowledge are in order to identify instances of knowledge, or else we must assume that we can identify instances of knowledge in order to determine what the criteria for knowledge are. Methodists opt for the first assumption over the second, claiming that we can, through philosophical reflection, determine what the criteria of knowledge are without needing to refer to any particular instances of knowledge. *See also* **particularism**; **criterion, problem of**.

Mill, John Stuart (1806–73)
See p. 130.

Moore, G. E. (1873–1958)
See p. 142.

Mooreanism
Mooreanism is the name given to the strikingly direct response to the problem of radical scepticism often attributed to G. E. Moore (1873–1958). This response involves arguing that since we do indeed know a great deal about the world, it follows that we must also know the denials of sceptical hypotheses as well, since such hypotheses are known to be inconsistent with most of our knowledge of the world. So, for example, since I know that I have two hands, and I know that if I have two hands then I cannot be a (handless) brain in a vat, it follows that I must also know that I am not a brain in a vat. So construed, Mooreanism seems to be making use of the

principle of closure. What is problematic about the view, however, is that many find it highly intuitive to suppose that we *can't* know the denials of sceptical hypotheses. It is thus incumbent on the proponent of Mooreanism to explain how this could be possible after all. To this end, recent defences of Mooreanism have appealed to the safety principle as a way of explaining how we could know the denials of sceptical hypotheses. *See also* **scepticism**.

Moral expressivist

Moral expressivists hold that moral statements do not express facts but rather perform a very different role instead, such as expressing one's support for a certain action, or one's desire to stop certain actions from taking place.

Other minds, problem of

The problem of other minds concerns the fact that it seems as if we don't actually observe other minds in the way that we observe objects in the world like trees and cars. After all, one's mind seems to be something that *underlies* one's body and one's bodily behaviour such that, although one's behaviour manifests one's mind, simply observing an agent's behaviour is not the same as observing their mind. Accordingly, the thought runs, in order to know that someone is minded we have to do more than merely observe their behaviour; we also have to infer that there is something underlying that behaviour and giving rise to it – namely, a mind. The reason why this is a problem is that it is not obvious what entitles us to this inference. *See also* **argument from analogy**.

Paradox

A paradox is an apparently valid argument which proceeds from premises which seem entirely intuitive, but which generates an absurd conclusion.

Particularism

A term coined by Roderick Chisholm (1916–99) to describe one historically popular way of responding to the problem of the criterion. According to this problem, if we try to understand what knowledge is, we immediately face a dilemma. Either we must assume that we can independently come to know what the criteria for knowledge are in order to identify instances of knowledge, or else we must assume that we can identify instances of knowledge in order to determine what the criteria for knowledge are. Particularists opt for the first assumption over the second, claiming that we can identify instances of knowledge without first having a grasp of what the criteria for knowledge are. *See also* **methodism**; **criterion, problem of**.

Pascal's wager
See p. 44.

Plato (*c.* 427–*c.* 347 BC)
See p. 13.

Popper, Karl (1902–94)
See p. 104.

Primary/secondary qualities
This is a distinction that was drawn (in modern times) by the philosopher John Locke (1632–1704). A primary quality is a feature of an object that the object has independently of anyone perceiving the object, whilst an object's secondary qualities are dependent upon the perception of an agent. A good example of a primary quality is shape, in that the shape of an object is not in any way dependent upon anyone perceiving that object. Compare shape in this respect with colour. The colour of an object is a secondary quality in that it depends upon a perceiver. If human beings were kitted-out with different perceptual faculties, then colours would be discriminated very differently.

Problem of other minds
See **other minds, problem of**.

Problem of the criterion
See **criterion, problem of the**.

Problem of the external world
See **external world, problem of the**.

Proposition
A proposition is what is stated by a declarative sentence. For example, the sentence 'The cat is on the mat' states that something is the case; namely, that the cat is on the mat, and this is the proposition expressed by this sentence. Notice that the same proposition will be expressed by an analogue declarative sentence which is in a different language, such as French, just so long as what is stated by that sentence is the same.

Propositional knowledge
This is *knowledge that* something (i.e., a proposition) is the case. It is typically contrasted with ability knowledge, or *know-how*. The two types of knowledge are treated differently because, intuitively at least, one might know how to do something (e.g., swim) without having any relevant propositional knowledge (e.g., without knowing that you can swim, perhaps because you forgot that you could until you fell in the water). *See also* **ability knowledge**.

Quine, W. V. O. (1908–2000)
See p. 35.

Radical scepticism
See **scepticism**.

Realism
See **anti-realism/realism**.

Reductionism
Reductionism is primarily a thesis as regards the epistemology of testimony that is usually attributed to David Hume (1711–76). Reductionism holds, in contrast to

credulism, that in order for a testimony-based belief to be justified, it is essential that the agent concerned is able to offer independent grounds in favour of that belief – that is, grounds which are not themselves further testimony-based beliefs. A similar position is also available as regards the epistemology of memory. Such a view holds that in order for a memory-based belief to be justified, it is essential that the agent concerned is able to offer independent grounds in favour of that belief – that is, grounds which are not themselves further memory-based beliefs. *See also* **credulism**; **testimony**.

Reid, Thomas (1710–96)
See p. 84.

Relativism
The kind of relativism that we have discussed in this book – there are other varieties that come under this name – concerns truth. This type of relativist holds that what you think is true is true. Thus, if I think that Paris is the capital of France, and you think that Paris is not the capital of France, on this view we are both right.

Reliabilism
A reliable belief-forming process is any process which tends to produce true beliefs rather than false beliefs. For example, in normal conditions, our perceptual faculties (e.g., our eyesight) are reliable belief-forming processes, enabling us reliably to form true beliefs about our immediate environment. According to a simple form of reliabilism, knowledge is just reliably formed true belief. More complex forms of reliabilism, such as certain types of virtue epistemology, hold that knowledge is true belief that arises out of the operation of one's reliable epistemic virtues or cognitive faculties. Both simple and complex forms of reliabilism are species of epistemic externalism, in that they hold that an agent can sometimes have knowledge even while lacking good grounds in support of her belief, just so long as certain other 'external' conditions hold (e.g., that her belief was in fact formed reliably). *See also* **epistemic externalism/internalism**; **virtue epistemology**.

Safety principle
The safety principle holds that if an agent knows a proposition, then that agent's true belief in that proposition must be *safe* in the sense that it couldn't have easily been false. (Alternatively, were the agent to continue believing that proposition in similar circumstances, then the belief would almost always still be true.) For example, provided circumstances are normal, your belief right now that you are reading this book is safe, since it is a belief that couldn't have easily been false. That is, it is not just that you happen to have a true belief in the particular circumstances in which you find yourself; instead, you would tend to form true beliefs about this subject matter across a range of relevantly similar circumstances. What is striking about the safety principle is that our beliefs in the denials of sceptical hypotheses may well be safe, and so if safety is (at least sometimes) all there is to knowing, it follows that it might be possible to know the denials of sceptical hypotheses after all, contrary to intuition. For example, my belief, in normal circumstances, that I am not a brain in a vat seems to

be safe, since there is no relevantly similar situation to this one in which I believe this proposition and yet what I believe is false. *See also* **Mooreanism**.

Sceptical hypotheses

A sceptical hypothesis is a scenario in which you are radically deceived about the world and yet your experience of the world is exactly as it would be had you not been deceived. Consider, for example, the fate of the protagonist in the film *The Matrix*, who comes to realise that his previous experiences of the world were in fact being 'fed' into his brain whilst his body was confined to a large vat. Accordingly, whilst he seemed to be experiencing a world rich with interaction between himself and other people, in fact he was not interacting with anybody or any *thing* at all (at least over and above the tubes in the vat that were 'feeding' him his experiences), but was instead simply floating motionlessly. The problem posed by sceptical hypotheses is that we seem unable to know that they are false. After all, if our experience of the world could be exactly as it is and yet we are the victims of a sceptical hypothesis, then on what basis could we ever hope to distinguish a genuine experience of the world from an illusory one? Sceptical hypotheses are thus used to motivate scepticism. *See also* **scepticism**.

Scepticism

To advance scepticism about a certain subject matter is to argue that it is impossible to have any knowledge of that subject matter. For example, scepticism about the existence of other minds would be the view that it is impossible to know that there exist other minds. Radical scepticism is a form of scepticism which targets a very broad subject matter. For example, one form of radical scepticism argues that we are unable to know anything at all about the external world (i.e., a world that is 'external' to our experience of it). Although it is natural to speak of radical scepticism as being a philosophical position, it is not usually advanced in this way but is rather put forward as a challenge to existing theories of knowledge to show why they don't generate the type of radical scepticism in question.

Secondary qualities

See **primary/secondary qualities**.

Sensitivity principle

The sensitivity principle states that if an agent knows a proposition, then that agent's true belief in that proposition must be *sensitive* in the sense that, had that proposition been false, she would not have believed it. For example, provided circumstances are normal, your belief that you are reading this book right now is sensitive since, had this not been true (but everything else remained the same), then you wouldn't believe that you were reading this book, but would believe that you were doing something else instead (e.g., reading another book or taking a nap). Some beliefs, in contrast, seem to be by their nature insensitive. Consider my beliefs in the denials of sceptical hypotheses, for example, such as my belief that I am not a brain in a vat. Were this belief to be false (i.e., were I to be a brain in a vat), I would be in a situation in which I would be deceived about whether I was a brain in a vat, and so would continue to believe that I wasn't a brain in a vat regardless. Thus, if sensitivity is a prerequisite of knowledge, it follows that we are unable to know the denials of **sceptical hypotheses**.

Soundness A sound argument is a valid argument that has true premises. *See* **validity**.

Testimony
In this book we have understood the notion of testimony quite broadly to include not just the formal verbal transmission of information that one finds taking place in, say, a courtroom, but also the intentional transmission of information in general – whether verbally or through books, pictures, videos, and so on.

Transcendental idealism
Transcendental idealism is a version of idealism proposed by Immanuel Kant (1724–1804). Kant agrees with the simple idealist that it is impossible to ever experience the external world (i.e., a world that is independent of our experience of it). Nevertheless, unlike the idealist, he argues that we are required to suppose that there is an external world that gives rise to this experience since, without this supposition, we would not be able to make any sense of such experience. On the face of it, such a view might look like a version of indirect realism since, like indirect realism, it appears to make our knowledge of the external world inferential. What is key to the view, however, is that we cannot gain knowledge of a world that is independent of experience through experience *at all*, directly or otherwise. It is in this sense that transcendental idealism is a form of idealism. *See also* **idealism**.

Validity
A valid argument is an argument where the premises *entail* the conclusion (i.e., where it is not possible for the premises to be true and the conclusion false). All good deductive arguments are valid. If a valid argument has true premises, then it is sound. *See also* **deduction**; **soundness**.

Value
See **instrumental value**; **intrinsic value**.

Virtue epistemology
A virtue epistemology is any theory of knowledge which holds that knowledge is true belief that is gained as a result of the operation of reliable epistemic virtues or cognitive faculties. One version of this thesis is simply a refinement of a simple form of reliabilism. Whereas reliabilism in its most basic form holds that one can gain knowledge through *any* reliable belief-forming process, the virtue epistemologist of this sort claims that only certain reliable belief-forming processes are knowledge-conducive (i.e., those which are epistemic virtues or cognitive faculties of the agent). In common with reliabilism, this form of virtue epistemology is a form of epistemic externalism, in that it holds that an agent can have knowledge simply by forming a true belief via one of her reliable cognitive faculties, even if she lacks good grounds to back up that belief. In contrast, there are versions of virtue epistemology which are allied to epistemic internalism rather than epistemic externalism, and so claim that it is essential that a knowing agent is able to offer good grounds in favour of what she

believes. This form of virtue epistemology holds that it is essential that one gains one's true belief via one's epistemic virtues, the thinking being that one cannot correctly employ one's epistemic virtues without thereby acquiring good grounds in favour of what one believes. *See also* **cognitive faculties**; **epistemic virtues**; **reliabilism**.

glossary of key examples

Lucky punter (p. 5): Harry forms his belief that the horse Lucky Lass will win the next race purely on the basis that the name of the horse appeals to him. Luckily for Harry, his belief is true, in that Lucky Lass does win the next race.

The moral: Harry has a true belief, but he lacks knowledge; one can't gain knowledge that a horse will win a race by forming one's belief on this aesthetic basis. Hence, true belief is not sufficient for knowledge.

Broken clock (p. 24): John comes downstairs one morning and sees that the time on the grandfather clock in the hall says '8.20'. On this basis, John comes to believe that it is 8.20am. This belief is true, since it is 8.20am. Moreover, John's belief is justified in that it is based on excellent grounds. For example, John usually comes downstairs in the morning about this time, so he knows that what the grandfather clock says is roughly correct. Furthermore, this clock has been very reliable at telling the time for many years and John has no reason to think that it is faulty now. He thus has good reasons for thinking that the time on the clock is correct. Crucially, though, the clock is broken; it stopped 24 hours earlier at 8.20am.

The moral: John has a justified true belief, but he lacks knowledge; one can't come to know what the time is by looking at a broken clock. Hence, justified true belief is not sufficient for knowledge. This is thus a **Gettier case**.

Hidden sheep (p. 26): Gayle, a farmer, forms her belief that there is a sheep in the field by looking at a shaggy dog which just happens to look very like a sheep. As it turns out, there is a sheep in the field, hidden from view behind the dog, and hence Gayle's belief is true. Moreover, her belief is justified too, since she has very good grounds for believing that there is a sheep in the field (the shaggy dog does look very like a sheep, after all).

The moral: Gayle has a justified belief, but she lacks knowledge, and so justified true belief is not sufficient for knowledge. This is thus a **Gettier case**. What is interesting about this Gettier case, however, is that Gayle doesn't seem to be making a false presupposition in gaining her true belief (as often happens in Gettier cases); rather, she just spontaneously forms the true belief that there is a sheep in the field.

Mr Phone Book (p. 45): Telly spends his days memorising as many phone numbers as he can from the phone book. In this way, he gains an awful lot of true beliefs. But Telly neither owns a phone (and has no intention of getting one), nor does he know anyone who has a phone. These true beliefs are thus completely useless to him.

The moral: Telly's passion for forming lots of true beliefs in this way seems irrational, but that seems to suggest that rationality is not merely a matter of maximising one's true beliefs.

Conscientious stooge (p. 48): Nell forms her belief with great care, and follows the epistemic norms of her community very closely. She has no reason to think that these norms are in any way epistemically faulty. Unfortunately, she has been taught the wrong epistemic norms (e.g., that one can determine a defendant's guilt by tossing a coin).

The moral: Nell's beliefs are in one sense at least responsibly formed, since she is doing the best she can by her lights, but given that she is following the wrong norms it is not clear that they are rational. *See* **deontic epistemic rationality**.

Trusting child (p. 50): Ethan is a small child who forms a belief that there is a toy in front of him because that is what he sees. He does see a toy, and so his belief is true, and circumstances are normal.

The moral: Arguably, Ethan knows that a toy is before him. If that's right, however, then it would seem to follow that knowledge does not require responsible, and thus rational, belief since Ethan merely believes what he sees and exercises no rational control over his believing. One could thus argue that this case shows that knowledge does not require even **deontic epistemic rationality**. Given that Ethan is unable to offer reasons in favour of his belief, this case also seems to lend support to **epistemic externalism**.

Broken thermometer (p. 56): Temp is forming his beliefs about the temperature in the room by looking at a thermometer on the world. Forming one's beliefs about the temperature in the room by looking at this thermometer is very reliable, in that it will invariably lead to a true belief, yet unbeknownst to Temp the thermometer is broken and is randomly fluctuating within a given range. The twist to the case is that there is someone hidden in the room next to the thermostat who is making sure that whenever Temp goes to consult the thermometer, the temperature in the room corresponds to the reading on the thermometer.

The moral: Temp is forming true beliefs in a very reliable fashion, yet he lacks knowledge since one cannot gain knowledge of the temperature of a room by looking at a broken thermometer. This case thus shows that reliable true belief is not sufficient for knowledge, and hence poses a problem for **reliabilism**.

Chicken-Sexer (p. 60): Chucky has an unusual natural trait in that by virtue of being raised around chickens, he is able to reliably distinguish between male and female chicks. But he doesn't have any good grounds that he can offer in favour of his beliefs. He doesn't, for example, know how he can distinguish between the chicks, nor does he know that he is reliable in this regard (though it is).

The moral: If you think that Chucky knows that, say, the chicks before him are of a different sex, then one will be very tempted to endorse epistemic externalism and so claim that knowledge does not require that the agent in question is able to offer good grounds in favour of his belief. In contrast, you might think that Chucky does not have knowledge in this case. If so, then you will be very tempted by the opposing proposal, epistemic internalism. In particular, you will most likely think that the reason why Chucky lacks knowledge is because he is unable to offer good grounds in favour of his belief, where this is necessary for knowledge. *See* **epistemic externalism/internalism**.

Lost in the desert (p. 69): Beau is lost in the desert, and in his dehydrated state he hallucinates that there is an oasis in front of him. Since this is just a mirage, Beau's experiences are not a good guide to the way the world is. But if Beau really had seen an oasis, his experiences would have been completely subjectively indistinguishable.

The moral: Cases like this seem to suggest that experiences fall short of the world in an important respect: whether one's experiences are a good guide to the world is not something that one can 'read-off' the experiences themselves. Some conclude from this point that we should be indirect realists about perceptual knowledge and so treat such knowledge as essentially inferential. *See* **argument from illusion**; **direct realism**; **indirect realism**.

Brain in a vat (p. 137): Neo has, unbeknownst to him, been abducted. His brain has been removed from his body and is now floating in a vat hooked up to super-computers. The supercompers are 'feeding' him experiences which are, as far as he knows, an authentic guide to the external world. So, for example, he has experiences which seem to be about trips to see his friends, experiences which are completely illusory given that he is in fact floating in a vat.

The moral: Cases like this are often thought to lend support to radical scepticism. The reason for this is that there seems no way in which we could exclude the possibility that we are not being deceived in this way, yet if we were the victim of such a deception most of what we believe would not amount to knowledge. So what is our basis for supposing that we know a great deal about the external world right now? *See* **sceptical hypotheses**; **scepticism**.

INDEX

(NB. If an entry is in **bold**, this indicates that this term appears in the glossary).

Abduction 96–8, **163**
Ability knowledge 3–4, 7, 8, **163**, 174
Adler, J. 90
Agrippa 34, 41, **163**
Agrippa's trilemma 33–40, **163–4**, 166, 170, 171
Alcoff, L. 161
Alexander the Great 59
Allen, W. 113, 116
Alston, W. P. 53
Annas, J. 18
Anti-realism/realism 151–7, **164**
A posteriori knowledge *See* a priori/empirical knowledge
A priori/empirical knowledge 91–4, 98–100, **164**
Argument from analogy 130–2, 135–6, **164**, 173
Argument from illusion 79–87, **164–5**, 168, 169, 171, 181
Aristotle 59–60, **165**
Audi, R. 125, 159
Avramides, A. 136
Ayer, A. J. 116, **163**

Baehr, J. 65
Bailey, A. 41
Baldwin, T. 149
Barnes, J. 64
Battaly, H. 64
Berkeley, G. 72, 73–4, 78–9, **165**, 170
Bernecker, S. 89, 159, 161

Bett, R. 40
Bird, A. 110
Blaauw, M. 159
Black, T. 149
Blackburn, S. 8, 157
Boghossian, P. 157
Bonjour, L. 41, 64, 78, 79, 100, 110, 160
Brueckner, T. 149

Campbell, R. 125
Casullo, A. 100
Chappell, T. 18
Chicken-sexer 60–4, 122, **165**, 168, 181
Chisholm, R. 21–3, 30, 40, 160, **165**, 172, 173
Classical foundationalism 36–40, 118–20, 124–5, **165–6**, 170
Closure principle **139–49**, 166
Coady, C. A. J. 89
Cognitive faculty 58–64, 122, **166**, 178
Cohen, S. 149
Coherentism 35–6, 39, 40, 41, 120–1, 164, **166**
Conee, E. 149
Contextualism 145–7, 148, 149, **166–7**
Craig, E. 159, 160, 162
Credulism 84–9, **167**, 175
Criterion, problem of the 22–5, 30–2, **167**, 172, 173
Cruz, J. 160

Dancy, J. 78, 159, 160
David, M. 54
Deduction 94–6, 99–100, 105, 109–10, **167**, 171, 177
DeRose, K. 149, 162
Deontic epistemic rationality 48–53, **167**, 180
Descartes, R. 22, 37–41, **167**
Deutscher, M. 89
Diogenes Laertius 34
Direct realism 76–8, 121, 134, **168**, 171, 181
Dowden, B. 9, 158
Downing, L. 79
Dretske, F. 149, 161
Dunn, J. 78

Empirical *See* **a priori/empirical knowledge**
Empirical knowledge *See* **a priori/empirical knowledge**
Empiricism 72, 74, 83, **168**
Eng, D. 90
Epistemic externalism/internalism 53–9, 67–71, 95–9, 115–16, 122, 123, 145, 165, **168**, 169–70, 175, 177, 180, 181
Epistemic internalism *See* **epistemic externalism/internalism**
Epistemic norm 48–53, 167, **168**, 180
Epistemic rationality 42–54, 108, 167, **168–9**, 180
Epistemic virtue 65, 69–71, 122, 124, 166, **169**, 177–8
Epistemology 3, **169**
External world, problem of 73, **169**

Fallibilism 151–4, 156–7, **169**, 171
Fallibility 38, 70, 134, **169**, 171
Falsification 103–6, 109, 110, **169–70**
Feldman, R. 160
Foley, R. 53, 54

Foundationalism 36–40, 118–25, 164, 165–6, **170**
Fumerton, R. 149, 160

Gemes, K. 110
Gendler, T. S. 161
Gettier cases 23–30, 50, 56–8, 63–4, 141, **170**, 179
Gettier, E. 23–4, 29
Glanzberg, M. 9, 158
Greco, J. 18, 65, 148, 149, 159
Green, C. 90
Groake, L. 41
Guyer, P. 78

Haddock, A. 18
Hawthorne, J. 149, 161
Hajek, A. 54
Hetherington, S. 29, 160
Hookway, C. 41
Huber, F. 111
Huemer, M. 161
Hume, D. 72, 74, 82–4, 101–3, 109, 168, **170**, 171, 174
Hyslop, A. 136

Idealism 73–8, **170**, 177
Indirect realism 71–3, 77–8, 164–5, 168, 169, **170–1**, 181
Induction 95–100, 101–11, 163, 167, 169–70, **171**
Induction, problem of 101–11, 169–70, **171**
Infallibilism 140, 169, **171**
Infallibility 38, 39, 139, 169, **171**
Inference to the best explanation *See* **abduction**
Infinitism 34, 39–41, 164, **171**
Instrumental value 10–19, **171**, 172
Intrinsic value 15–18, 171, **172**
Introspection 93–4, 99, **172**
Invasion of the Body Snatchers 133, 136
Irwin, T. H. 64–5

Jenkins, C. 100

Kant, I. 75, 78, 170, **172**, 177
Kaplan, M. 110
Kind, A. 100
Klein, P. 41, 150
Korcz, K. 162
Kornblith, H. 54, 65
Kraut, R. 18
Kvanvig, J. 18, 54

Lackey, J. 89
Landesman, C. 160
Lehrer, K. 21, 54, 160
Lemos, N. 125
Lipton, P. 100
Locke, J. 71–2, 74, 78–9, 83, **172**
Luper, S. 149
Lynch, M. 8, 157, 158

Martin, C. B. 89
Marxism 104
Matrix, The 138, 149, 176
Methodism 21–3, 29, 167, **172**, 176
Mill, J. 130
Mill, J. S. 130, 136, 164, **172**
Millar, A. 18
Miller, A. 158
Moore, G. E. 142–3, 149, **172**
Mooreanism 142–5, 147–8, **172–3**,
    176
Moral epistemology 112–25
Moral expressivism 115–16, 124, **173**
Morris, W. E. 90
Morton, A. 160
Moser, P. K. 159, 161

Neta, R. 161
Newman, L. 41

O'Brien, D. 79
O'Grady, P. 158
Other minds, problem of 129–36, 164,
    173

Pappas, G. 54
Paradox 139, **173**
Particularism 21–3, 30, 167, 172, **173**
Pascal, B. 44–5
Pascal's wager 44–5, 54, 108, 110, **173**
Plato 13–14, 18, 19, 59, **173**
Pojman, L. P. 160, 161
Pollock, J. 54, 160
Popper, K. 103–6, 109–11, 169–70, **173**
Poston, T. 54
Primary/secondary qualities 71–2,
    77–8, **174**
Pritchard, D. H. 8, 18, 19, 149–50, 159,
    160, 161
Problem of other minds *See* **other
    minds, problem of**
Problem of the criterion *See* **criterion,
    problem of**
Problem of the external world *See*
    external world, problem of
Proposition 3, **174**
Propositional knowledge 3–4, 7–8, 163,
    174
Psychoanalysis 104
Pyrrhonism 34, 40

Quine, W. V. O. 35, 41, **174**

Radical scepticism *See* **scepticism**
Realism *See* **anti-realism/realism**
Reductionism 82–90, 167, **174–5**
Reichenbach, H. 107–10
Reid, T. 84–5, 167, **175**
Relativism 155–8, **175**
Reliabilism 55–65, 165, **175**, 178, 180
Robinson, H. 78
Russell, Bertrand 142
Russell, Bruce 100
Ryle, G. 9

Safety principle 143–5, 148–9, **175–6**
Sayre-McCord, G. 125
Sceptical hypotheses 37, 137–48, **176**,
    177, 181

Scepticism **37,** 83, 85, 129–36, 137–50, 151–2, 155–7, 167, 173, **176,** 181
Schofield, M. 18
Schroeder, M. 19
Scruton, R. 78
Secondary qualities *See* **primary/secondary qualities**
Senor, T. 90
Sensitivity principle 140–1, 147–8, **176–7**
Sextus Empiricus 34
Sherlock Holmes 97, 100
Shope, R. K. 8, 29, 30
Shwartz, R. 78
Sinnott-Armstrong, W. 125
Skorupski, J. 136
Socrates 13
Sosa, D. 78
Sosa, E. 21, 54, 64, 89, 149, 159, 161
Soundness 94, 99–100, **177**
Steup, M. 9, 30, 54, 149, 159, 160
Sutton, J. 90
Swartz, N. 9, 158
Swinburne, R. 110
Swoyer, C. 158

Testimony 80–90, 167, 175, **177**
Thomas, A. 18
Thornton, S. 111, 136
Thorsgud, H. 41
Tomberlin, J. 162
Touching the Void 107, 111

Tramel, P. 125
Transcendental idealism 74–6, 77–8, 170, **177**
Truman Show, The 81–4, 90
Truncellito, D. 9, 30

Utilitarianism 130
Uzgalis, W. 79

Validity 94–5, 99, **177**
Value *See* **instrumental value; intrinsic value**
Vander Nat, A. 161
Vickers, J. 110
Villanueva, E. 161
Virtue epistemology 57–65, 122–4, 169, 175, **177–8**
Vogel, J. 100, 149

Warfield, T. 149
Webb, M. 90
Welbourne, M. 160
Williams, B. 44
Williams, M. 40, 161
Wilson, F. 136
Wittgenstein, L. 142
Wolterstorff, N. 54

Yaffe, G. 90

Zagzebski, L. 18, 30
Zimmerman, M. 19